Not Your Granny's Grammar

An Innovative Approach to Meaningful and Engaging Grammar Instruction

Patty McGee

Tim Donohue

CORWIN

FOR INFORMATION:

Corwin
A SAGE Company
2455 Teller Road
Thousand Oaks, California 91320
(800) 233-9936
www.corwin.com

SAGE Publications Ltd.
1 Oliver's Yard
55 City Road
London EC1Y 1SP
United Kingdom

SAGE Publications India Pvt. Ltd.
Unit No 323-333, Third Floor, F-Block
International Trade Tower Nehru Place
New Delhi 110 019
India

SAGE Publications Asia-Pacific Pte. Ltd.
18 Cross Street #10-10/11/12
China Square Central
Singapore 048423

Vice President and Editorial Director: Monica Eckman
Director and Publisher: Lisa Leudeke
Senior Acquisitions Editor: Liz Gildea
Content Development Editor: Melissa Rostek
Product Associate, Content and Product: Zachary Vann
Project Editor: Amy Schroller
Copy Editor: Diana Breti
Typesetter: C&M Digitals (P) Ltd.
Proofreader: Lawrence W. Baker
Cover Designer: Scott Van Atta
Marketing Manager: Margaret O'Connor

Printed and bound by CPI Group (UK) Ltd, Croydon, CR0 4YY

Library of Congress Cataloging-in-Publication Data

Names: Donohue, Timothy J., author. | McGee, Patricia, 1953- author.

Title: Not your granny's grammar : an innovative approach to meaningful and engaging grammar instruction / Timothy J Donohue, Patty Grawehr McGee.

Description: Thousand Oaks, California : Corwin, 2025. | Includes bibliographical references and index. |

Identifiers: LCCN 2025003318 | ISBN 9781071941676 (paperback) | ISBN 9781071989661 (epub) | ISBN 9781071989678 (epub) | ISBN 9781071989685 (pdf)

Subjects: LCSH: English language—Grammar—Study and teaching (Elementary)

Classification: LCC LB1576 .D6343 2025 | DDC 372.61—dc23/eng/20250429
LC record available at https://lccn.loc.gov/2025003318

This book is printed on acid-free paper.

25 26 27 28 29 10 9 8 7 6 5 4 3 2 1

Contents

PART THREE: LESSONS FOR THE JOURNEY: IMMERSION, EXPLORATION, TRANSFER

CHAPTER FOUR

CHAPTER FIVE

CHAPTER SIX

CHAPTER SEVEN

CHAPTER EIGHT

PART FOUR: YOUR GRAMMAR REFRESHER: ALL YOU NEED TO KNOW ABOUT GRAMMAR AND STANDARDS

Note From the Publisher: The authors have provided video and web content throughout the book that is available to you through QR (quick response) codes. To read a QR code, you must have a smartphone or tablet with a camera. We recommend that you download a QR code reader app that is made specifically for your phone or tablet brand.

Videos and web content may also be accessed at links under the QR codes.

Acknowledgments

FROM PATTY

Not Your Granny's Grammar exists because of the compassionate and clever people who make up my tribe. With deepest gratitude I thank the people listed below:

My family: The delight you share in my creations is a daily buoy. Your cleverness shows up time and time again in my writing, reminding me of why I write in the first place.

My educator friends over the decades: Thank you for showing me what innovative instruction looks like. I am deeply grateful for your brilliance and commitment to curiosity, equity, and allyship.

My friends (who may or may not be educators): You remind me to step away and play. Thank you for making play a priority.

My mentors: You guide(d) me even when I am a cringe-worthy, overconfident rookie, which was in my early years and every year since. I promise to pay your wisdom forward.

Tim Donohue: Your brilliance in grammar and so many other areas is rare and inspirational. You create spreadsheets out of sketch notes and add order to wild ideas. We imagined this book years ago when we were writing curriculum, and here it is! Thank you for fixing my grammar as we were writing, even though AI thought it was okay.

FROM TIM

It's always been my dream to write a book, and I would not be where I am today without the following people in my life:

My family: Thank you to my family for all of your unwavering support throughout this journey. Katherine, I could not have done this without your constant encouragement and guidance. You are my partner, my best friend, and my greatest supporter. Chris, Jake, and Ryan—you are a constant source of joy and inspiration. From assisting as grammar explorers to keeping me energized when writing was tough, you helped in so many ways with this book.

My parents and sister: Thank you to my parents, Janet and Kevin, who inspired me at an early age with their love of language and teaching and who passed down to me their grammar lineage. Your support throughout this process has been invaluable. And thank you, Lauren, for instilling in me the power to dream. May we forever silently correct people's grammar.

My students: Thank you to all of my former students who helped me grow as a teacher and as a person. My experiences with you in the classroom helped inform much of this work. Whether you were trying out different sentence destroyers, critiquing my cheesy puns, or exploring the role of the individual in society through your writing, I am forever grateful for our time together and what you taught me. There is no spoon.

Dorry Ross: Thank you to my college professor Dorry Ross at the University of Delaware who led the most intense, fun, and challenging course on teaching grammar. To say I was prepared to teach grammar and writing following that course is an understatement. My entire approach to teaching writing throughout my career has been grounded in the ideas and strategies emphasized in that course.

Patty McGee: I could not have asked for a better partner or friend for this collaboration. You have taught me so much over the years about how to lead with kindness and inspire others. Watching you work your magic with students and teachers has inspired me to continuously refine my craft. I've always considered it a privilege just to learn from you and to now work alongside you, I consider it an honor. I never imagined that I could become an author until you saw something in me before I saw it in myself. I am forever grateful for your mentorship and guidance and abundance of positivity that I often leaned on to help make this dream come true.

FROM BOTH OF US

We are both deeply grateful for the educators who tried this work on for size. We thank you for giving this a whirl and sharing your insights with us. In many cases, we both were able to visit classrooms to teach and witness the delight of students engaging in Grammar Study. Thank you also to the school leaders who created conditions for grammar to be learned in an entirely new way.

Editors! It is often said that the editors' names should be on the cover of a book as a co-author. We feel the same with this book, too. So, to all who have touched this book from proposal to publication, we hope you see your fingerprints in the words on these pages.

Having the force of Corwin Literacy uplifting our voice makes us stand taller. The faith you show in the promise and possibility of a novel grammar approach is evidence of your commitment to the strongest instruction possible for all learners. You keep educators and students in focus as you weave your magic.

PUBLISHER'S ACKNOWLEDGMENTS

Corwin gratefully acknowledges the contributions of the following reviewer:

Connie Obrochta
Reading Recovery teacher leader and adjunct instructor for Reading and Language Dept., National Louis University
Chicago, IL

About the Authors

Patty McGee is a nationally recognized literacy consultant, speaker, and educator with a passion for transforming classrooms into spaces where language and learning come alive. With decades of experience as a teacher, coach, and advocate for delightful literacy practices, Patty has worked alongside educators across the country, partnering to unlock the full potential of their students through innovative and practical teaching strategies. *Not Your Granny's Grammar* is her third book. Connect with Patty at www.pattymcgee.org.

Tim Donohue is a passionate educator and lifelong learner who lives for those "aha" moments when a student's eyes light up with understanding. A grammarian at heart and a lover of all things language, Tim is passionate about empowering students to use language and writing as tools for self-discovery and critical thinking. He is a former English teacher and curriculum director who currently serves in the role of assistant superintendent, coordinating all aspects of district curriculum and instruction. Tim holds master's degrees in English (Writing Studies) and Educational Leadership from Montclair State University. He has presented at numerous state and local conferences, sharing his expertise and enthusiasm for teaching and learning with other educators.

Patty:

To my father, who believed in second chances—for people and poorly constructed sentences.

To my mother, who has shown me that puns are the glue of language; they compound meaning and stick with you forever (I am world serious).

Tim:

To Katherine, Chris, Jake, and Ryan—my source of love and joy.

PART ONE

Grammar Remodel

iStock.com/Alona Horkova

CHAPTER ONE

Not Your Granny's Grammar

The greater part of the world's troubles are due to questions of grammar.

This lament sounds familiar, huh? Like something you might hear in the faculty room or mumble to yourself when reading student writing. But, lo and behold, these words were written by Michel de Montaigne, a 16th-century French philosopher. Grammar feels like a "now" problem. Alas, Michel shows us that it is a centuries-long problem that has not yet been resolved.

Throughout history we can mark moments when grammar has been at the forefront of literacy concerns. One notable grammar movement was at Harvard University during the Industrial Revolution. With the burgeoning middle class lifting many into wealth that they never had before, the newly rich wanted a high-class education. They descended on the classrooms at Harvard to the dismay of many professors and upper-crust scholars who found their writing to be atrocious; the professors actually started a movement to purge what they called "linguistic barbarisms" from the new students' writing.

Fast-forward to today. You probably picked up this book because you feel the same angst about grammar usage today as so many have across history. Maybe you feel that grammar is a forgotten foundational skill, lost in the shuffle of literacy instruction. Perhaps you feel torn about how to teach grammar, even if it is something that you agree needs to be explicitly taught. There are often myriad reasons why we feel this tension about teaching grammar. Very often, teachers are torn because they are grammarians themselves and uphold a set of expectations that they do not see students meet. Other teachers feel wobbly with grammar, unsure of how grammar works, and therefore unsure of how to teach it. Most educators we have come across did not have the most delightful experience learning grammar when they were young and want something different for their students. They want a grammar refresh, something entirely different from their experience as a student, their parents' experience as a student, and even their grandparents' because, with very few exceptions, grammar instruction has remained the same for generations. This book from 1819 (see Photo 1.1) shows a clear resemblance to some grammar resources today! We like to think of this traditional way of teaching grammar as our Granny's Grammar.

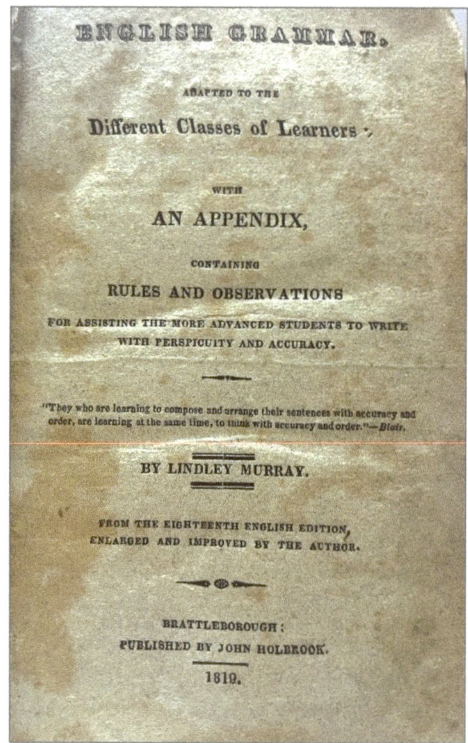

ENGLISH GRAMMAR,

ADAPTED TO THE

Different Classes of Learners;

WITH

AN APPENDIX,

CONTAINING

RULES AND OBSERVATIONS

FOR ASSISTING THE MORE ADVANCED STUDENTS TO WRITE WITH PERSPICUITY AND ACCURACY.

"They who are learning to compose and arrange their sentences with accuracy and order, are learning at the same time, to think with accuracy and order."—*Blair.*

BY LINDLEY MURRAY.

FROM THE EIGHTEENTH ENGLISH EDITION, ENLARGED AND IMPROVED BY THE AUTHOR.

BRATTLEBOROUGH:
PUBLISHED BY JOHN HOLBROOK.
1819.

Photo 1.1. Title page from the 1819 edition of *English Grammar*

Feeling this same angst and tension, and knowing grammar will never go out of style in education (pun intended), we have developed Grammar Study, which has become our favorite approach to teaching grammar. We come from differing grammar backgrounds but have found common ground in revolutionizing grammar instruction. Patty's background included years of grammar instruction as a student only to find herself with big grammar gaps in both writing and the teaching of grammar. Although Patty felt strong about teaching in her literacy block, grammar was the clear exception. Tim studied grammar deeply as an English major in college, which helped to fill in gaps that remained following high school. As a teacher, Tim utilized his deep knowledge of grammar while teaching writing, beginning all writing instruction at the sentence level and helping students to build upon that essential foundation. And so, we have teamed up to provide a resource for you that resets how grammar is taught. Suffice it to say, this book will guide you step by step, lesson by lesson, through nurturing grammar knowledge and usage for both you and your students.

TIME TRAVELING THROUGH GRAMMAR

Read the quotes from each century in Table 1.1, starting back in the 16th century. Notice how the grammar has changed over time. It's not just the vocabulary that feels different. It is also the use of capital letters, punctuation, and syntax.

Table 1.1

CENTURY	AUTHOR	QUOTE
16th	Michel de Montaigne (the guy we quoted earlier who was none too happy about grammar usage in the 16th century)	Nature has with a Motherly Tenderness observed this, that the Action she has enjoyned us for our Necessity should be also pleasant to us, and invites us to them, not only by Reason, but also by Appetite: and 'tis Injustice to infringe her Laws.
17th	Margaret Cavendish	For disorder obstructs: besides, it doth disgust life, distract the appetites, and yield no true relish to the senses.
18th	Hannah Cowley	The common events of this little dirty world are not worth talking about, unless you embellish them!
19th	Oscar Wilde	My own business always bores me to death. I prefer other people's.
20th	W.E.B Dubois	Education must not simply teach work—it must teach Life.
21st	Joseph Bruchac	One of the things I've been taught by Native American elders is the importance of patience, of waiting to do things when the time is right.

WHAT GRAMMAR DOES

Let's begin by answering the question, "Why do we teach grammar in the first place?"

We think these t-shirts pictured on Tim and his son, Chris, share at least one reason (see Photos 1.2 and 1.3).

Photo 1.2.
Tim proudly wears a shirt given to him by his parents who are language lovers and grammarians in their own right.

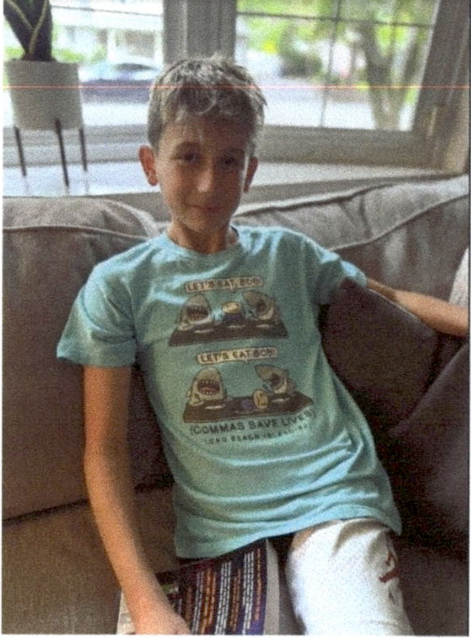

Photo 1.3.
Tim's son, Chris, wears a shirt that he picked out while on vacation in Long Beach Island. Of course he chose a grammar shirt! In Tim's family, grammar humor is an heirloom passed down from generation to generation.

> **Grammar Nerd Alert!**
>
> Still wondering about who vs. whom? In this case, following the preposition *about*, the objective case pronoun *whom* is used. More on all of this later!

There are many more reasons why we teach grammar. Here are the grounds from which we champion grammar learning.

1. Grammar is to writing as a paintbrush is to a painter. It is a tool for self-expression and meaning building. *It is not grammar and style. Grammar is style.*

2. Grammar makes writing more powerful and with this power, people go places. There is rarely a profession in which a person does not use some grammar.
3. Knowing grammar well helps one break the rules intentionally, just as Picasso was a fine artist before he became the artist we know today.
4. The majority of students are not considered proficient in writing, and this has been the case for the last 30 years. (National Assessment of Educational Progress, 2016)

Before we introduce our approach to grammar instruction, we want to share some important foundational concepts.

WHAT GRAMMAR IS

1. Grammar is not a static set of rules. It is ever-evolving. This quote from the website *The English Club* says it perfectly.

   Grammar is the system of a language. People sometimes describe grammar as the "rules" of a language, but in fact no language has rules. If we use the word "rules," we suggest that somebody created the rules first and then spoke the language, like a new game. But languages did not start like that. Languages started by people making sounds which evolved into words, phrases, and sentences. No commonly spoken language is fixed. All languages change over time. What we call "grammar" is simply a reflection of a language at a particular time. (Essberger, n.d.)

2. Grammar differs from community to community. There is no *superior* grammar. We have both traveled around the country, and each community we visit has its own unique grammatical style. However, there is a set of grammar standards that we as teachers are obliged to teach. Each state has decided what those standards are.
3. There is a difference between spoken grammar and written grammar. How we speak doesn't entirely line up with the grammar standards. Book grammar is also different from grammar standards. Writers use grammar to craft their writing and very often, very intentionally, do not conform to the standards.
4. There is no consensus on correct grammar usage. Among the many style guides, the most popular are the *Publication Manual of the American Psychological Association*

Scan the QR code to see a breakdown of the grammar standards by grade in the Common Core.

qrs.ly/hzge09d

To read a QR code, you must have a smartphone or tablet with a camera. We recommend that you download a QR code reader app that is made specifically for your phone or tablet brand.

(APA), the Modern Language Association's *MLA Handbook*, and *The Chicago Manual of Style* (CMOS).

5. The purpose of grammar instruction is to benefit writing. Identification of parts of speech, sentence types, and grammar rules isn't a necessity for learning grammar. Identification has, however, been the first step in teaching grammar. We have often heard statements like, "Students can't even identify a noun so how can they use them?" Students are using nouns and other parts of speech long before they even know the names of them. Take, for example, the piece of writing from a fourth grader shown in Figure 1.1. Review the notations and notice all of the grammatical moves they are making; the student would likely be unable to name all of these moves by solely using grammatical lingo. But they used grammar correctly and used it for meaning-making.

Figure 1.1 • Students Can Use Sophisticated Grammar Even Though They Can't Name the Grammar Terms

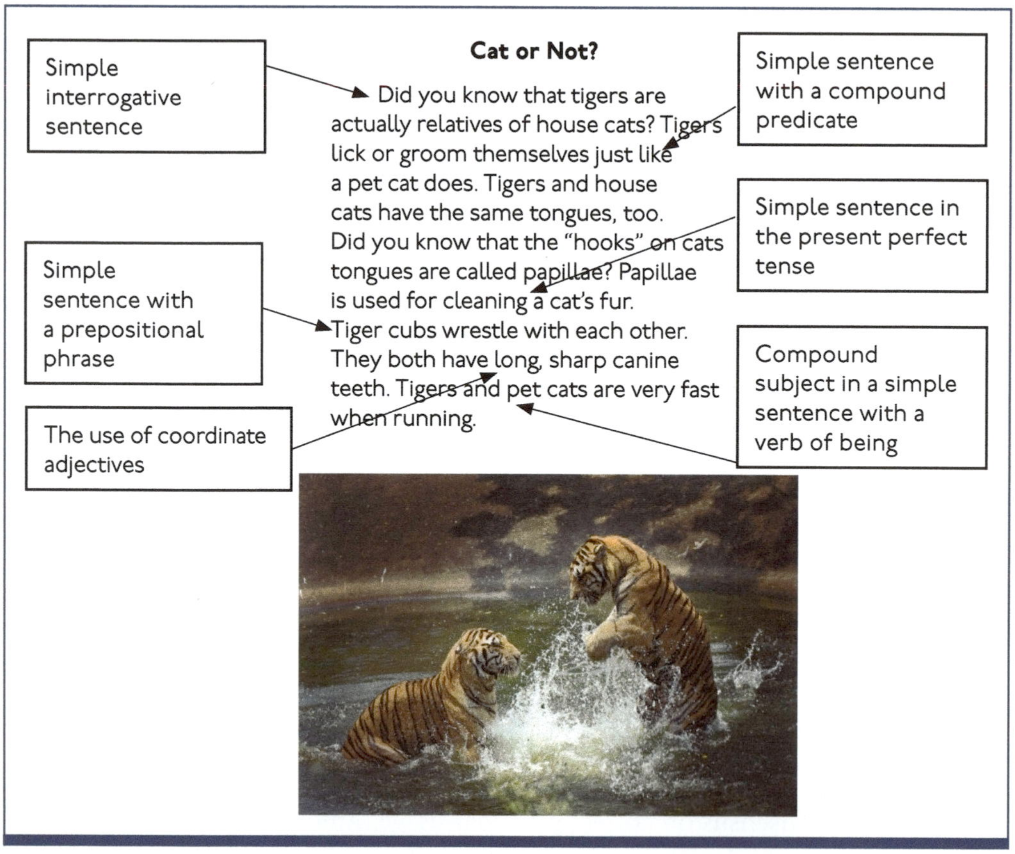

Simple interrogative sentence

Simple sentence with a compound predicate

Cat or Not?

Did you know that tigers are actually relatives of house cats? Tigers lick or groom themselves just like a pet cat does. Tigers and house cats have the same tongues, too. Did you know that the "hooks" on cats tongues are called papillae? Papillae is used for cleaning a cat's fur. Tiger cubs wrestle with each other. They both have long, sharp canine teeth. Tigers and pet cats are very fast when running.

Simple sentence in the present perfect tense

Simple sentence with a prepositional phrase

Compound subject in a simple sentence with a verb of being

The use of coordinate adjectives

iStock.com/hxdbzxy

RESEARCH

There have been decades of research devoted to the efficacy of grammar instruction. Instruction differs widely. Yet grammar practices have remained largely the same.

Research has indicated that traditional practices of teaching grammar are ineffective. These traditional practices often include out-of-context exercises, such as worksheets about identifying parts of speech, which separates grammar from the writing process itself. As long ago as 1963, Braddock et al. found that, "the teaching of formal grammar has a negligible or, because it usually displaces some instruction and practice in actual composition, even a harmful effect on the improvement of writing" (p. 49). Hillocks (1986) shared his meta-analysis results on grammar instruction: "If schools insist upon teaching the identification of parts of speech, the parsing or diagramming of sentences, or other concepts of traditional grammar (as many still do), they cannot defend it as a means of improving the quality of writing" (p. 138). Hillocks and Smith (1991) shared, "Research over a period of nearly 90 years has consistently shown that the teaching of grammar has little or no effect on students" (p. 591).

What does work, then, in grammar instruction is teaching in service of writing (DiStefano & Killion, 1984; Ehrenworth & Vinton, 2005; Harris, 1962; Weaver, 1996). Further findings demonstrate that teaching grammar in context will enhance sentence sense, variety, and syntactic fluency; promote the use of appropriate conventions; develop rich content by developing details about abstract ideas via grammatical constructions; improve organization through a focus on transitions and connectors; and enrich voice and style "appropriate to purpose, content, and audience" (Weaver & Bush, 2008).

In a compelling research article entitled "Playful explicitness with grammar: A pedagogy for writing" (Myhill et al., 2013), the authors demonstrated that explicitly teaching grammar enhances student writing, particularly when teachers adopt a playful approach that emphasizes lively discussion and strong links to the writing tasks students are engaged in. Exactly the kinds of instruction we can implement with a few instructional shifts!

The most recent research we have found is Stephen Graham and colleagues' (2023) meta-analysis on writing treatments. In advocating for instruction at the sentence level, Graham et al.

identify "examples of sentence instruction" that "ranged from sentence combining (O'Hare, 1971) to explicitly teaching students how to construct specific sentence structures through explanation, models, and practice (Kennedy, 2008). Such instruction produced statistically detectable ESs [effect sizes] of 0.73 for all writing outcomes...and 0.75 for writing quality" (p. 46). In other words, teaching sentence combining and construction is the way to go.

In addition, *The Writing Rope* by Joan Sedita (2023) outlines a framework for explicit writing instruction, and one of the threads of this rope is The Syntax Strand, which includes grammar and syntactical awareness, sentence elaboration, and punctuation. Sedita notes the explicit relationship that exists between reading and writing and how knowledge of syntax—the ways in which words, phrases, and clauses are organized to create sentences—is critical for students as they read for meaning and write with purpose. Beginning writing instruction at the sentence level provides students with a common language connected with elements of syntax that can be utilized in the context of authentic writing and reinforced through various reading experiences (e.g., shared reading).

Further recommendations for grammar instruction from a variety of thought leaders emphasize the importance of sentence construction, combining, and expansion (Graham, 2006; Graham & Hebert, 2011; Graham et al., 2015; Hochman et al., 2017; Sedita, 2023).

We took all of this into account, as well as our combined 50+ years as educators, to design our approach to grammar instruction that we call Grammar Study, which we'll explore and share with you throughout this book.

WHAT IS GRAMMAR STUDY?

As we developed this approach, we dug into the etymology of the word *study* because it is nuanced and learner-centered. In the 12th century, "study" meant to "strive toward, devote oneself to, cultivate." In the 14th century, it meant to "reflect, muse, think, ponder." Though "study" now has multiple definitions and can be used as both a noun and verb, we prefer to define it as something detailed and active, fueled by curiosity.

When we study something, particularly outside of school, we seek out a variety of experiences. Tim studies guitar (and grammar, of course). This study of guitar has been a decades-long experience in which he has

- **sought out experts** by learning to play some of his favorite Dave Matthews Band songs.
- asked for **feedback** from other guitar players and guitar teachers.
- **memorized** notes, chords, scales, and finger placements.
- **questioned** the playing techniques used by others and **hypothesized** how to incorporate those techniques himself.
- **experimented** with these new techniques when practicing individually and when playing with others.
- **reflected** on what he has learned about guitar and how the songs he has played can sound even better.

These are the multilayered experiences that make true study so powerful. Grammar Study takes a similar approach. We create an experience for students where they can *seek out experts, ask for feedback, memorize, question, hypothesize, experiment (play),* and *reflect on* grammar—not all in one day, of course, but through intentionally designed units. As you can see in Table 1.2, which compares Granny's Grammar with Grammar Study, our approach provides learners with opportunities to learn grammar in bite-size interactions with written language that matters to them.

Table 1.2 • A Side-by-Side View of Your Granny's Grammar vs. Grammar Study

YOUR GRANNY'S GRAMMAR	GRAMMAR STUDY
RULE IV. The noun of multitude, or signifying many, may have a verb or pronoun agreeing with it, either of the singular or plural number: yet not without regard to the import of the word, as conveying unity or plurality of idea: as, "The meeting *was* large;" "The parliament *is* dissolved;" "The nation *is* powerful;" "My people *do* not consider: *they* have not known me;" "The multitude eagerly *pursue* pleasure as *their* chief good;" "The council *were* divided in *their* sentiments." We ought to consider whether the term will immediately suggest the idea of the number it represents, or whether it exhibits to the mind the idea of the whole as one thing. In the former case, the verb ought to be plural; in the latter, it ought to be singular. Thus it seems improper to say, "the peasantry *goes* barefoot, and the middle sort *makes* use of wooden shoes." It would be better to say, "The peasantry *go* barefoot, and the middle sort *make* use," &c. because the idea in both these cases, is that of a number. On M 2 Photo 1.4 Grammatically dense and wordy explanations given for grammar usage.	 Photo 1.5 Simplified, actionable instruction is given in bite-sized pieces.
Name: ____________ **Nouns** **Underline the noun in each sentence.** 1. The robin flew away. 2. My cat jumped onto the bed. 3. Amir liked his new soccer coach. 4. The tea was very hot. 5. Janie loved to listen to music. Photo 1.6 Isolated worksheet completion is done alone and disconnected from composing writing.	 Photo 1.7 Collaborative, playful learning is fueled by inquiry and curiosity with an eye for usage.

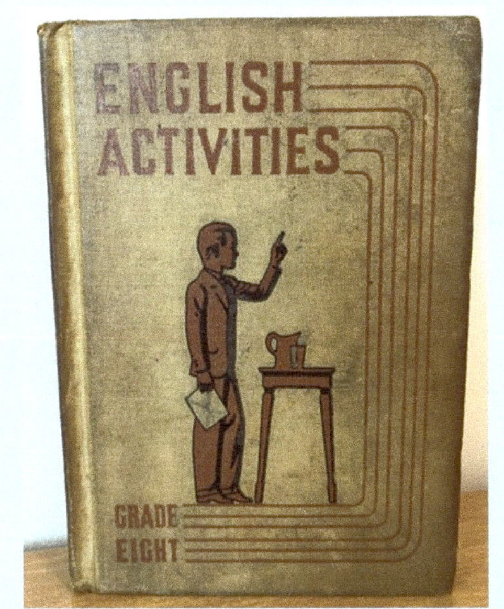

Photo 1.8
Lengthy grammar lessons focus on the teacher.

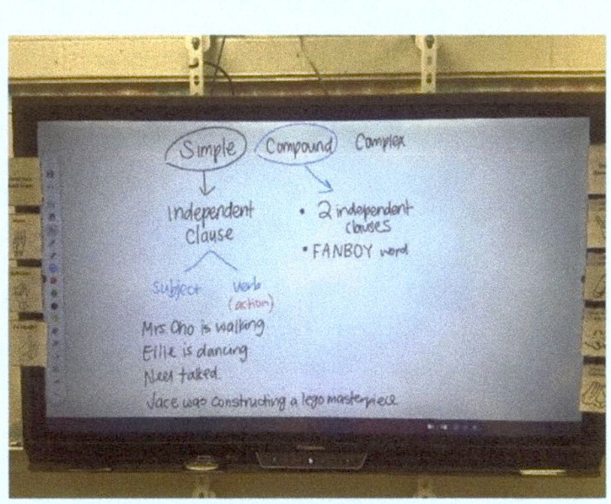

Photo 1.9
Quick explicit lessons teach how to use a grammar concept in writing.

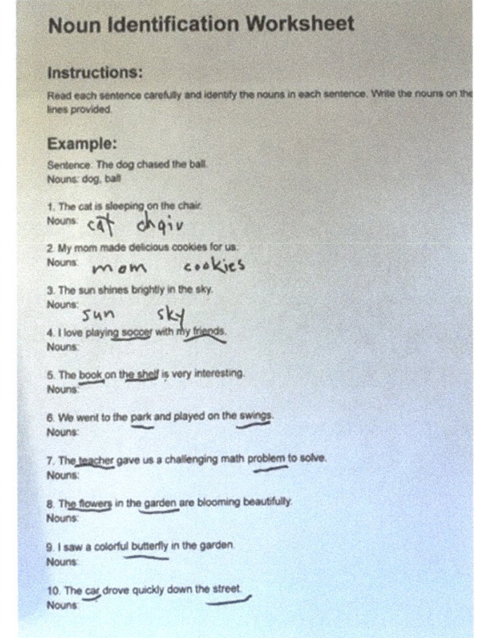

Noun Identification Worksheet

Instructions:

Read each sentence carefully and identify the nouns in each sentence. Write the nouns on the lines provided.

Example:

Sentence: The dog chased the ball.
Nouns: dog, ball

1. The cat is sleeping on the chair.
Nouns: cat chair
2. My mom made delicious cookies for us.
Nouns: mom cookies
3. The sun shines brightly in the sky.
Nouns: sun sky
4. I love playing soccer with my friends.
Nouns:
5. The book on the shelf is very interesting.
Nouns:
6. We went to the park and played on the swings.
Nouns:
7. The teacher gave us a challenging math problem to solve.
Nouns:
8. The flowers in the garden are blooming beautifully.
Nouns:
9. I saw a colorful butterfly in the garden.
Nouns:
10. The car drove quickly down the street.
Nouns:

Photo 1.10
The class moves on after completing a worksheet.

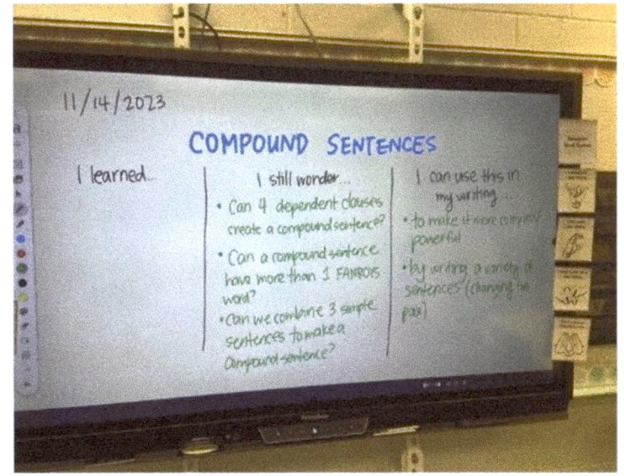

Photo 1.11
Time is taken to reflect on wonderings and curiosities.

THE GRAMMAR LOVERS' BOOK NOOK

Throughout the book, you'll find these book nooks, highlighting our favorite grammar books for teachers and students. We hope you'll choose one or two to read on your grammar journey!

For Teachers: *Mechanically Inclined* by Jeff Anderson (2023)

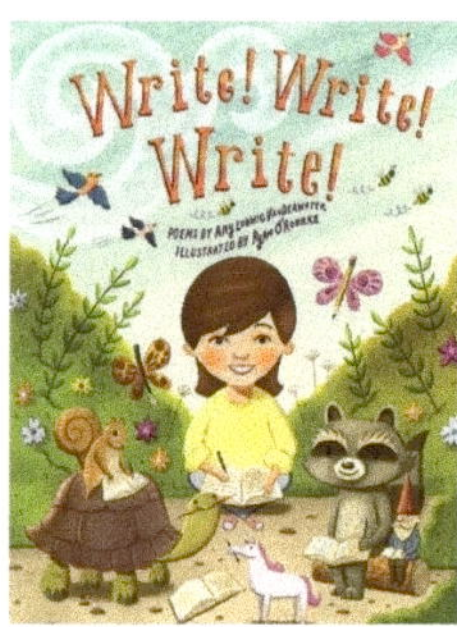

For Students: *Write! Write! Write!* by Amy Ludwig Vanderwater (2020)

A SUCCINCT OVERVIEW OF A GRAMMAR STUDY UNIT

In Grammar Study, each grammar unit has three phases spread over five to six weeks, creating multiple opportunities for students to seek out experts, ask for feedback, memorize, question, hypothesize, experiment (play), and reflect on grammar. The three phases are

Immersion

Focus Areas

Transfer

These phases reflect Hattie and Donoghue's (2016) work on the three phases of learning—surface, deep, and transfer—and reflect how people learn over time.

The units and lessons in this book are organized by these phases (see Figure 1.2). Each lesson is meant to be 10–15 minutes and taught 3–5 times per week.

Figure 1.2 • Three Phases of a Grammar Unit

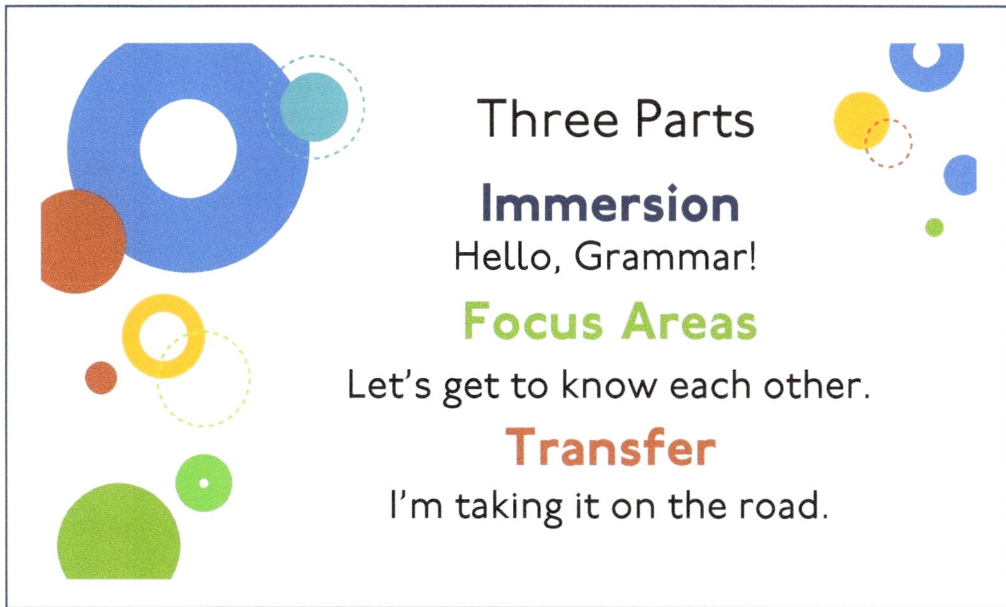

Phase 1: Immersion: Hello Grammar! (2–4 Days)

You'll see this lightbulb icon next to the Immersion lessons in this book.

We begin by introducing students to the focus of the unit in the Immersion phase. This "surface learning" is the first phase of learning and introduces students to the grammatical concepts that will be the focus of the unit. We do this through a study of mentor texts using inquiry questions to guide the exploration.

Phase 2: Focus Areas: Let's Get to Know Each Other (3–4 Weeks)

You'll see this magnifying glass icon next to the Focus Area lessons in this book.

The Focus Areas phase of the unit enables students to deepen their grammatical knowledge across time and takes up the bulk of the time we will be studying a particular grammar concept. During these three or four weeks, the areas of focus change so that students have myriad opportunities to develop grammar know-how. There are three types of experiences students will take part in, as shown in Table 1.3.

Table I.3 • Three Parts of a Grammar Unit

Explore: Hypothesize and Play. These days are full of inquiry, play, and experimentation. The majority of days in this deep learning time will be Explore days. In this book, Explore lessons are categorized into "Explore and Hypothesize" and "Explore and Play."
Explicit Teaching. These days, teachers explicitly model the steps for using a particular grammatical concept.
Reflection. This is a time to pause and consider what we have learned thus far about the focus of the unit and share what we still wonder.

Phase 3: Transfer: I'm Taking It on the Road

You'll see this pencil and notebook icon next to the Transfer lessons in this book.

The Transfer phase begins at this point in the grammar unit (and continues throughout the year in all pieces of writing) by creating tools that will support students in applying their new grammar knowledge.

This is a quick overview of the phases, but we promise that the rest of the book will dive deeply into unit design and share lessons galore for each phase.

KNITTING THIS CHAPTER TOGETHER

We ask you to think of this grammar reset and book as a virtual trust fall. We have worked in countless classrooms with brilliant educators, and it is remarkable what happens when students are invited into a true study of grammar. The engaged and curious disposition they take on as they work with partners or in groups to question, hypothesize, and experiment with grammatical concepts and use explicitly taught strategies is enchanting to witness. It is learning alive right in front of us. This work builds a common language around grammar that is cultivated in this type of classroom community. As we embark on this novel approach to grammar, let's keep our eye on the prize. We want students to learn grammar in such depth and detail that they, over time, become fluent users of grammar.

HOW THIS BOOK IS ORGANIZED

This book is organized to empower you to implement a Grammar Study approach. A brief description of each chapter follows.

Chapter 2: Setting Up the Classroom for Grammar Study will help you get all that you need ready for Grammar Study to go smoothly.

Chapter 3: Start With a Study of Sentences will give you one full unit that you can use just as is, day by day.

Chapter 4: Immersion Lessons: Mentor Texts and Tips begins our "choose your own adventure" portion of the book. You will mix and match the resources from Chapters 4, 5, 6, and 7. Chapter 4 includes mentor texts to use during Phase 1: Immersion.

Chapter 5: Explore Lessons: Hypothesize and Play includes options for students to play with grammar to build grammar know-how. These are usually used in the Explore lessons, which are part of Phase 2: Focus Areas.

Chapter 6: Explicit Lessons: Anchor Charts and How-Tos is a set of lessons and anchor charts for you to use when teaching lessons explicitly and for students to use when applying to their writing. These will be lessons taught in explicit teaching sessions, which are part of Phase 2: Focus Areas.

Chapter 7: Transfer Lessons: Tools and Schedules builds a launch pad for the transfer of grammar learning into everyday writing. These bring you into Phase 3: Transfer.

Chapter 8: Assessment: For Learning and of Learning gives you simple and informative methods to assess *for* learning and assessments *of* learning.

But that's not all! A significant portion of this book gives a glimpse into Tim's grammar brain in *Part 4: Your Grammar Refresher: All You Need to Know About Grammar and Standards.* He has a deep and detailed understanding of grammar and conventions, and he has put this into a digestible format for any grammar refresher you might need. See Part 4 of the book to read this incredible resource; we hope you'll use it as a quick grammar guide as you read this book and as you plan grammar instruction. You may even want to review it first before you begin diving into the other chapters!

Scan this QR code to watch Tim's series of videos that break down key grammar concepts!

qrs.ly/rogkpqy

Many of the resources in the book are available online for download on the companion website; scan the QR codes next to each downloadable resource to retrieve them. The online Appendix, also available on the companion website, shows how Your Grammar Refresher and the chapters of this book align with most state standards.

GRAMMAR SCOPE AND SEQUENCE FOR GRADES 2–8

To give you a bird's eye view of how a year may unfold for your grade level, we wanted to end this chapter by sharing a suggested scope and sequence with you. Although we fully support teachers creating their own grammar scope and sequence, we know it can take some time. To streamline this, we have put together suggested units from Grades 2–8 (see Table 1.4). You will notice that we really like to start off any grammar experience with sentences. The science of writing indicates that constructing, combining, and expanding sentences is the most useful grammar instruction. From there, feel free to change the order of the other units as you so choose.

Table 1.4 • A Suggested Progression of Units for Grades 2–8

GRADE 2				
UNIT 1	**UNIT 2**	**UNIT 3**	**UNIT 4**	**UNIT 5**
Designing all Sorts of Sentences (sentence types, expanding sentences, conjunctions)	Punctuation Power (end marks, commas)	The "Who" and "What Did They Do": A Study of Nouns and Verbs	Painting With Words: How to Use Adjectives, Adverbs, and Pronouns	Capitalization and More Punctuation (capitals, articles)
GRADE 3				
UNIT 1	**UNIT 2**	**UNIT 3**	**UNIT 4**	**UNIT 5**
Essential Sentences: Designing and Combining the Three Most Common Sentence Types	Can We All Just Agree? (agreement and prepositional phrases)	Describing Words (and the Words They Describe) (nouns, pronouns, adjectives, adverbs, and verbs)	The Art of Punctuation (commas, conjunctions, apostrophes, quotations)	Oh, My Stars! A Study of Capitals, Punctuation, and Interjections

GRADE 3				
UNIT 1	**UNIT 2**	**UNIT 3**	**UNIT 4**	**UNIT 5**
(simple, compound, complex sentences)				(capitals, articles, complete sentences, punctuation for effect, interjections)
GRADE 4				
UNIT 1	**UNIT 2**	**UNIT 3**	**UNIT 4**	**UNIT 5**
Blueprints of Language: Mastering Sentence Structure (simple, compound, complex sentences, coordinating and subordinating conjunctions, prepositional phrases)	The Past, Present, and Future Walked Into a Room: It Was Tense (verb tenses)	Shall We Agree? Fitting Sentences Together Like Puzzle Pieces (agreement, run-ons, splices, double negatives, adjective order, all sorts of nouns and pronouns)	Building a Punctuation Toolkit (punctuation and quotes)	Capitals, Apostrophes, Commas, and More! (capitals, commas, articles, apostrophes, in possessives)
GRADE 5				
UNIT 1	**UNIT 2**	**UNIT 3**	**UNIT 4**	**UNIT 5**
The Anatomy of a Sentence: Understanding Structure (simple, compound, complex sentences, coordinating and subordinating conjunctions, prepositional phrases)	Let's Quote! Using Quotations and Punctuation in Lots of Different Types of Writing (quotations for dialogue, citing text, capitalization, hyphens)	Word Choice for the Win! (all sorts of nouns, pronouns, adjectives, adverbs, and verbs, more agreement, plural possessives)	Choosing and Using Sentences With Purpose (agreement and prepositional phrases, modal auxiliaries, correlative conjunctions)	Edit Like an Artist: Redesigning Sentences (run-ons, fragments, shifts in verb tenses, commas in a series, capitalizing/underlining/italicizing titles of works, comma to offset tag words, direct address)

(Continued)

(Continued)

GRADE 6				
UNIT 1	**UNIT 2**	**UNIT 3**	**UNIT 4**	**UNIT 5**
Sentence Architectures: Designing Clear Communication (simple, compound, complex sentences with prepositional phrases and pronouns)	Marks of Meaning: A Journey Through Punctuation (end marks, commas, parentheses, dashes)	Pronoun Possibilities: Exploring Personal, Possessive, and More	Why So Tense? Exploring Agreement of Verb Tenses	Odds and Ends: Crafting Sentences With Parts of Speech and Intentional Design (synthesize what was learned in the other units to consolidate learning)
GRADE 7				
UNIT 1	**UNIT 2**	**UNIT 3**	**UNIT 4**	**UNIT 5**
From Simple to Compound-Complex: Exploring Sentence Structure (simple, compound, complex, and compound-complex)	Who Are You Calling a Misplaced Modifier? (phrases, clauses, and dangling modifiers)	Advancing Adjectives and Adverbs in Sentence Design (adjectives, adverbs, coordinate adjectives, conjunctive adverbs)	Punctuation in Practice: From Commas to Colons	Common Confusables (Practice with homophones, quotation punctuation, sentence agreement)
GRADE 8				
UNIT 1	**UNIT 2**	**UNIT 3**	**UNIT 4**	**UNIT 5**
Sentence Architectures: Designing Clear Communication (simple, compound, complex, and compound-complex sentences that include intentional use of phrases and clauses)	What on Earth Is a Verbal? (using gerunds, participles, and infinitives)	Geesh, Those Verbs are Moody! (active and passive voice, indicative, imperative, interrogative, and subjunctive mood)	Punctuation Precision: Fine-Tuning Your Writing (commas, ellipses, dashes)	Voice & Mood: The Dynamic Duo of Effective Writing (using verbs in the active and passive voice and the conditional and subjunctive mood for effect)

CHAPTER TWO

Setting Up the Classroom for Grammar Study

English can be weird. It can be understood through thorough thought, though.

—Anonymous

Oh, we love a good playful grammar quote, if you have not noticed! This one is both clever and intuitive. It moves us to want to provide students with time to go deep with grammar learning to build nuanced grammar know-how. To make this possible, we first need a few structures, materials, and routines (see Figure 2.1). In this chapter, we will explore the following:

- building in time for grammar exploration
- setting up the classroom to amplify learning
- using grammar notebooks to think, try, and apply
- maximizing peer power with grammar partnerships
- coaching into grammar growth

Figure 2.1 • The Key Elements to Consider When Setting up Your Grammar Unit

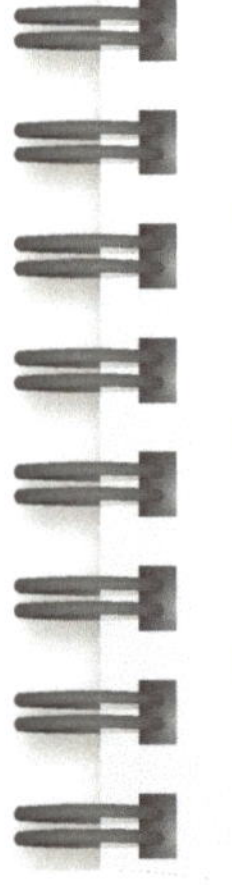

TIPS FOR INTERACTING WITH THIS CHAPTER

- Many of the suggestions in this chapter may already be in place in your classroom. Zoom in on the parts that you may want to spend a little time setting up or refining.
- The environment you create will support the collaborative, creative, and playful tone that is Grammar Study. You can always return to this chapter for ideas as Grammar Study is up and running.
- An organized classroom with solid routines is the framework of bountiful learning. The simpler it all is, the better.

BUILDING IN TIME FOR GRAMMAR EXPLORATION

We get it—teachers' plates are full. Many educators tell us that with all the emphasis on teaching reading, there is no time to teach writing, let alone grammar. But as this book goes to press, we sense a promising shift; more educators and researchers are talking about best practices in writing instruction. Professional conversations on the reading and writing connection are here again! And perhaps most noteworthy is that thought leaders often speak of *efficiency* along with effectiveness. The science of literacy and learning meets the science of cognitive psychology and productivity. The take away? We must see that a school schedule isn't set in indelible ink. Nor is it sacred. Schedules reflect our priorities. We can examine them; we can pick up an eraser, so to speak, and erase what isn't working. We can craft instructional time. We can teach grammar.

Our inspiration for this concept of time crafting is productivity expert Mike Vardy (2020). Ever since we read his book *Timecrafting*, we've become better at aligning our wishes and values to how we spend our time, so that our intentions get our attention. As Vardy says, "True mastery is not in the multitude of things we juggle, but in discerning what deserves our attention and courageously letting go of the rest."

In the classroom, we apply Vardy's principles by reminding ourselves that teachers are problem solvers, creatives by nature, well-suited to this work of molding time. Let's turn now to a few key ideas for integrating Grammar Study into the schedule.

THE GRAMMAR LOVERS' BOOK NOOK

For Teachers: *Grammar Matters* by Lynn Dorfman and Diane Dougherty (2023)

For Students: *Exclamation Mark* by Amy Krouse Rosenthal and Tom Lichtenheld (2022)

Tips for Success: Managing Your Time, Managing Your Mindset

To manage your time and your mindset as you bring grammar exploration into your classroom, consider the following tips.

Managing Your Time

- **Carve out 10 minutes of time three to five times per week**. Write this into a schedule. When it is in a schedule, there is a greater likelihood that Grammar Study happens. In terms of where you schedule grammar, it can be in the writing block but does not have to be. Just like word study, Grammar Study can stand alone in its own space yet will be intentionally integrated into writing down the road a piece.
- **End at 10 minutes (15 minutes, tops):** A hard stop is necessary. If the session feels like it needs more time, extend the lesson into the next scheduled time. Creating connected pockets of grammar learning across time is the key to its efficacy.

- **Lengthen grammar units**. Methods of our granny's grammar instruction included quick bursts of grammar focused worksheets, quizzes, and tests that created the illusion that everyone was able to use grammar accurately. By contrast, grammar units lasting five or six weeks that go deep into related concepts allow for learning over time.

Managing Your Mindset

- **Remember that each interaction with a grammar concept will build grammar know-how, but mastery is not the goal at the get-go.** Be okay with uncertainty and approximation at the end of a grammar session. Trust that grammar is being learned bit by bit over time. Heck, when we think about it, most of us (including Patty but not Tim. Tim knows it all!) are still developing our understanding of grammar usage. Think of it as a snowball effect. Every time that snowball rolls, it collects more snow.
- **Keep it simple:** This approach to grammar instruction frees you from all the correcting and grading of grammar (more on this in a later section of this chapter on grammar coaching). When you see the upcoming lessons, you will notice that there is very little bling. No slide decks, online games, or other froufrou. The materials are simple, straightforward, and low tech. This is intentional.

When timecrafting schedules, one needs to pull out all the creativity (and sometimes calculus) possible. For inspiration or imitation, note a few ways to manipulate the grammar units so that they can fit more easily into your existing schedule.

- Teach grammar 3 to 5 times per week for 10-15 minutes. The unit will take you about eight weeks to complete, but it will still feel cohesive.
- Teach grammar five times per week tucked into your schedule. Tucking this in may mean you might not hold a Grammar Study at the same time, but that will make no difference to the learning.

- If you have a 45-minute writing block, take 10–15 minutes at the end of the of the block to teach grammar. You can do this anywhere from three to five times per week.
- If you have a 90-minute block or more, you are making many other teachers quite jealous of you. In this case, we like to use Grammar Study as a break between reading and writing.
- You may also consider scheduling in cycles by taking away the Monday-Friday constraint and instead designing a six-day cycle and a six-week unit schedule.

Finding time in a school day for anything, including grammar, can be tricky. But with these ideas we hope you have some tools and inspiration to squeeze it in.

SETTING UP THE CLASSROOM TO AMPLIFY LEARNING

Preparing a classroom as a workspace dedicated to learning and productivity will enable you and students to capitalize on every minute of grammar learning time. We like to keep in mind some wisdom from the book *The Space: A Guide for Educators* (Hare & Dillon, 2016). They write, "We are not decorating learning spaces. We are designing them to amplify learning."

They suggest that teachers and students co-design learning spaces to include the following:

1. spaces to collaborate
2. spaces to create
3. spaces to showcase learning
4. spaces for quiet

In the subsections that follow, we'll outline characteristics of these spaces that will support a Grammar Study.

Photo 2.1. A space for collaboration

Spaces to Collaborate

During virtually every grammar learning experience, students will be working in partnerships or trios. The how-to of partnerships comes later in this chapter. So for now, remember, Grammar Study happens out loud in collaboration with classmates. Making sure there is space in the classroom for these collaborations may include the following:

- Designating space around the room for partnership meet-ups
- Designing space to meet as a whole class community for sessions in which everyone collaborates
- Having tables, chairs, beanbags, yoga mats, ottomans, carpets, or other such seating options to provide flexible learning experiences
- Establishing routines for moving among spaces to maximize time and ease of use

Photo 2.2. Students sharing ideas from their grammar notebooks

Spaces for Materials

To make the most of collaboration, students will have spaces with simple materials that they can access as needed. In some cases, you may want to establish routines for getting materials needed and returning them so that they are ready to use at any time. Designate certain areas of your classroom for these materials:

- grammar notebook (more about this in a minute)
- easel and chart paper for whole group experiences
- dry-erase boards and markers
- writing materials such as pens, markers, and colored pencils
- sentence strips
- word cards in baggies (more in Chapter 3 about word cards)
- sticky notes
- clipboards
- scissors

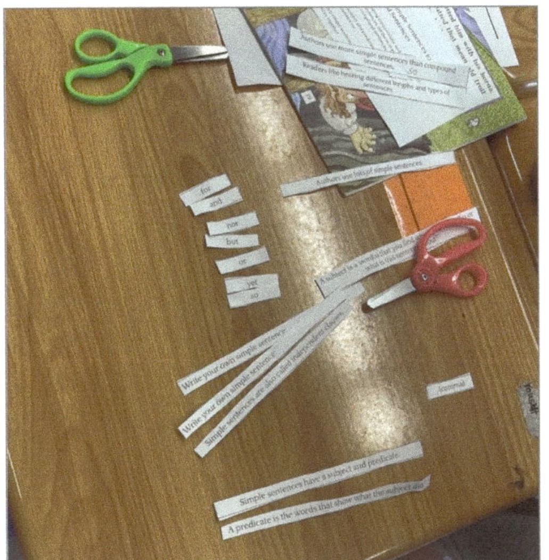

Photo 2.3. Students cut out sentences and conjunctions to create compound sentences.

Spaces to Showcase Learning

Showcasing learning is different from taking student work and displaying it on a board. Showcasing learning is interactive and shows learning progress. Consider showcasing

- Student's questions, hypotheses, and conclusions
- Anchor charts that explicitly teach how to use a particular grammar concept
- Sample pages of strong grammar notebooks
- Photos of grammar learning in action
- Shared reflections of learning and lingering curiosities
- Co-created tools to help transfer grammar learning to writing

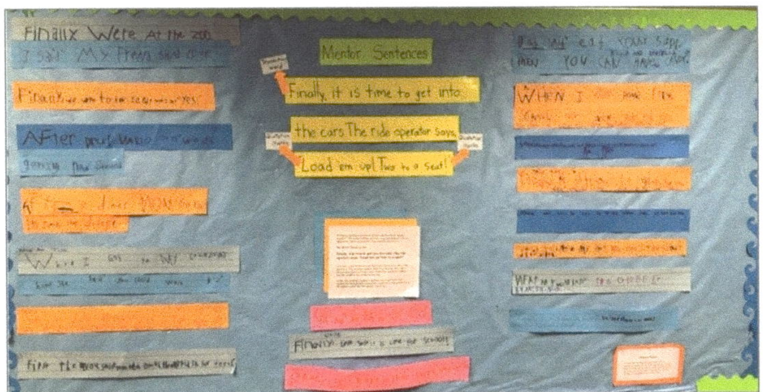

Photo 2.4. Showcase of student learning. Imagine what else you might add to the board from the list.

Spaces for Quiet

Classrooms are often places where busy collaborations are happening, but students also need serene, solo time, free from digital distractions and other noises that tend to creep into some rooms (e.g., chairs scraping on the floor, loud conversation, noise from outside the window or classroom door). Consider using these quiet spaces when

- Students are browsing their grammar notebooks to theorize, draw conclusions, and reflect on learning
- Students are taking part in pre- and post-assessments (see ideas for these in Chapter 8)
- Students are writing independently and using the tools learned from Grammar Study in their own writing

Photo 2.5.
One student using a grammar notebook to jot down what she learned that day.

USING GRAMMAR NOTEBOOKS TO THINK, TRY, AND APPLY

Even in this digital world where a plethora of technology is at our fingertips, we recommend the very simple and powerful paper notebook for Grammar Study. There really is no substitute for it at this juncture. The pages of the notebook become filled with musings, playful experimentations, sketches, notes, reminders, reflections, and more. The most conducive and rich place for this is in a paper notebook.

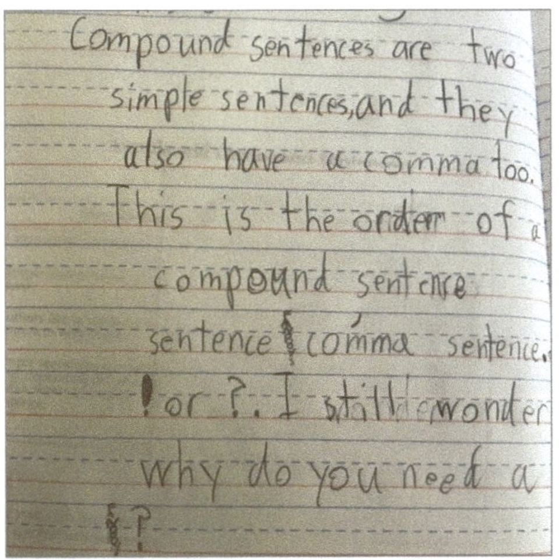

Photo 2.6.
A written reflection of what a student learned and is wondering about

The pages of the notebook become filled with musings, playful experimentations, sketches, notes, reminders, reflections, and more.

Photo 2.7.
Student jotting down the sentence she created from grammar word cards

Following are a few pointers for using the Grammar Notebook:

1. If possible, establish a composition notebook that is dedicated to Grammar Study (more in just a bit on how to introduce the notebooks to students). Some teachers use an entire notebook or a part of a notebook for this purpose. We suggest that this notebook does not leave the classroom because of the potential for it getting lost. It is too precious a resource that is built across (and maybe even beyond) a school year.
2. Choose a place where they can be kept and easily retrieved as needed.

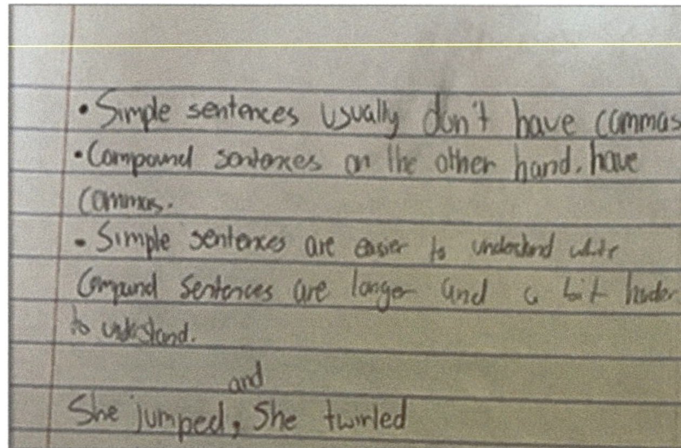

Photo 2.8.
Student jotting down their hypotheses of the differences between simple and compound sentences

3. Think of the notebooks as a thinking space that will eventually become a personal grammar handbook that students can use when writing. Ideally, it is a sidekick for each learner to record learning and build cohesion between Grammar Study times. Students will

   - Jot what they think they know about the grammar topic
   - Jot what they are learning
   - Jot questions about the grammar concepts
   - Write theories when posed with an inquiry experience
   - Jot sentences and other grammar concepts with labels to guide further learning and usage
   - Jot to connect one day's learning to the next
   - Co-create tools with partners or with the class to use during writing time
   - Record or glue in anchor charts that teach about grammar usage
   - Record any other use that students discover and create themselves

We recommend that you also keep your own grammar notebook so that students see how this protected space holds boundless options for building grammar knowledge.

Introducing the Grammar Notebook

When introducing a grammar notebook to students, keep it simple. Here are a few easy steps to follow:

1. Title the notebook, or section of a notebook, with the words Grammar Study Notebook.
2. Write the title of each unit on a sticky note tab, folded page, or tab created in some other way.
3. Ask students to have their notebooks open for each grammar session. Whatever the lesson is that day, remind students (when appropriate) to jot in their notebooks.
4. When ending a unit, students may look over what they wrote and highlight the most important things to remember from that unit.
5. When starting a new unit, create a new tab with the name of the unit.

Photo 2.9.
Students using an anchor chart from their grammar notebook, along with some simple sentences, to write complex sentences

MAXIMIZING PEER POWER WITH GRAMMAR PARTNERSHIPS

Can you remember the absolute silence that grammar instruction required of us as students? I mean, talking was often forbidden. Grammar learning was a solo task of finishing grammar worksheets or diagramming sentences. Yes, we were given directions and lots of well-intended support, but grammar learning was solitary.

Grammar Study is, in contrast, quite social. It's an ongoing, collaborative experience in which learners co-construct an understanding of how standard English grammar works. Partnerships are critical to a true Grammar Study. In the spirit of Grammar Study's conversational vibe, we share how-tos for sustaining partnerships in a Q & A format.

Figure 2.2 • One Classroom's Long-Term Grammar Partnerships

GRAMMAR PARTNERSHIPS	
Jace & Gus	Sophie & Joshua & Alexis
Pedro & Matteo	Noah & Adnan
Skylah & Sadie	Tahn & Lorenzo
Ellie & Avery	Neel & Jan
Estella & Caleb	Mayson & Miina

Long-term partnerships in grammar are ideal. Students can stick together for a while, which may be a unit, a trimester, or even the entire year.

Commonly Asked Questions & Answers

Q: **What are grammar partnerships?**

A: Grammar partnerships are small groups of two or three students who stick together for a while (a unit, a trimester, a year). They build conversations, pose questions, explore answers, and use grammar aloud (see Figure 2.2).

Q: **How do we pair students?**

A: We like to experiment with partnerships a bit. No partnership is set in stone, and it can always be reworked. Ideally, we try to pair students who are conversationally compatible. Do they have a comfortable enough relationship with each other to talk? The partnerships that we have seen *not* work are those who have some tension because of some significant conflict. We have also seen partnerships not work when they both have great affection for one another, including the best of friends and requited crushes. Ultimately, you, the teacher, will make the final decisions on who will be partnered together.

Q: **How do we pair students who have some conversational challenges?**

A: Yes, we will always have students who may be new speakers of English, may have some social challenges, or have expressive language difficulties. These students truly benefit in a group of three. They may not be contributing as much to the conversation, but they are still there for it.

Q: **Why do we have grammar partnerships?**

A: Remember, standard English grammar is most often found in books that we read silently, and hearing grammar used aloud is irreplaceable. When speaking using standard grammar, learners build familiarity and fluidity. Grammar partners co-build a deeper, more complex knowledge of grammar usage.

Photo 2.10.
Grammar partners reflecting with one another on what they have learned thus far in the unit

Q: What do grammar partnerships do?

A: Partnerships use talk as the vehicle for learning. They talk about confusions and questions that arise and seek out answers together. They hypothesize, experiment, and play with grammatical concepts. In one instance, grammar partners were super curious about prepositions and prepositional phrases. They posed the question, "Does a prepositional phrase turn a sentence into a complex sentence?" They searched for examples of sentences with prepositional phrases in them, compared sentences, brought in what they had already learned about the different types of sentences, and concluded all types of sentences can include prepositional phrases.

Partnerships learn together, and they can

- Co-build grammar know-how
- Experiment with a hypothesis
- Explore questions that arise
- Speak using "book" grammar
- Give and receive feedback
- Try a few things out together that have been directly taught
- Reflect on learning and curiosities
- Co-create tools that can be used in writing

Q: When do we use grammar partnerships?

A: Virtually every day of Grammar Study, students work in partnerships or whole group collaborations. The pre- and post-assessment days are the exception. Each lesson in this book suggests times and ways partnerships can work together.

The more partnerships work together, the more grammar learning will deepen and develop. It is an essential part of Grammar Study.

SOME WORDS OVERHEARD IN PARTNERSHIP CONVERSATIONS

"Simple sentences stand on their own—I get it now—that's why they're called independent!" —Shae & Asia

" . . . and, but, or—is that the 'con' in conjunction? Con means 'with' right? Conjunction and commas combine two simple sentences." —Sho & Lukan

"'The bird chirped merrily' could be its own sentence but instead it gets put together with 'the flowers' sentence. I think it makes it sound more descriptive—if there were too many sentences on their own it might sound weird." —Lilian

"Doesn't *while* usually go in the middle of a sentence?" —Leon

"I never thought of a sentence as something that you build, but when it says sentence 'construction' that makes me think about it differently." —Rachelle

Grammar Nerd Alert!

Words like *while* and *because* (subordinating conjunctions) can be used to combine sentences and also begin sentences. When we teach students to begin sentences this way, we are helping them to develop more versatility and complexity in their writing and their ideas.

COACHING INTO GRAMMAR GROWTH

Author created using Imgflip AI tool

Perhaps one of the biggest shifts from traditional grammar instruction to Grammar Study is the role of the teacher. Students are at the center of Grammar Study: their curiosity, their theories, their usage, and their craft. When students are at the center, the teacher's role shifts from the traditional "holder of all grammar knowledge" to one who coaches learners through a variety of experiences. When you put on the coaching hat and support students as they play with grammar, use the following guidelines.

1. **Grammar coaches support exploration.**

   Kelly McGrath (2015), the chief learning officer at Planet3, defines exploration-based learning as "an active learning approach. Students' abilities are dynamically balanced with difficulty level in the system to provide exhilarating and fulfilling learning experiences. The visually and intellectually compelling storylines within the environment challenge each student to leverage their own curiosity and passion to solve complex problems using data and evidence to form arguments and reach conclusions." Grammar *and* exhilarating, fulfilling experiences that leverage curiosity and passion? Yes, please! Here are few tips on how to coach into exploration.

   - **Say as little as possible.** Sometimes we teachers, in our desire to be helpful and supportive, insert ourselves too much into student exploration. When it's time for exploration in grammar, pose some questions and see what happens. It is not necessary to frontload a whole lot of information. Take, for example, a lesson in which students are studying how an author uses punctuation. We want to avoid telling students everything there is to know about punctuation. Instead, we pose a question such as, "What is this author doing with punctuation? What can we learn from how this author uses punctuation?" And then encourage discussion in partnerships. If conversation lags, give it a minute or two. A little wait time to process the experiences is often all students need. If they need a little nudging, let it be just that. A few words to focus or guide such as, "Look at the punctuation here and here. What does this show us about how to use punctuation?"

- **Allow for space and time to grapple with grammar.** When exploration happens, students (ideally) do not find one quick answer or conclusion. We see some productive struggle (the process of effortful learning that develops grit and creative problem solving), and this is super healthy for learning and their brains (MIND Education, 2024). This means that perhaps all of the 10 minutes of a grammar session is students taking on an inquiry stance and not actually coming to a definitive conclusion. In fact, this is the glue that holds Grammar Study together: limiting linear, definitive conclusions about grammar and instead, creating a deep understanding of how grammar and conventions work by engaging with grammar in a variety of ways.

- **Pose questions to encourage student inquiry.** You may find that deliciously deep questions come from student partnerships, such as "Why are there commas in only some complex sentences?" or "Do prepositional phrases make a sentence complex?" Partnerships can explore these questions, which can act as an inquiry question that guides all partnerships in the class. These questions are grammar gold.

- **Formatively assess as students are learning.** Grammar learning happens across time and contexts, so it is best to take the pulse of student learning as it is happening. Teachers consistently ask themselves, "What do these students know, almost know, or not yet know?" and given the answer, they provide experiences to nurture learning growth. Mastery will happen eventually, but the progression to mastery may be an unpredictable road. By coaching to point the way, you will pave a path full of learning for your students. Much more on this in Chapter 8.

2. **Grammar coaches provide some direct instruction.**

Perhaps you are thinking, "What do you mean *some* direct instruction? This is grammar. Shouldn't it all be direct instruction?" Hear us out. We are all for direct, explicit, clear instruction (see a comprehensive collection of explicit lessons in Chapter 6). But we know that teacher instruction cannot be the only grammar experience. We have found that the more kids have the opportunity to play and experiment with what we have taught directly, the more students learn. So, yes, direction and explicit grammar instruction is a necessity in and among a variety of learning experiences.

Effective direct instruction holds some vital characteristics.

- It must be brief. We like our direct instruction to last about 10 minutes or less.
- It must be practical. When we teach directly, we like to include specific steps a student writer can follow to use what we are teaching. (More specifics on this in the next chapter.)
- It must be crystal clear. When we share each step a student writer can follow, we show what each step looks like in action.

3. **Grammar coaches build time for reflection.**

Reflection is the stickiest glue for the brain. Or, as John Dewey (2008) said, "We do not learn from experience. We learn from reflecting on experience." Coaches know this deep down and preserve time to reflect. Use reflection opportunities to

Photo 2.11. Students composing aloud using their grammar notebooks as guidance

- Pause to name what has been learned. Periodically (daily or every few days) take a few minutes to pause and think, "What have we learned so far that is important to hold onto and remember?" List that out, or ask students to talk with a partner (or both!)

  AND

- Assess what has been learned. When we, as grammar coaches, are able to note what students have learned, are starting to learn, and have yet to learn, we adjust our teaching accordingly.

KNITTING THE CHAPTERS TOGETHER

As you are setting up the environment for Grammar Study, there are a few steps you might want to take next:

- Audit your schedule for times to build in Grammar Study
- Gather materials for a grammar workspace
- Designate a grammar notebook space
- Establish grammar partnerships
- Shore up coaching practices
- Read over the suggested scope and sequence for your grade level
- Check out Your Grammar Refresher in Part 4 of this book if you could use a brush up on grammar concepts before you go further!

In the next chapter, we have provided one soup-to-nuts unit on sentences. It will take you step by step through one unit of Grammar Study.

PART TWO

Lessons to Begin

iStock.com/Alona Horkova

CHAPTER THREE

Start With a Study of Sentences

Sentences actively create sense in language. And the business of the study of sentences is grammar.

—David Crystal (2004)

The quotation above drives home the point of this entire chapter and the reason we feel so strongly about the study of sentences being the very first unit that students experience. It is backed by significant research as well. At the time that this book is being written, we are in the wake of the science of reading movement, which is now emphasizing the science of writing for students to grow into fully literate adults. Natalie Wexler and Judith Hochman (Amplify, 2024b) emphasize the importance of sentence construction, combining, and expansion. This is backed by a multitude of studies by Stephen Graham and his colleagues (see, e.g., Graham, 2006; Graham & Hebert, 2011; Graham et al., 2015; Graham et al., 2023) and referenced by thought leaders in *Science of Writing: A Primer* (Amplify, 2024a). All indicators, from both formal and anecdotal studies, point us toward sentences.

But before we continue, let's take a moment to knit the first two chapters to this mega chapter.

- Chapter 1 established a conceptual understanding of a new method of Grammar Study in which students learn grammar through exploring, hypothesizing, talking, experimenting, playing, reflecting, and so much more. This chapter also introduced the phases of a unit, types of experiences found in each phase, and a proposed scope and sequence for Grades 2–8.
- Chapter 2 built a classroom environment to support Grammar Study.

Chapter 3 is designed to make those concepts more concrete and walk you and your students through a progression of lessons. *Keep in mind that the order of these lessons is intentional.* We have titled this unit Essential Sentences.

In this chapter, we will

- Share a unit that moves through three phases: Immersion, Focus Areas, and Transfer (see Chapter 1 for a reminder on this).
- Provide you with guidance and materials to use for each 10- to 15-minute grammar lesson.
- Recommend simple, low tech moves to build understanding of simple, compound, and complex sentences.

We always choose sentences as the very first study. Here's why.

- **Sentences are the containers that hold all parts of speech.** When we study sentences, we are also inextricably studying so much more.
- **Sentences are a wonderful way to nurture curiosity about grammar**. There's so much to know about sentences that students can explore them indefinitely, envisioning new possibilities each time.
- **Sentences are the building blocks of writing.** Research has shown that sentence construction is the most useful grammar instruction (Graham, 2023).

TIPS FOR INTERACTING WITH THIS CHAPTER

- ☐ Take off your teacher hat and partake as a grammar learner. This means that you can use this chapter as a grammar learning experience that will, in turn, become a grammar unit that you will teach your students.
- ☐ Trust us and follow the unit closely. It is intentionally designed in this order and has been classroom tested.
- ☐ If any grammatical concept is confusing, check out Part 4, which will give a clear explanation of that concept.

This chapter and Chapters 4–6 that follow include lessons that span the three phases: Immersion, Focus Areas, and Transfer. Each lesson provided throughout the book employs the following consistent structure for ease of use:

Lesson Title & Type of Lesson: This will include a specific title in relation to the grammatical concept. It will also describe the lesson type, including Explore, Explicit Teaching, and Reflection. There are also days for assessment.

What's Happening: We share a quick summary of the lesson to help you envision what will unfold during those 10–15 minutes.

You Will Need: To make the grammar lesson run smoothly, we suggest materials. This may include something to project, something to photocopy, or an anchor chart. Each chart can be utilized as is or reproduced/modified by you to fit your students.

Lesson Steps: We walk you through how to proceed with the grammar lesson. It may also include background/context that is required for the students, one or more strategies for students to use, and opportunities for additional practice.

Why This Lesson?: This section provides the teacher with a rationale for when and why this lesson might be taught. This rationale can be communicated to students to explain how this particular grammatical concept will fit within their writing (and reading).

Tips: We offer relevant tips and suggestions that either provide a brief refresher about the concept or outline other strategies that might be utilized when teaching it. The tips often refer to Your Grammar Refresher in Part 4 of the book, which provides a greater level of detail (and sample sentences) about the topic.

This chapter contains 19 lessons! A full list of the lesson progressions and their phase and type are available in Table 3.1.

Why 3 Focus Areas? Scan the QR code to learn more.

qrs.ly/q5gkprg

Table 3.1 • Lesson Progression in This Chapter

LESSON NUMBER	PHASE OF THE UNIT	TITLE OF LESSON	TYPE OF LESSON	PAGE NUMBER
1	Immersion	Show What You Know	Pre-Assessment	51
2	Immersion	Sentence Sleuths	Inquiry	53
3	Immersion	Sentence Sleuths Probe Deeper	Inquiry	56
4	Immersion	Sentence Sleuths Side by Side	Reflection	59
5	Deep Learning Focus Area 1	Simple and Compound Sentences	Explore and Hypothesize	62
6	Deep Learning Focus Area 1	FANBOYS	Explicit Teaching	65
7	Deep Learning Focus Area 1	Compound Sentence Construction	Explore and Play	68
8	Deep Learning Focus Area 1	Pause and Ponder	Reflection	71
9	Deep Learning Focus Area 2	Simple? Complex? Make Your Best Guess!	Explore and Hypothesize	73
10	Deep Learning Focus Area 2	Sentence Destroyers	Explicit Teaching	76
11	Deep Learning Focus Area 2	Complex Sentence Construction	Explore and Play	78
12	Deep Learning Focus Area 2	Pause and Ponder	Reflection	82
13	Deep Learning Focus Area 3	Three's a Charm	Explore and Hypothesize	84
14	Deep Learning Focus Area 3	Sentence Types and Comma Rules	Explicit Teaching	87
15	Deep Learning Focus Area 3	Sentence Construction	Explore and Play	89
16	Deep Learning Focus Area 3	Pause and Ponder	Reflection	91
17	Transfer	Grammar Tools	Transfer	94
18	Transfer	Sentence Reno	Transfer	97
19	Transfer	Show What You Know Now	Post-Assessment	99

Ooooooo! This is exciting! You and your students are about to embark on a road yet traveled. Kick this time off with great excitement as you introduce the concept of Grammar Study. To get started, share

What Grammar Study is (a deep dive into how Standard English language works and how we can use it in our writing like an artist)

Why Grammar Study (it is the most effective and, dare we say, fun way to learn grammar)

How Grammar Study works (a mix of grammar inquiry, experimentation, teaching, and conversation built into three parts)

Before we begin, a few things to remember: The lessons in this chapter are intended to be taught in the order we have placed them. The first section of lessons are the Immersion lessons. These lessons are marked by the lightbulb icon and a dark blue heading. The second section of lessons are the Focus Areas. These lessons are marked by the magnifying glass icon and a green heading. The final section of lessons are the Transfer lessons. These lessons are marked by the pencil icon and an orange heading. Future chapters will have lessons that you can mix and match for whatever you'd like to study next, but we recommend proceeding through this chapter in order. Let's begin!

THE GRAMMAR LOVERS' BOOK NOOK

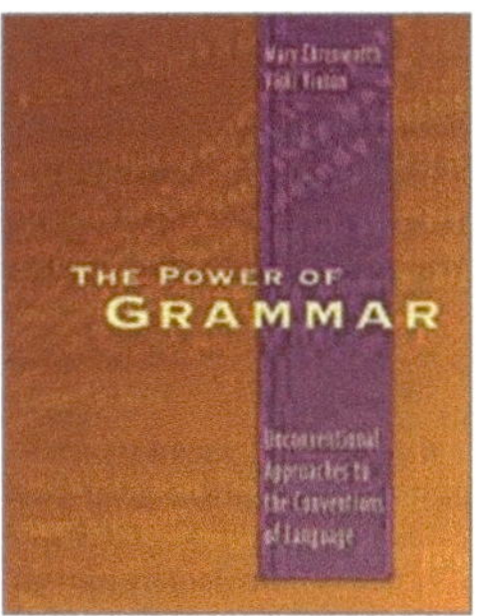

For Teachers: *The Power of Grammar* by Mary Ehrenworth and Vicki Vinton (2005)

For Students: *Punctuation Celebration* by Elsa Knight Bruno (2012)

GRAMMAR STUDY OF THREE TYPES OF SENTENCES

Phase 1 of the Unit: Immersion Lessons

Introducing Students to Sentences

LESSON NUMBER	TITLE OF LESSON	TYPE OF LESSON	PAGE NUMBER
1	Show What You Know	Pre-Assessment	51
2	Sentence Sleuths	Inquiry	53
3	Sentence Sleuths Probe Deeper	Inquiry	56
4	Sentence Sleuths Side by Side	Reflection	59

Lesson 1: Show What You Know

Type: Immersion

WHAT'S HAPPENING

Students will take a pre-assessment (see Handout 3.1) that will show what knowledge they already have about sentence grammar. Even if this pre-assessment feels like you are not gleaning much information, it becomes a rich progress monitoring tool that you give again at the end of the unit. It's thrilling to see the difference in what students know now and then.

YOU WILL NEED

- One copy of the pre-assessment for every student (Handout 3.1)
- A writing utensil for each student

LESSON STEPS

Scan this QR code to access a printable version of Handout 3.1, the pre-assessment sheet.

qrs.ly/lxge09i

1. Distribute one pre-assessment to every student.
2. Read aloud the directions and the sentences.
3. Ask students to write everything they know about each sentence for the next five minutes.

WHY THIS LESSON?

It is always sound to pre-assess to find out what students know, almost know, and do not yet know before instruction. This will help you make plans for the rest of the unit.

TIPS

- While students are taking the assessment, walk around to encourage and support them. They may feel like they don't know much about sentences, and that is quite alright.
- Try not to give too much information about the answers to the assessment. If you do, jot that down as something to revisit in the unit.

HANDOUT 3.1: PRE-ASSESSMENT

Gathering What We Know About Sentences

Below are different types of sentences. Take some time to jot down what you know about these sentences already. This may include the type of sentence, the parts of speech, punctuation, or anything else you know or notice.

Sentence #1: Dolphins use echolocation to navigate and find food.	Sentence #2: Dolphins use echolocation to navigate, and they also use it to find their favorite snacks.
Sentence #3: The birds chirped merrily while the flowers swayed in the breeze.	Sentence #4: As Lily delved deeper into the world of sentences, her grasp of grammar became stronger.

Lesson 2: Sentence Sleuths

Type of Lesson: Inquiry

WHAT'S HAPPENING?

Students will partner up and talk using one or both of the following guiding questions:

- What do you notice about how sentences are built in this text?
- How does this author design sentences or structure sentences?

For most lessons in this book, students will work in pre-established long-term grammar partnerships. Refer to Chapter 2 for more on how to create these collaborative peer partnerships.

Scan this QR code to access a printable version of Handout 3.2, the mentor text worksheet for this lesson.

qrs.ly/6cge09l

YOU WILL NEED

- Long-term grammar partnerships
- Mentor Text #1 (Handout 3.2)
- Grammar notebooks

LESSON STEPS

1. Give partnerships a copy of the mentor text or project the mentor text for all to see. Read the mentor text aloud to the class.
2. Share something you notice about sentence structure. For example, "There are a variety of lengths of sentences."
3. Invite students to get curious about the sentences in the mentor text and to jot down their thoughts in their grammar notebooks.
4. Visit around the room and listen in to what students are saying
5. Wrap up the lesson by sharing out some ideas that groups had. This may sound like, "Some groups noticed that sentences all had punctuation. Others noticed that there were often commas when there were connecting words."

(Continued)

(Continued)

WHY THIS LESSON?

Students begin a study of grammar by first looking at how sentences are used in context and creating theories about different types of sentences.

TIPS

- The hardest part of immersion lessons is knowing that students are theorizing and hypothesizing, not mastering a grammatical concept. Rest assured that this inquiry lays the foundation for discovery and learning later in the unit.
- Students who are new to the concept of Grammar Study are likely to notice the content of the sentences rather than the design. That is something that will become more and more developed over time.
- It may feel odd to end after just a few minutes. Consider this an introductory activity; future lessons will build upon this.

Photo 3.1. A long-term partnership jotting down in their grammar notebooks their theories of three types of sentences

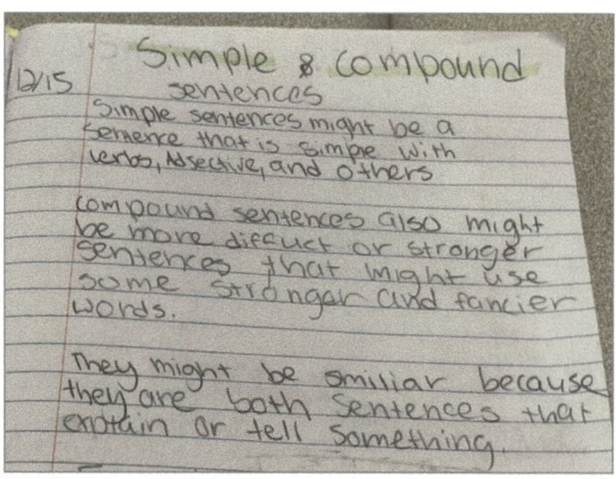

Photo 3.2. One grammar notebook with theories about sentences

HANDOUT 3.2: MENTOR TEXT #1

Talk with your partner and share what you notice about the sentences in Dolphins: Dive In!

Simple sentences are in plain text.

Compound sentences are underlined.

Complex sentences are in italics.

Dolphins: Dive In!

Let's dive into the world of dolphins and have a splash of fun with sentences that'll flip your fins!

Dolphins are oceanic creatures. Dolphins are oceanic mammals, and they're also known for their playful nature. *Although dolphins are oceanic mammals, they manage to turn the waves into their own water playground.*

Their sleek bodies glide through the water effortlessly. *Because their sleek bodies are perfectly adapted to aquatic life, they can glide through waves and underwater.* Dolphins can glide through the water easily, and they can leap into the air with incredible grace.

Even though dolphins live in water, they need to come up for air, which makes their blowhole a unique adaptation. Dolphins use echolocation to navigate and find food. Echolocation is the ability to use playful clicks and whistles that sound like a secret code. Dolphins use echolocation to navigate, and they also use it to find their favorite snacks. *Because dolphins rely on echolocation, they can find tiny fish even in the vast ocean expanse.*

Dolphins use clicks and whistles to chat with pals, and they also use body language to express their feelings. *After observing dolphins, it becomes clear that they have a complex social structure, which adds to their intriguing charm.* They are often very interested in humans. Dolphins often ride the bow waves created by boats, and this seems to be their version of a water roller coaster.

iStock.com/ALesik

Lesson 3: Sentence Sleuths Probe Deeper

Type of Lesson: Inquiry

WHAT'S HAPPENING?

Using a second mentor text, students will partner up and talk about what they are noticing about sentences.

YOU WILL NEED

- Long-term grammar partnerships
- Mentor Text #2 (Handout 3.3)
- Grammar notebooks

Scan this QR code to access a printable version of Handout 3.3, the mentor text worksheet for this lesson.

qrs.ly/mtge09m

LESSON STEPS

1. Give partnerships a copy of the mentor text or project the mentor text for all to see. Read the mentor text aloud.
2. Point out the way simple, compound, and complex sentences are identified in the mentor text (plain text, italics, or underlined).
3. Invite students to get curious about the sentences in the mentor text and to jot down their thoughts in their grammar notebooks.
4. Visit around the room and listen in to what students are saying.
5. Wrap up the lesson by sharing out some ideas that groups had. This may sound like, "Some groups noticed that the simple sentences were usually shorter. I wonder if that is the case all the time. Others noticed that there were joining words in sentences. Some have even called them conjunctions."

WHY THIS LESSON?

After a day of getting curious about sentences, this mentor text focuses less on content and more on structure by identifying types of sentences. Most teachers find that at this point, students are looking for grammatical constructions.

TIPS

- Bring your notebook around with you as you listen to the conversations. Write down what you are hearing to help you refer to this lesson in the future.
- Encourage students to come up with as many hypotheses as they can by simply asking "What else do you notice?"
- Many of the hypotheses will be slightly accurate or inaccurate. That is just what we want. We will test those hypotheses soon.

Photo 3.3. Students getting curious about the three types of sentences using a mentor text

HANDOUT 3.3: MENTOR TEXT #2

Talk with your partner and share what you notice about the sentences in Lily the Grammar Guru.

Simple sentences are in plain text.

Compound sentences are underlined.

Complex sentences are in italics.

Lily the Grammar Guru

In the town of Grammaville, punctuation danced in the streets and verbs mingled at cafes. There lived a girl named Lily. *Lily adored language and often embarked on grammatical adventures that led her to unravel the mysteries of sentences.*

One sunny morning, Lily strolled into the local library, her eyes widening at the sight of shelves lined with books about grammar. *As she browsed, she discovered a dusty book titled "Sentencica: A Grammarian's Tale."* Lily inhaled deeply. She opened the book, and her journey into the world of sentences began.

The opening lines introduced Lily to simple sentences. These held the power to convey concise thoughts. Feeling inspired, she grabbed her notebook and wrote, "The sun shines brightly." This simple sentence warmed her heart. She decided to nickname simple sentences "independent clauses." After all, they are a collection of words that can stand independently on their own.

But Lily's grammatical journey didn't stop there. *She learned about compound sentences, which have two independent clauses joined by a cool collection of words called coordinating conjunctions.* One afternoon, she scribbled, "The birds chirped merrily, and the flowers swayed in the breeze." Lily realized that coordinating conjunctions, such as "and," "but," and "or," were the bridge connecting these clauses.

However, Lily hungered for more complexity in her sentences. *Her reading led her to discover complex sentences, in which an independent clause is accompanied by a dependent clause.* Yes, you guessed it. A dependent clause cannot stand on its own. It needs to lean on something more, well, independent! Eager to experiment, she penned, "*While the rain poured outside, I enjoyed a warm cup of tea.*"

As Lily delved deeper into the world of sentences, her grasp of grammar became stronger. She reveled in constructing writing pieces that combined simple, compound, and complex sentences. Her friends and family marveled at her talent, and they asked for guidance when they stumbled over sentence construction.

Lily's fame as a grammarian spread far and wide as time passed. She hosted workshops in the library, teaching the townspeople the art of crafting sentences. The library, once quiet, became a hub of excitement as people gathered to explore the wonders of grammar.

Lesson 4: Sentence Sleuths Side by Side

Type of Lesson: Inquiry

WHAT'S HAPPENING?

Students will lay the two mentor texts next to each other and look for similarities between the way authors used sentences. This will give them even more opportunity for discovery as well as time to revise their hypotheses.

YOU WILL NEED

- Long-term grammar partnerships
- Both Mentor Texts #1 and #2 from the previous lessons (Handouts 3.2 and 3.3)
- Grammar notebooks

LESSON STEPS

1. Students set the two mentor texts side by side with their grammar notebooks open to the theories they jotted down.
2. Partnerships compare the two pieces and the theories they wrote. Ask, "What else do we notice about the three types of sentences?"
3. Students jot these ideas down in the grammar notebook.
4. Partnerships reflect on the questions, "Have any of my theories/ideas changed? Been confirmed? Sparked questions or wonderings?"
5. Students jot these down as well.

WHY THIS LESSON?

Comparing two different authors' use of sentences conveys a more holistic picture of sentence structure that students can use for multiple text types or genres. One mentor text is a story and the other is informational. Both use the three types of sentences.

(Continued)

(Continued)

TIPS

- You may be starting to see a more detailed way of thinking about sentences. Try not to affirm or correct students at this point. Rather, like scientists do, propose some hypotheses as points of future learning with a "this may or may not be true" stance.
- Eavesdrop on the conversations, jotting down anything notable to inform future lessons.
- This may be day three for you of feeling a bit uncomfortable with this approach to grammar. Breathe. We've got you!

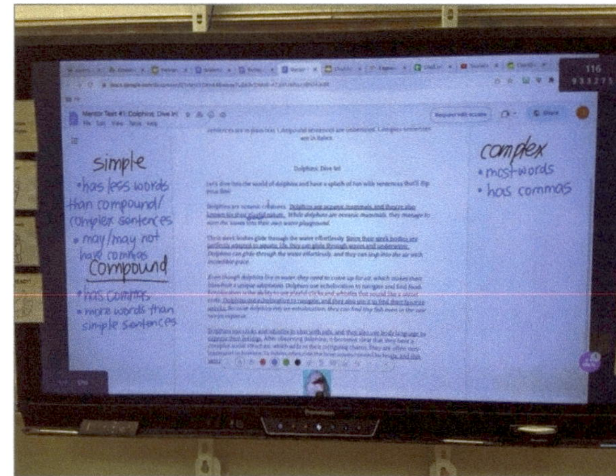

Photo 3.4. A whole class debrief of what students are noticing about different types of sentences when comparing the two mentor texts

DEEP LEARNING

Phase 2 of the Unit: Focus Area Lessons

LESSON NUMBER	TITLE OF LESSON	FOCUS AREA	TYPE OF LESSON	PAGE NUMBER
5	Simple and Compound Sentences	Focus Area 1	Explore and Hypothesize	62
6	FANBOYS	Focus Area 1	Explicit Teaching	65
7	Compound Sentence Construction	Focus Area 1	Explore and Play	68
8	Pause and Ponder	Focus Area 1	Reflection	71
9	Simple? Complex? Make Your Best Guess!	Focus Area 2	Explore and Hypothesize	73
10	Sentence Destroyers	Focus Area 2	Explicit Teaching	76
11	Complex Sentence Construction	Focus Area 2	Explore and Play	78
12	Pause and Ponder	Focus Area 2	Reflection	82
13	Three's a Charm	Focus Area 3	Explore and Hypothesize	84
14	Sentence Types and Comma Rules	Focus Area 3	Explicit Teaching	87
15	Sentence Construction	Focus Area 3	Explore and Play	89
16	Pause and Ponder	Focus Area 3	Reflection	91

Lesson 5: Simple and Compound Sentences

Type of Lesson: Explore and Hypothesize

WHAT'S HAPPENING?

Partnerships will have the opportunity to compare simple and compound sentences. Through this comparison, students will start to notice more specific commonalities between the sentence types and theorize what makes them different.

YOU WILL NEED

- Simple and Compound Sentences, projected or printed for each partnership (Handout 3.4)
- Grammar notebooks
- Long-term grammar partnerships

Scan this QR code to access a printable version of Handout 3.4, Simple and Compound Sentences.

qrs.ly/xcge09u

LESSON STEPS

1. Share the collection of sentences in Handout 3.4, either by providing a printed copy for each partnership or by projecting it. Read aloud the two groups of sentences.
2. Ask partners to compare the two sets of sentences and hypothesize (make their best guess) what makes them simple sentences and compound sentences.
3. Ask partners to explore the relationship between the two types of sentences.
4. Ask partners to jot down these ideas in their grammar notebooks.
5. Walk around and collect their theories and ideas to use for the direct teaching day.

WHY THIS LESSON?

This type of exploration experience prepares students to continue to theorize, even revise, their theories about the differences between simple and compound sentences. Notice the clues found in each sentence to give some direction on some theories that bubble up.

TIPS

- As the grammar coach, gather the theories you are hearing students share. Highlight the ones that are on track and inspire students to dig deeper.
- Resist the temptation to correct their thinking. Similar to a science experiment, this type of experience creates a curiosity that builds the motivation for inquiry.
- Remember, mastery will come in time. This is part of the snowball of learning that will layer upon itself with deep, nuanced understanding of grammar

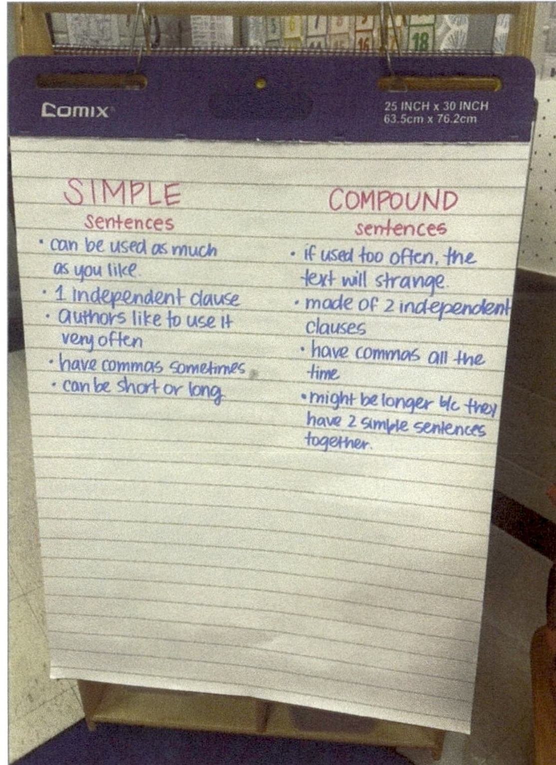

Photo 3.5. This classroom decided to collect the ideas partners came up with as they compared simple and compound sentences.

HANDOUT 3.4: SIMPLE AND COMPOUND SENTENCES

What Do You Notice?

SIMPLE SENTENCES	COMPOUND SENTENCES
I am a simple sentence. Simple sentences are not always short. Authors like to use simple sentences very often. Simple sentences can be short or long, depending on the writer's purpose.	Compound sentences combine two simple sentences, and each simple sentence is also called an independent clause. Authors use compound sentences sometimes, but they are careful not to use them in every sentence. Too many compound sentences make the writing sound strange, and no one wants their writing to sound strange.

Guiding Questions:

Make your own discoveries, of course. But if you are not sure where to start, use these questions to inspire you.

Compare the two types of sentences. What are you noticing?

Can you find simple sentences inside compound sentences? Compound sentences inside simple sentences?

Are simple sentences always shorter than compound sentences?

Lesson 6: FANBOYS

Type of Lesson: Explicit Teaching

WHAT'S HAPPENING?

This is a time to build upon the explore day to confirm, expand, and/or override compound sentence knowledge. You will be introducing FANBOYS, an acronym for coordinating conjunctions:

For

And

Nor

But

Or

Yet

So

This flows like a traditional minilesson where you introduce the purpose of the lesson, model the steps of using coordinating conjunctions to create a compound sentence, and then ask students to try.

YOU WILL NEED

- Long-term grammar partnerships
- The FANBOYS anchor chart on how to create compound sentences (Photo 3.7)
- Two sets of simple sentences (we love to use sentence strips for this)
- Grammar notebooks

LESSON STEPS

1. Introduce the lesson by explaining that you will be sharing steps on how to make compound sentences out of two simple sentences.

(Continued)

(Continued)

2. Tell students that the acronym FANBOYS is a way to remember the words we use to make compound sentences. Read each word in the acronym.
3. Using an anchor chart like the one provided in Photo 3.7, show how to take two simple sentences, choose a FANBOYS, and create a compound sentence. You may use these simple sentences or choose your own to jazz it up a bit: *Dolphins swim. Dolphins breathe air.*
4. Give students a chance, in partnerships, to try using predetermined simple sentences. You may use these simple sentences or write your own for students to try: *There are a number of different types of sentences. Compound sentences are one type of sentence.*
5. Ask students to jot down the compound sentence and label how they made it.

WHY THIS LESSON?

This lesson is the first step in getting super practical on how to create compound sentences. This step-by-step process will be used over and over again throughout the writing life of your students, and having something as accessible and useful as the acronym FANBOYS will be a very useful tool long term.

TIPS

- Make this lesson a super scaffolded experience with compound sentences. Provide the simple sentences for students to more easily create a compound sentence. You will release these scaffolds along the way throughout the unit and the year, but for this lesson, use these supports.
- You may be inclined to include a lesson on independent and dependent clauses. If you do, it may be best to split the lesson into two.

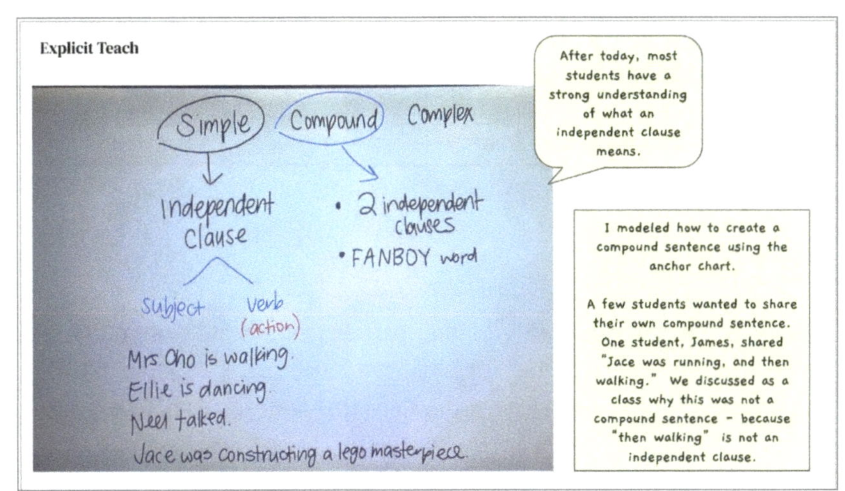

Photo 3.6.
You may want to pause and do what Ms. Cho and Ms. London did to clarify what independent clauses are.

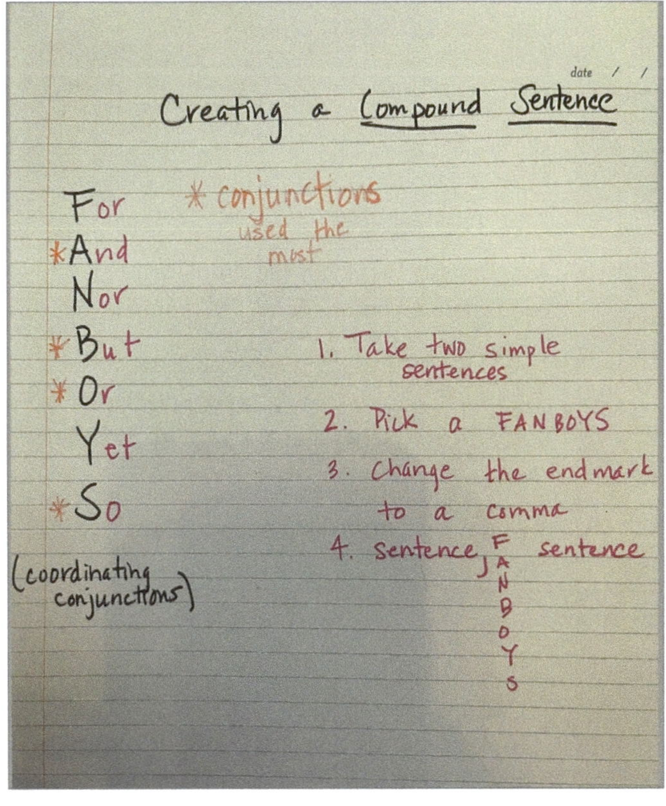

Photo 3.7.
Creating a compound sentence anchor chart

Lesson 7: Compound Sentence Construction

Type of Lesson: Explore and Play

WHAT'S HAPPENING?

Students will work with their grammar partners and create compound sentences using pre-made sentence strips. They will need to refer to the FANBOYS anchor chart (Photo 3.8) to follow the steps that were demonstrated.

YOU WILL NEED

- Long-term grammar partnerships
- Scissors
- Copies of Presto Change-o! for each student (Handout 3.5)
- Grammar notebooks
- Writing utensil

Scan this QR code to access a printable version of Handout 3.5, Presto Change-o!

qrs.ly/4vge0a0

LESSON STEPS

1. Provide each long-term partnership with one copy of the handout.
2. Ask students to cut out the simple sentences, coordinating conjunctions, and comma from the document.
3. Ask students to construct compound sentences using the simple sentences and paste them into their grammar notebook.
4. Ask students to label the parts they made sure were included in a compound sentence.
5. Repeat as time allows.

WHY THIS LESSON?

By using sentence strips of simple sentences, students engage in a scaffolded and creative experience to design sentences using the ingredients needed.

The conversations that happen, along with the example compound sentences that students create, will be foundational for greater independence in sentence design.

TIPS

- Allow for lots of conversation between partners as they construct compound sentences.
- Coach students as they build compound sentences by saying, "Yes, that is a compound sentence (when it is). How do you know?" or "What if I took this word out (take out the subject)? Would it still be a compound sentence? Why or why not?"
- Repeat this lesson as needed to be sure students can create compound sentences from simple sentences.

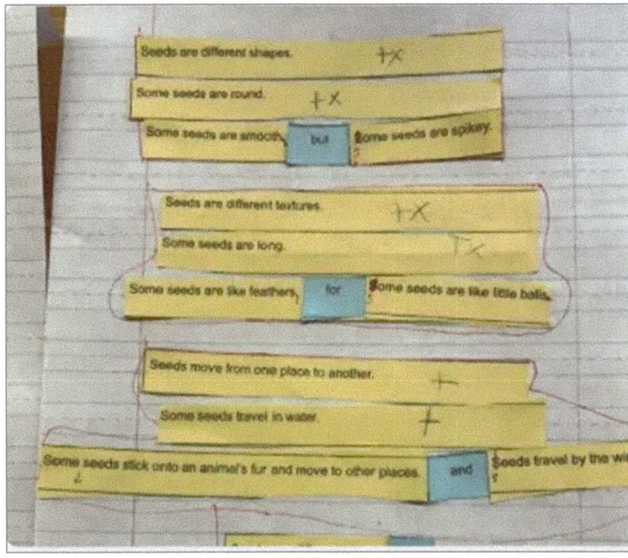

Photo 3.8. One student's grammar notebook

HANDOUT 3.5: PRESTO CHANGE-O!

Using Simple Sentences to Design Compound Sentences

Cut out the sentence strips, the coordinating conjunctions, and the commas. Use what you have cut out to make compound sentences. Paste them in your grammar notebook and list what you did to make the compound sentences.

Example: Simple sentences have a subject and predicate, and authors use more simple sentences than compound sentences.

- Two simple sentences
- Comma connecting the two simple sentences
- FANBOYS link the sentences together

<table>
<tr><td colspan="7">Simple sentences are also called independent clauses.</td></tr>
<tr><td colspan="7">Simple sentences have a subject and a predicate.</td></tr>
<tr><td colspan="7">A subject is a word(s) that you find when you ask, "Who or what is this sentence about?"</td></tr>
<tr><td colspan="7">A predicate is the words that show what the subject did.</td></tr>
<tr><td colspan="7">Authors use lots of simple sentences.</td></tr>
<tr><td colspan="7">Authors use more simple sentences than compound sentences.</td></tr>
<tr><td colspan="7">Readers like hearing different lengths and types of sentences.</td></tr>
<tr><td colspan="7">Write your own simple sentence:</td></tr>
<tr><td colspan="7">Write your own simple sentence:</td></tr>
<tr><td>for</td><td>and</td><td>nor</td><td colspan="4">but</td></tr>
<tr><td>or</td><td>yet</td><td>so</td><td>,
(comma)</td><td>,
(comma)</td><td>,
(comma)</td><td>,
(comma)</td></tr>
</table>

Lesson 8: Pause and Ponder

Type of Lesson: Reflection

WHAT'S HAPPENING?

This is a moment to pause and reflect on everything students have learned thus far. Reflecting on learning helps it stick and also builds opportunities for inquiry. In partnerships, students will look back over the charts, notes, and sentences they have designed to consider what they know about simple and compound sentences and what they are still curious about.

YOU WILL NEED

- Long-term grammar partnerships
- Grammar notebooks
- Chart paper/doc camera/whiteboard or some other place to write the reflections students share

LESSON STEPS

1. Ask long-term partnerships to browse their grammar notebook and point out what they have learned thus far.
2. Ask partnerships to discuss these two questions:
    a. What do you know about simple and compound sentences?
    b. What are you still curious about or wondering about simple and compound sentences?
3. Listen to student conversations, and jot down both learning and wonderings. Share these with the entire class.

WHY THIS LESSON?

Reflection is the stickiest glue for the brain. Or, as John Dewey said, "We don't learn from experience. We learn from reflecting on experience." When students pause and reflect, they solidify their grammar learning. This also sets them up for future inquiry based on the questions they still have.

(Continued)

(Continued)

TIPS

- You decide what to write down and share with the class. Some pretty cool wonderings arise during these conversations such as, "Can a sentence have three independent clauses?" If the discussion is not this elevated, but there is learning going on, that's just fine.
- You may want to take a break from our progression of lessons and use a few questions from the reflection time to guide you in an inquiry about grammar. Some of the best learning happens with spontaneous grammar questions.

Lesson 9: Simple? Complex? Make Your Best Guess!

Type of Lesson: Explore and Hypothesize

WHAT'S HAPPENING?

We are shifting from compound sentences for a bit and moving into complex sentences. Students begin by hypothesizing or theorizing the difference between simple and complex sentences. They do this in partnerships and jot their thoughts down in their grammar notebook.

YOU WILL NEED

- Long-term grammar partnerships
- Simple or complex sentences, projected or printed for each partnership (Handout 3.6)
- Grammar notebooks

Scan the QR to access a printable version Handout 3.6, Simple or Complex Sentences.

qrs.ly/j2ge0a5

LESSON STEPS

1. Share the collection of sentences in the Simple or Complex Sentences handout. Read aloud the two groups of sentences.
2. Ask partners to compare the two sets of sentences and hypothesize (make their best guess) what makes them simple sentences and complex sentences.
3. Ask partners to explore the relationship between the two types of sentences.
4. Ask partners to jot down these ideas in their grammar notebooks.
5. Walk around and collect their theories and ideas to use for the direct teaching day.

(Continued)

(Continued)

WHY THIS LESSON?

This type of exploration experience prepares students to theorize the differences between different types of sentences. Notice the clues found in each sentence to give some direction on some theories that bubble up.

TIPS

- As the grammar coach, gather the theories you are hearing students share. Highlight the ones that are on track and inspire students to dig deeper.
- Resist the temptation to correct their thinking. Similar to a science experiment, this type of experience creates a curiosity that builds the motivation for inquiry.
- Remember, mastery will come in time. This is part of the snowball of learning that will layer upon itself with deep, nuanced understanding of grammar

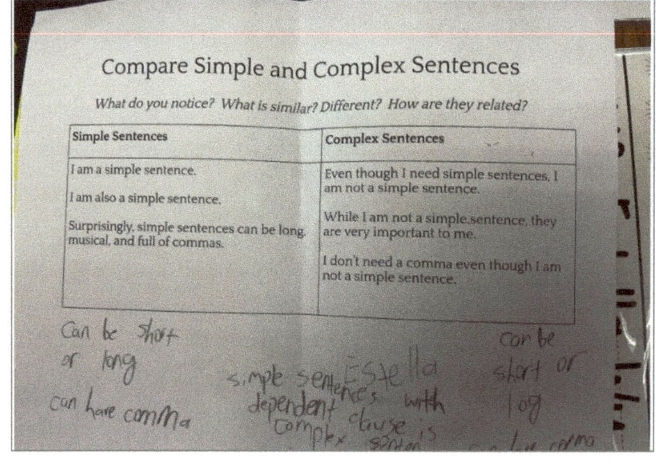

Compare Simple and Complex Sentences

What do you notice? What is similar? Different? How are they related?

Simple Sentences	Complex Sentences
I am a simple sentence. I am also a simple sentence. Surprisingly, simple sentences can be long, musical, and full of commas.	Even though I need simple sentences, I am not a simple sentence. While I am not a simple sentence, they are very important to me. I don't need a comma even though I am not a simple sentence.

Photo 3.9. In this instance, students were able to recognize right away that complex sentences have an independent and dependent clause.

HANDOUT 3.6: SIMPLE AND COMPLEX! WHAT'S THE DIFFERENCE? MAKE YOUR BEST GUESS!

What do you notice? What is similar? Different? How are they related?

SIMPLE SENTENCES	COMPLEX SENTENCES
I am a simple sentence. I am also a simple sentence. Surprisingly, simple sentences can be long, musical, and full of commas.	Even though I need simple sentences, I am not a simple sentence. Although I am not a simple sentence, they are very important to me. I don't need a comma even though I am not a simple sentence.

Lesson 10: Sentence Destroyers

Type of Lesson: Explicit Teaching

WHAT'S HAPPENING?

This is a time to build upon the Explore day to confirm, expand, and/or override complex sentence knowledge. You will be introducing "sentence destroyers," which is a nickname for subordinating conjunctions: after, although, as, when, while, unless, because, before, if, since. This flows like a traditional mini-lesson in which you introduce the purpose of the lesson, model the steps of using subordinating conjunctions to create a complex sentence, and then ask students to try.

YOU WILL NEED

- The anchor chart on how to create complex sentences (see Photo 3.10)
- Two sets of simple sentences (we love to use sentence strips for this)
- Grammar notebooks
- Long-term grammar partnerships

LESSON STEPS

1. Introduce the lesson by explaining that you will be sharing steps on how to make complex sentences out of two simple sentences
2. Using an anchor chart like the one shown in Photo 3.10, show how to take two simple sentences, choose a "sentence destroyer," and create two different complex sentences. You may use these simple sentences or choose your own to jazz it up a bit: *It was late March. Spring was in the air. Because it was late March, spring was in the air. Spring was in the air while it was late March.*
3. Give students a chance, in long-term partnerships, to try using predetermined simple sentences. You may use these simple sentences or write your own for students to try: *There are different types of sentences. Authors use them all when they write.*
4. Ask students to jot down the complex sentence and label how they made it.

WHY THIS LESSON?

This lesson is the first step in getting super practical on the "how-to" of complex sentences. This step-by-step will be used over and over again throughout students' writing lives, and having something as accessible and useful as the concept of sentence destroyers will be an asset in the long term.

TIPS

- Make this lesson a super scaffolded experience with complex sentences. Provide simple sentences for students to more easily create two complex sentences. You will release these scaffolds along the way throughout the unit and the year, but for this lesson, use these supports.
- Wondering why we call them "sentence destroyers"? Because when you add them to an independent clause, they turn it into a dependent clause. Essentially, they destroy sentences.

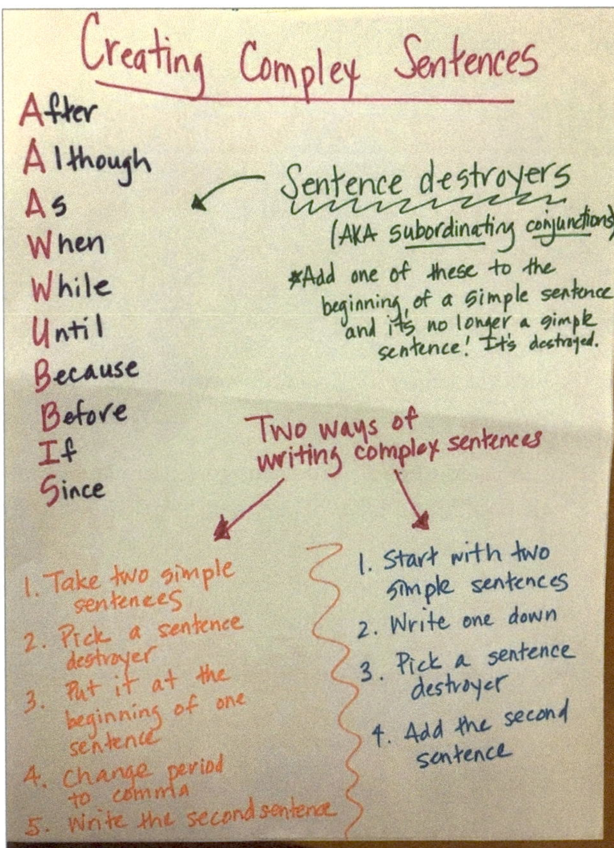

Photo 3.10. Anchor chart for writing two different types of complex sentences

Lesson 11: Complex Sentence Construction

Type of Lesson: Explore and Play

WHAT'S HAPPENING?

First, students will cut out the word cards. Students will work with their grammar partners and create complex sentences using word cards. They will need to refer to the complex sentence anchor chart (Photo 3.10) to follow the steps that you demonstrated.

YOU WILL NEED

- Long-term grammar partnerships
- Scissors for each student/partnership
- Copies of the word cards (Handout 3.7)
- Envelopes or baggies
- Crayons or markers
- Grammar notebooks
- Writing utensil

Scan the QR code to access a printable version of Handout 3.7, full-size versions of the word cards.

qrs.ly/ijge0a9

LESSON STEPS

1. Provide a copy of the word cards handout to each partnership.
2. Ask them to pick a color duo in either crayon, marker, or both. Color the back of the word cards in this duo. This will help when (not if) cards land on the ground and they are not sure which group to return them to.
3. Direct students to cut out the word cards.
4. Then ask them to
    - Collect the sentence destroyers in a pile
    - Create a complex sentence using the word cards
    - Write the sentence down in their notebook and label the parts

5. Repeat as time allows.
6. Give each group an envelope or baggie to store their word cards.

WHY THIS LESSON?

By using word cards, students engage in a scaffolded and creative experience to design sentences using the ingredients needed. The conversations that happen, along with the example of complex sentences that students create, will be foundational for greater independence in sentence design. These word cards can be used throughout the school year.

TIPS

- Stretch this lesson over two to three days. Cutting out the cards may take a while. We promise it is worth the time investment. You can use these all year long.
- Coach students as they build complex sentences by saying, "Yes, that is a complex sentence (when it is). How do you know?" or "What if I took this word out (take out the subject)? Would it still be a complex sentence? Why or why not?"
- The sheer number of words may be overwhelming for some students. Cut out just the first few pages to get started. Later on, add more words to the bag.

Photo 3.11. Different groups of students working on building sentences with word cards

HANDOUT 3.7: WORD CARDS

snake	chair	day
cat	parents	mice
shelter	sister	brother
trait	animal	photo
bird	feather	forest
park	food	night

ing	ed	st
s	ful	ly
less	er	est
or	ness	ist
ion	ment	able
ible	en	ies

. (period)		?	!	
, (comma)		' (apostrophe)	"	"
;		:	-	
(	)	of	in	
above		under	around	
on		behind	through	

eat	sleep	dance
is	are	run
cry	study	learn
write	wash	look
jump	keep	catch
taste	love	agree
am	are	was
were	be	have

them	theirs	many
whose	yourself	this
whom	our	ourselves
mine	neither	either
myself	nobody	no one
anything	everyone	everything

he	she	they
we	it	them
us	you	our
ours	I	Who
whom	someone	anyone
anything	anyone	another

jealous	beautiful	adorable
lazy	sleepy	joyful
gigantic	colorful	sad
happily	quickly	sleepily
gladly	slowly	playfully
mysteriously	generously	peacefully

and	but	or
nor	for	so
yet	beneath	beyond
until	into	from
from	up	down
a	an	the
after	although	as
when	while	until
because	before	if
since	. (period)	, (comma)

Lesson 12: Pause and Ponder

Type of Lesson: Reflection

WHAT'S HAPPENING?

This is a moment to pause and look back over everything that you have learned thus far. Reflecting on learning helps it stick and also builds opportunities for inquiry. In partnerships, students will look back over the charts, notes, and sentences they have designed to consider what they know about simple and complex sentences and what they are still curious about.

YOU WILL NEED

- Long-term grammar partnerships
- Grammar notebooks
- Chart paper/doc camera/whiteboard or some other way to record the class reflections

LESSON STEPS

1. Ask partnerships to browse their grammar notebook and point out what they have learned thus far.
2. Ask partnerships to discuss these two questions:
   a. What do you know about simple and complex sentences?
   b. What are you still curious about or wondering about simple and complex sentences?
3. Listen to student conversations and jot down both learning and wonderings. Share these with the entire class.

WHY THIS LESSON?

You've read this reasoning before. Reflection is the stickiest glue for the brain. When students pause and reflect, they solidify their grammar learning. This also sets up for future inquiry based on the questions we still have.

TIPS

- You decide what to write down and share with the class. Some pretty cool wonderings arise during these conversations such as, "Does a sentence become a complex sentence if you add a prepositional phrase?" If the discussion is not this elevated, but there is learning going on, that's just fine.

- You may want to take a break from the progression of lessons in this chapter and use a few questions from the reflection time to guide you in an inquiry about grammar. Some of the best learning happens with spontaneous grammar questions. The question above helped a fifth-grade class discover that prepositional phrases could be found in all types of sentences.

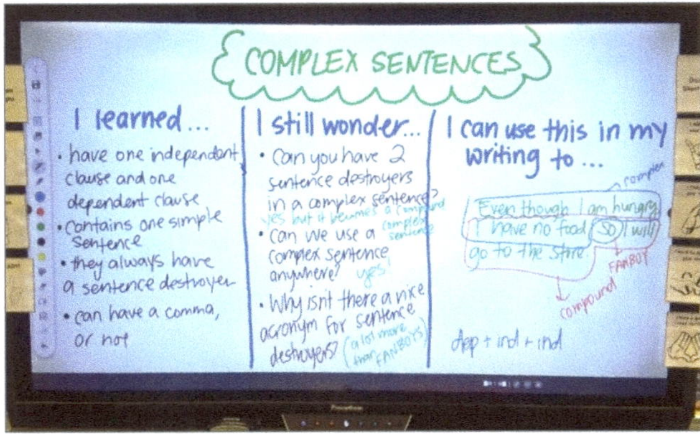

Photo 3.12. One classroom's reflections about sentences. These reflections were collected and revisited across the unit.

Lesson 13: Three's a Charm

Type of Lesson: Explore and Hypothesize

WHAT'S HAPPENING?

To round out the unit, it is helpful to study the three types of sentences together to truly drive home the relationship between them. Students begin by comparing simple, compound, and complex sentences. They do this in partnerships and jot their thoughts down in their grammar notebook.

YOU WILL NEED

- Three's a Charm, projected or printed for each partnership (Handout 3.8)
- Grammar notebooks
- Long-term grammar partnerships

Scan this QR code to access a printable version of Handout 3.8, Three's a Charm.

qrs.ly/llge0ad

LESSON STEPS

1. Share the Three's a Charm handout with the collection of sentences. Read aloud the three groups of sentences.
2. Ask partners to compare the three sets of sentences and note the differences and similarities.
3. Ask partners to jot down these ideas in their grammar notebooks.
4. Walk around and support this work.

WHY THIS LESSON?

This type of exploration experience sets students up to be able to build even deeper knowledge of the relationship between the three types of sentences.

TIPS

- As the grammar coach, remind students of what they have learned thus far. Encourage students to look back in their notebooks or anchor charts as needed.

- You will witness knowledge of the three types of sentences begin to coalesce.
- Encourage students to wonder. Their thinking will be deeper and more nuanced in this part of the unit.

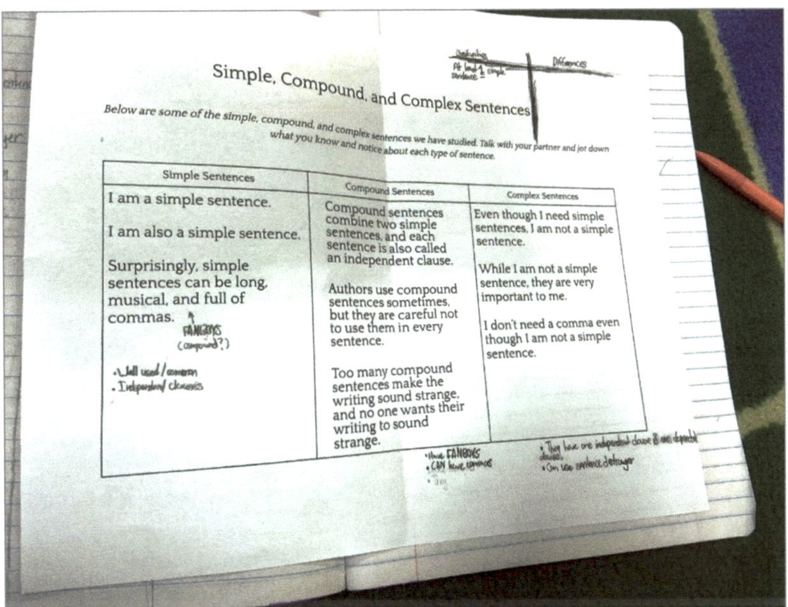

Photo 3.13.
Jennifer Cho, the teacher, shared that Student A and Student E thought this sentence was a compound sentence due to the "and" (FANBOYS word). They discussed what a compound sentence has—two independent clauses and a FANBOYS word—and realized that this is not a compound sentence. However, they realized that simple sentences can use FANBOYS words, too! They also noticed that all three sentence types contain at least one simple sentence.

HANDOUT 3.8: THREE'S A CHARM

Simple, Compound, and Complex Sentences

Below are some of the simple, compound, and complex sentences we have studied. Talk with your partner and jot down what you know and notice about each type of sentence.

SIMPLE SENTENCES	COMPOUND SENTENCES	COMPLEX SENTENCES
I am a simple sentence. I am also a simple sentence. Surprisingly, simple sentences can be long, musical, and full of commas.	Compound sentences combine two simple sentences, and each simple sentence is also called an independent clause. Authors use compound sentences sometimes, but they are careful not to use them in every sentence. Too many compound sentences make the writing sound strange, and no one wants their writing to sound strange.	Even though I need simple sentences, I am not a simple sentence. Although I am not a simple sentence, they are very important to me. I don't need a comma even though I am not a simple sentence.

Lesson 14: Sentence Types and Comma Rules

Type of Lesson: Explicit Teaching

WHAT'S HAPPENING?

Simple, compound, and complex sentences have different comma rules. This lesson makes them even more clear.

YOU WILL NEED

- Long-term grammar partnerships
- The anchor chart on when to use commas when combining sentences (see an example in Photo 3.14)
- Two sets of simple sentences (we love to use sentence strips for this)
- Grammar notebooks

LESSON STEPS

1. Introduce the lesson by explaining that you will be sharing steps on where to add commas when combining simple sentences.
2. Using an anchor chart like the one shown in Photo 3.14, show when and where to include a comma. Use the sample sentences provided or your own sentences that may be more relevant to students.
3. Give students a chance, in partnerships, to try using predetermined simple sentences. You may use these simple sentences or write your own for students to try:

   The piano played quietly in the background. The crowd entered the theater.
4. Ask students to jot down three different combinations of the two sentences and mark on each sentence where the comma is inserted.

WHY THIS LESSON?

The use of commas in the three types of sentences can be tricky, especially because these rules are not always followed in published books. The trick in knowing where to put commas is to look at the dependent and independent clauses.

(Continued)

(Continued)

TIPS

- Students may be ready to make up their own simple sentences at this point. If it feels right, give them a chance to try that. They always have the option of using the sentences we give them if it is too difficult.
- If you are a second-grade teacher, we can use this lesson but not expect mastery yet. The use of complex sentences is a standard in third grade.

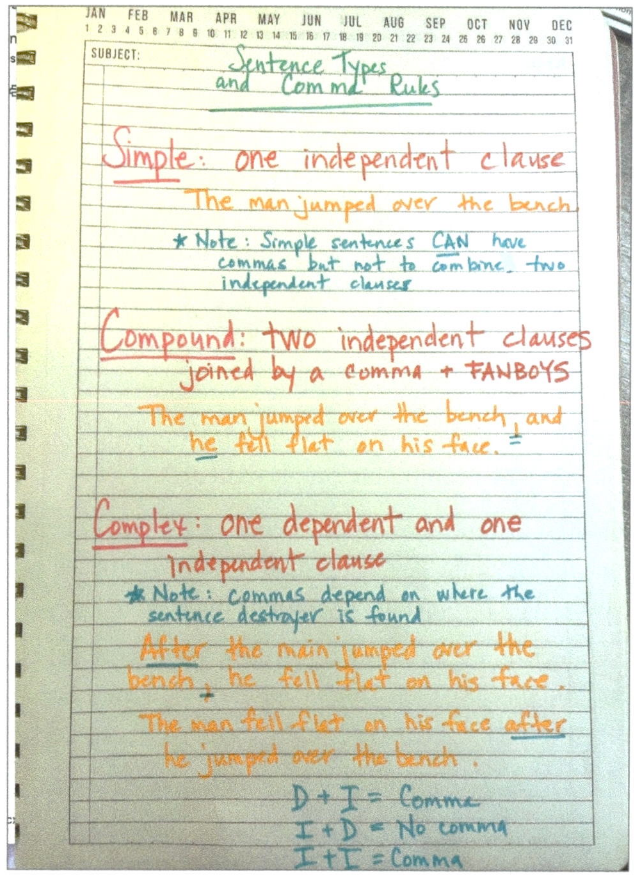

Photo 3.14. An anchor chart that helped students learn where to add commas

Lesson 15: Sentence Construction

Type of Lesson: Explore and Play

WHAT'S HAPPENING?

The word cards are put back to work here! Partnerships will build simple sentences and then turn them into either compound or complex sentences. Ideally, they will try all three designs of compound and complex sentences.

YOU WILL NEED

- Word cards
- Grammar notebooks
- Anchor charts that students can refer to

LESSON STEPS

1. Ask students to organize the word cards so that the subordinating and coordinating conjunctions are ready to be used.
2. Ask partners to create simple sentences that relate to each other.
3. Ask partners to redesign these sentences into compound and/or complex sentences.

WHY THIS LESSON?

Designing simple, compound, and complex sentences together can boost the skills that will be needed when students are revising their writing for sentence variety.

TIPS

- This is a great experience to repeat for a day or two.
- If the word cards seem like they have too many moving parts, you can use sentences from previous lessons or from the mentor text.

(Continued)

(Continued)

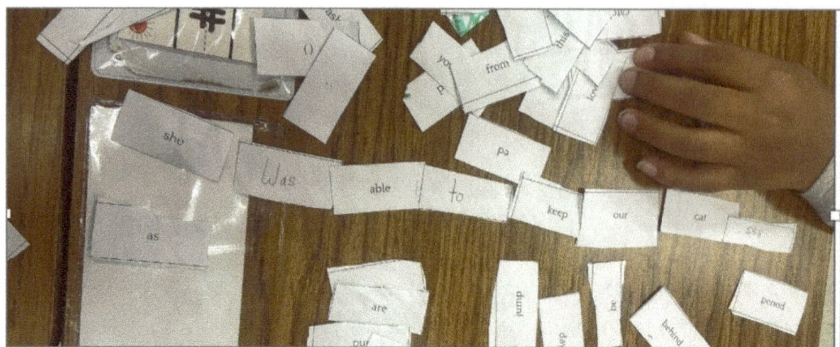

Photo 3.15.
One of the simple sentences students made

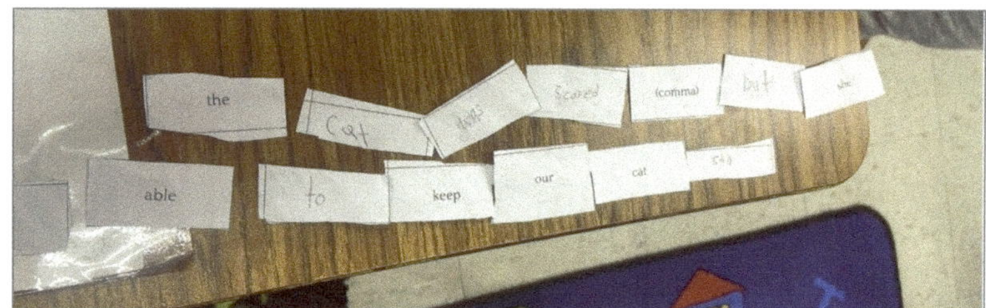

Photo 3.16.
The same students turned that simple sentence into a compound sentence.

Lesson 16: Pause and Ponder

Type of Lesson: Reflection

WHAT'S HAPPENING?

This lesson offers a moment to pause and look back over everything that has been learned thus far, which at this point is significant. In partnerships, students will look back over the charts, notes, and sentences they have designed to consider what they know about simple, compound, and complex sentences and what they are still curious about.

YOU WILL NEED

- Long-term grammar partnerships
- Grammar notebooks
- Chart paper/doc camera/whiteboard or some other way to record the reflections and questions

LESSON STEPS

1. Ask partnerships to browse their grammar notebook and point out what they have learned thus far.
2. Ask partnerships to discuss these two questions:
    a. What do you know about simple, compound, and complex sentences?
    b. What are you still curious about or wondering about simple, compound, and complex sentences?
3. Listen to student conversations and jot down both learning and wonderings. Share these with the entire class.

WHY THIS LESSON?

Pausing and reflecting is essential in helping grammar stick. You will be embarking on some transfer lessons next, and this will give you a sense whether students are ready to move on or need more time.

(Continued)

(Continued)

TIPS

- You decide what to write down and share with the class. Some pretty cool wonderings arise during these conversations such as, "What other types of sentences are there besides these three?"
- You may want to take a break from our progression of lessons and use a few questions from the reflection time to guide you in an inquiry about grammar. Some of the best learning happens with spontaneous grammar questions.

TRANSFER

Phase 3 of the Unit: Transfer Lessons

LESSON NUMBER	TITLE OF LESSON	TYPE OF LESSON	PAGE NUMBER
17	Grammar Tools	Transfer	94
18	Sentence Reno	Transfer	97
19	Show What You Know Now	Post-Assessment	99

Lesson 17: Grammar Tools

Type of Lesson: Transfer

WHAT'S HAPPENING?

This is the final phase of the unit, when students will consolidate what they have learned and create a resource to use in their writing. Co-create a tool that will help you all remember when and/or how to use the three types of sentences. This will take longer than one session. See page 95 for a sample tool that one class created.

YOU WILL NEED

- Grammar notebooks
- A place to create the tool digitally or on paper

LESSON STEPS

1. Decide on the document that you will create as a class: a shared doc, a chart, or some other type of resource that can be used when writing. The tool will be something used throughout the rest of the school year when students write.
2. Make this resource together. Students can suggest what to include in this tool while you gather and organize this information.
3. Pinpoint when it can be used, such as when editing a piece of writing or in other subject areas when they write.

WHY THIS LESSON?

This lesson will be worth its weight in gold. What you create here will be used over and over throughout writing assignments in writing instruction and beyond. No pressure, though; it can always be revisited and revised as needed. Think of it as a living document.

TIPS

- This tool may be on an anchor chart, a document, or some other resource that can be shared and used whenever students write.
- If you are in a self-contained classroom, be sure to use the tool in other subject areas. If you are in a departmentalized setting, be sure to share the tool with content area teachers. This way, students can improve their writing in all areas.

SAMPLE TOOL

SIMPLE SENTENCES

We can use this when

- We are making a list
- We are writing one sentence
- We used too many compound/complex sentences
- We want to explain or describe something

A simple sentence

- Can have a comma, lots of commas, or no commas at all
- Must make sense by itself
- Is one independent clause (a group of words that makes sense by itself)
- Can be short or long
- Can have a FANBOYS word (for, and, nor, but, or, yet, so)

COMPOUND SENTENCES

We can use this when

- We want to support our thesis with a detail(s)
- We want to put a lot of information into one sentence
- We want to combine two simple sentences

(Continued)

(Continued)

- We want to explain something in detail
- We have too many simple sentences and we want to make our writing fancy

A compound sentence

- Has two independent clauses (simple sentences)
- Includes a FANBOYS word in between two simple sentences
- Has a comma before the FANBOYS word

COMPLEX SENTENCES

We can use this when

- We want to provide multiple details in one sentence
- We want to explain our thinking
- We want to compare/contrast and explain ("although, while . . .")
- We want to show cause and effect ("because...")

A complex sentence

- Combines one independent clause and one dependent clause (a group of words that doesn't make sense on its own)
- Has a sentence destroyer (after, although, as, when, while, until, because, before, since) either at the beginning of the sentence or in between the two clauses
- May or may not have a comma, depending on the order of the clauses
    - Independent + Dependent = No comma
    - Dependent + Independent = Comma*

*If there is a comma, it goes after the dependent clause and before the independent clause.

Lesson 18: Sentence Reno

Type of Lesson: Transfer

WHAT'S HAPPENING?

Students go back to writing they have already completed and revise their sentences using the tool you co-created.

YOU WILL NEED

- Student writing sample
- Class tool created in Lesson 17

LESSON STEPS

1. Ask students to select a piece of their past writing (can be digital or hard copy). For example, they may use something in their writer's notebooks/journals, previously completed writing pieces, or writing that is in progress.
2. Direct students to keep the class-created tool nearby.
3. Ask students to revise their writing using the class tool. Encourage them to look closely at the sentences they have written and combine, break apart, or revise the sentences to include simple, compound, and complex sentences.

WHY THIS LESSON?

This is allowing students to dip a toe into how they will use the tool in the future. By test-driving this tool, you will be able to revise it if needed.

TIPS

- This will help improve writing but not perfect writing. Expect that student writing will still contain some grammatical mishaps. Focus just on sentence construction.
- If this is the first time they have revised writing based on sentences, some students may need extra support in using this tool. You can extend this lesson over a few days.

(Continued)

(Continued)

Photo 3.17. Students are looking at their opinion writing drafts while having their toolkits open to take stock of what kinds of sentences they used and to revise sentences as needed

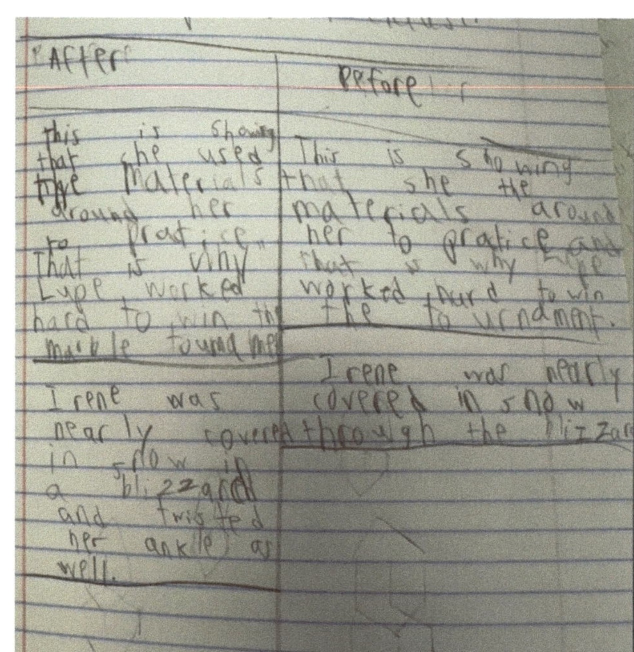

Photo 3.18.
Student listed some sentences from his writing that he had and what he changed them to. *Note from the teachers*: This activity was great for students to reflect and look back on their writing. It was interesting to notice that some students were focused on whether their sentences made sense or not, some were taking stock of what kind of sentences they had and tried to diversify, and some were focused on whether their punctuation was correct.

Lesson 19: Show What You Know Now

Type of Lesson: Post-Assessment

WHAT'S HAPPENING?

Students will go back to the pre-assessment that they took at the beginning of this unit and revisit it with the knowledge they have gained.

YOU WILL NEED

- Previously completed pre-assessments
- A writing utensil that is different from the one that was originally used
- Optional: Sticky notes for students to write their revised answers on

LESSON STEPS

1. Give students their previously completed pre-assessment.
2. Give students a different color writing utensil than was first used (or change the font color if done digitally).
3. Ask students to take the assessment again, describing the sentences with their current knowledge.

WHY THIS LESSON?

This is the best feeling for everyone involved. Students will see the growth they have made and you will too! You will all see just how much grammar learning has happened throughout the unit. It is a chance to celebrate!

TIPS

- Bask in a job well done!

(Continued)

(Continued)

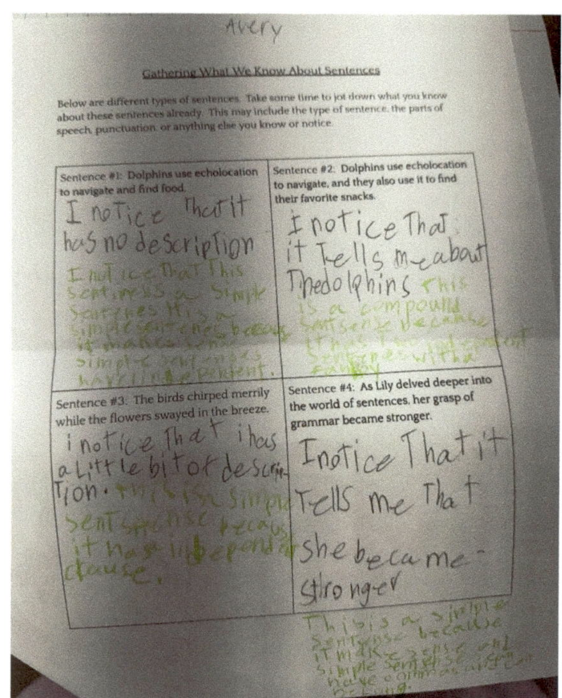

Photo 3.19. Notice the growth from the beginning of the unit!

Gathering What We Know About Sentences

Below are different types of sentences. Take some time to jot down what you know about these sentences already. This may include the type of sentence, the parts of speech, punctuation, or anything else you know or notice.

Sentence #1: Dolphins use echolocation to navigate and find food.	Sentence #2: Dolphins use echolocation to navigate, and they also use it to find their favorite snacks.
I notice the punctuation, the word Dolphins, navigate, and food, and echolocation. I notice how they tell us how Dolphin's are able to find food. I notice how this sentence is a simple sentence. I also notice that they put a capital letter on the word Dolphin.	I notice the punctuation, and how the use echolocation to help them find there food. I notice this sentence is a compound sentence and how there is a comma and a FANBOY words
Sentence #3: The birds chirped merrily while the flowers swayed in the breeze.	**Sentence #4: As Lily delved deeper into the world of sentences, her grasp of grammar became stronger.**
One of a few things I notice is the punctuation and swayed. I notice how this is a simple sentence and how there is animals.	I notice the grammar, and delved deeper. I also notice the word grasp. I notice the new charachter they put into the story. I notice this is a complex sentence

Photo 3.20. Students were amazed to see how much they learned

KNITTING THE CHAPTERS TOGETHER

How did it go? We are hoping that you saw how your classroom setup (Chapter 2) supports the Grammar Study in this chapter. We are also hoping you (and the students) have a new vision of what grammar instruction can look, sound, and feel like. Now that you have completed the first unit of Grammar Study, use the rest of the book to choose your own adventure. The chapters offer lessons and resources you can mix and match for whatever you'd like to study next.

PART THREE

Lessons for the Journey

Immersion, Exploration, Transfer

iStock.com/Alona Horkova

CHAPTER FOUR

Immersion Lessons

Mentor Texts and Tips

Doesn't it help to scrutinize that already assembled bookshelf display at Ikea before going home to those often-confusing instructions?

—Rebecca Alber (2014)

The image of examining a constructed bookshelf offers a clear example of how people of all ages learn through imitation and observation. When learning writing, students benefit more from studying well-crafted texts than from simply following a set of rules, guidelines, or directions. By observing strong writing and deconstructing "already assembled" texts, students learn how to construct their own sentences and texts.

As we have seen in previous chapters, the Immersion phase of a unit plays a critical role in building grammatical curiosity and knowledge by exposing students to language and concepts using an inquiry-based approach. Immersion provides multiple opportunities for students to examine grammar authentically in the context of writing. By utilizing carefully selected mentor texts, teachers can provide students with a window into how grammar functions in real-world contexts.

In grammar instruction, we also want to ensure that we use different text types (narrative, informational, etc.) so students can examine sentence structures, word choice, punctuation, and other grammatical concepts within these texts. By exploring different text types and the concepts contained and modeled within them, students develop a deep understanding of grammar and how grammatical concepts look across different genres of writing. This chapter, which focuses on the Immersion phase of the Grammar Study unit, provides the following:

- Four multi-use mentor texts and a teacher reference guide for each text
- A mentor text and companion lesson for each of the following topics: nouns and verbs, adjectives and adverbs, pronouns, commas
- An overview of how to create your own mentor text

Think about using this section of the book like you use a text when you plan shared reading activities. Because each mentor text addresses multiple grammatical concepts, you can utilize each text in multiple ways.

The lessons that follow use the same structure introduced in Chapter 3 and provide a primary use for the mentor text as outlined in the lesson title; however, each lesson plan contains additional ways to utilize the mentor text. Finally, following each mentor text, there is an overview and analysis of how the different grammatical concepts are utilized within the text. Each topic is also covered in detail in Part 4: Your Grammar Refresher.

THE GRAMMAR LOVERS' BOOK NOOK

For Teachers: *Grammar Keepers* by Gretchen Bernabei (2015)

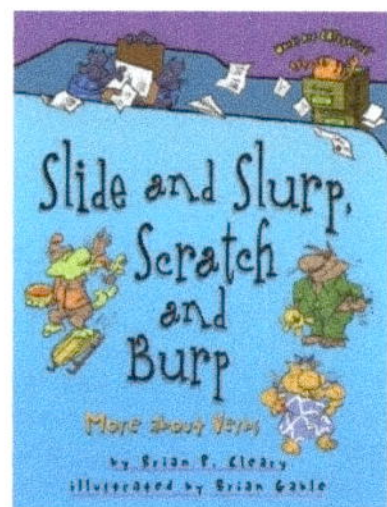

For Students: *Slide and Slurp, Scratch and Burp* by Brian Cleary (2007) (and any books from the Words are CATegorical series)

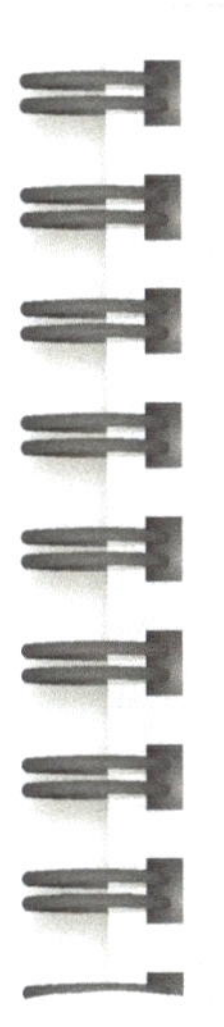

TIPS FOR INTERACTING WITH THIS CHAPTER

- Use the lessons and texts as ready-to-go Immersion activities.
- Adapt the lessons to meet your students' needs. If students have already mastered the skill of the identified lesson for the text, create your own lesson with a different focus. For example, if you notice that students need support with punctuating dialogue, narrow your lens of focus with the text to an inquiry of how dialogue is utilized. Continue to reuse the text for different purposes.
- Examine the same grammatical concepts or skill across multiple mentor texts.

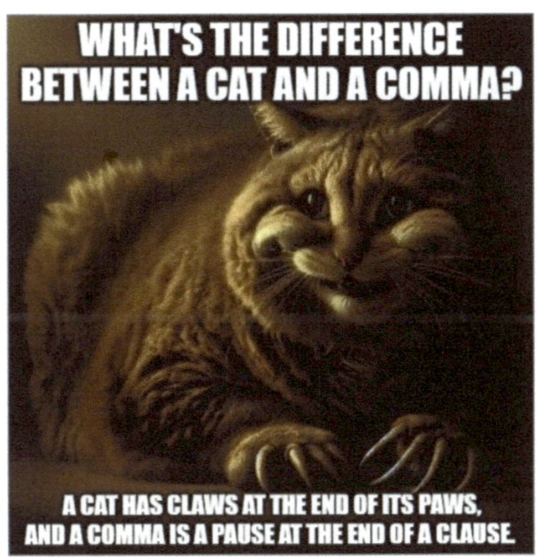

Author created using Imgflip AI tool

Speaking of clauses, let's get started by looking at how nouns and verbs come together to create them. The lessons that follow are detailed in Table 4.1.

Table 4.1 • Lesson Progression in This Chapter

LESSON NUMBER	TITLE OF THE LESSON	PAGE NUMBER
1	Nouns and Verbs	108
2	Adjectives and Adverbs	114
3	Pronouns	119
4	Commas (and Other Punctuation)	124

Lesson 1: Nouns and Verbs

Type of Lesson: Immersion

Time: 15 Minutes

WHAT'S HAPPENING?

Students will partner up and talk about either or both of the guiding questions:

- What do you notice about the types of nouns and verbs that are used?
- How are nouns and verbs connected in sentences?

YOU WILL NEED

- Long-term grammar partnerships
- Mentor text: "A Day at the Beach" (Handout 4.1)
- Grammar notebooks
- *For the teacher's reference only:* "A Day at the Beach" Mentor Text Reference Guide (see page 110). Use this to guide your prep and the class conversation.

Scan the QR code for a printable version of Handout 4.1, the mentor text and reference guide for this lesson.

qrs.ly/p9ge0ai

LESSON STEPS

1. Give each partnership one copy of the mentor text or project it for all to see. Read the mentor text aloud, while students follow along.
2. Share something you notice about nouns or verbs, such as, "Some nouns are capitalized, and others are not. Some verbs are action words, and others are not."
3. Invite students to get curious about the sentences in the mentor text. Pose the guiding questions above. Ask students to jot down their thoughts in their grammar notebooks.
4. Visit around the room and listen to what students are saying.
5. Wrap up the lesson by sharing out some ideas that groups had. This may sound like, "Some groups noticed that nouns often begin

sentences and verbs come after nouns. Others noticed that some nouns end in 's' or 'es.' Some nouns are capitalized. Some verbs end in 'ed.'"

WHY THIS LESSON?

Nouns and verbs are foundational components of grammar, and being able to identify and use them appropriately helps students develop a strong foundation for more complex writing and Grammar Study.

TIPS

- If this is initial work with nouns and verbs, you might simply focus on singular and plural nouns and present/past tense verbs.
- You might also focus one reading of the text only on nouns and a second reading only on verbs.

HANDOUT 4.1: NOUNS AND VERBS IMMERSION TEXT

A Day at the Beach

On a sunny morning at Camp Brightside, a team of camp counselors worked together as the excited campers boarded the yellow bus. Today was the annual beach trip to Shadow Bay—a day the campers look forward to all year! Sarah, one of the camp counselors, put on her glasses and checked her list one last time. “Emily, David, Michael, and Maria, are you all back there?” she called out. Another counselor responded, “Yes, they’re right here!” The kids cheered and waved their beach towels over their heads as happiness and joy spread throughout the bus.

As the bus rumbled down the road, the children sang songs and played games, tapping their feet in excitement. Michael and Maria played a game of tic-tac-toe; David made funny faces and caused two other campers to erupt in laughter; and Emily stared peacefully out the window at the leaves on the passing trees.

An hour later, the bus pulled into the Shadow Bay parking lot. Sarah led the group down a sandy path past a series of bushes to the beach where they spread out their towels. Michael’s shoes flew in the air as he immediately ran toward the water. The other kids quickly followed behind him. After dipping their toes in the water, they held hands and jumped in together!

Later, after hours of playing and swimming, the campers gathered to eat their sandwiches. It was a well-deserved break! They sat in a circle under their umbrellas and shared highlights from the day. Before long, they were quickly back to playing. By the time the sun began its descent, everyone was tired but happy. They had shared a wonderful day filled with laughter, teamwork, and memories that would last a lifetime.

As they boarded the bus for the return trip to Camp Brightside, Emily whispered to Maria, “I can’t wait to come back next year.”

Maria’s face lit up as she nodded and replied, “Me too. This was the best beach trip ever! I can’t believe it’s over!”

"A DAY AT THE BEACH" MENTOR TEXT REFERENCE GUIDE

Overview of Nouns

- **Singular Nouns:** bus, trip, beach, sun, sand, towel
- **Plural Nouns:** campers, towels, shells, games, seagulls, glasses, bushes, kids
- **Abstract Nouns:** laughter, excitement, happiness, joy, teamwork, highlights
- **Proper Nouns:** Camp Brightside, Shadow Bay, Emily, David, Michael, Maria, Sarah
- **Irregular Nouns:** children, feet, leaves
- **Possessive Nouns:** Michael's shoes, Maria's face
- **Collective Nouns:** a team of camp counselors
- **Gerunds:** playing, swimming

Overview of Verbs

- **Regular Verbs:** boarded, checked, called, responded, cheered, waved, spread, played, made, caused, stared, followed, jumped, gathered, shared, whispered
- **Irregular Verbs:** are, was, were, had, been, sang, sat, flew, ran, made, led, came, held, found, went, began
- **Future Tense:** will come, will last
- **Past Perfect Tense:** had shared
- **Modal Verbs:** would last, can't wait
- **Passive Voice:** "The day was filled with laughter, sandcastles, and teamwork."
- **Linking Verbs:** "everyone was tired"

Other Grammar Topics Included

Introductory Phrases:

- *On a sunny morning at Camp Brightside,* a team of camp counselors worked together . . .
- *An hour later,* the bus pulled into the Shadow Bay parking lot.
- *After dipping their toes in the water,* they held hands and jumped in together!
- *Before long,* they were quickly back to playing.

Dependent Clauses:

- *As the bus rumbled down the road,* the children sang songs and played games, tapping their feet in excitement.
    - D-I complex sentence (comma)
- Sarah led the group down a sandy path past a series of bushes to the beach *where they spread out their towels.*
    - I-D complex sentence (no comma)
- *By the time the sun began to set,* everyone was tired but happy.
    - D-I complex sentence (comma)

Semicolons:

- Michael and Maria played a game of tic-tac-toe; David made funny faces and caused two other campers to erupt in laughter; and Emily stared peacefully out the window at the leaves on the passing trees.

Frequently Confused Words

- To/Two/Too
    - . . . the annual beach trip **to** Shadow Bay
    - David made funny faces and caused **two** other campers to erupt in laughter
    - Maria's face lit up as she nodded and replied, "Me **too**. This was the best beach trip ever!"

- There/Their/They're
  - Emily, David, Michael, and Maria, are you all back **there**?
  - The kids cheered and waved **their** beach towels over **their** heads
  - After dipping **their** toes in the water, they held hands and jumped in together!
  - Another counselor responded, "Yes, **they're** right here!"
- It's/Its
  - I can't believe **it's** over!
  - By the time the sun began **its** descent . . .

Lesson 2: Adjectives and Adverbs

Type of Lesson: Immersion

Time: 15 Minutes

WHAT'S HAPPENING?

Students will partner up and talk about either or both guiding questions:

- What do you notice about what the adjectives and adverbs are describing?
- Where are adjectives and adverbs placed in sentences?

YOU WILL NEED

- Long-term grammar partnerships
- Mentor text: "Sunrise Adventure" (Handout 4.2)
- Grammar notebooks
- *For the teacher's reference only:* "Sunrise Adventure" Mentor Text Reference Guide (see page 116). Use this to guide your prep and the class conversation.

Scan the QR code for a printable version of Handout 4.2, the mentor text and reference guide for this lesson.

qrs.ly/t2ge0ap

LESSON STEPS

1. Provide each partnership with one copy the mentor text or project it for all to see. Determine whether you will focus on adjectives or adverbs in the first reading. With that lens in mind, read the mentor text aloud while students follow along. Adjectives are italicized and adverbs are bolded.
2. Share something you notice about adjectives or adverbs, such as, "Adjectives can be used to add details about things like size, shape, color; adverbs can describe details about actions."
3. Invite students to get curious about the sentences in the mentor text. Pose the guiding questions above. Ask students to jot down their thoughts in their grammar notebooks.
4. Visit around the room and listen to what students are saying.

5. Wrap up the lesson by sharing out some ideas that groups had. This may sound like, "Some groups noticed that adjectives can come before or after nouns but usually before. Adjectives can be used to compare things (bigger, faster). Sometimes two adjectives are listed next to each other (lengthy, scenic car ride), and sometimes they are separated by commas and other times not. Adverbs describe verbs. Some adverbs end in "ly." Some adverbs can describe adjectives (*breathtakingly* beautiful forest).

WHY THIS LESSON?

Adjectives and adverbs are essential parts of speech that help students write descriptively and with precision. This lesson builds upon students' knowledge of nouns and verbs. The entry point focus for younger students is identifying and examining adjectives and adverbs at the word level. A more complex analysis can look at adjective phrases and adverbial phrases and clauses (see Sections 4 (Phrases) and 5 (Clauses) of Part 4: Your Grammar Refresher for more information).

TIPS

- For adjectives, see if students start to ask the following questions about nouns: *What kind? How many?*
- For adverbs, see if students start to ask the following questions about verbs, adjectives, and other adverbs: *When? Where? How? Why? How often?*
- Use a comma to separate consecutive adjectives (coordinate) that describe the same noun and can be swapped in order and still make sense (the red, oversized truck)
    - Put the word "and" between the adjectives and see if the phrase makes sense
- Do not use a comma to separate cumulative adjectives (three yellow chickens)

HANDOUT 4.2: ADJECTIVES AND ADVERBS IMMERSION TEXT

Sunrise Adventure

When the sun began its *gentle* climb *early* that morning, the Garfield family could **barely** contain their *boundless* excitement. The *long-awaited* camping trip to Maine was **finally** here! After a *lengthy, scenic* car ride, they arrived at a **breathtakingly** *beautiful* forest with *towering* trees and a *babbling* stream **nearby**. They **swiftly** pitched their *spacious* tents and **meticulously** unpacked all of their *essential camping* supplies. They noticed that one tent was **slightly** *bigger* than the other.

Under the *twinkling* stars, the Garfields gathered **closely** around a *crackling* campfire and roasted marshmallows. The *crisp night* air was filled with *joyous* laughter and the *comforting* warmth of the fire.

Early the next morning, Emily—the *youngest* in the family—shook her parents **gently** from their *peaceful* slumber so that they could head off for a sunrise hike. They bundled up in *warm* clothes and followed her through the *tranquil* forest with their flashlights leading the way. Emily was **clearly** *more curious* than her brother who stayed behind everyone else.

Suddenly, they emerged from a clearing, and a *breathtaking* sight unfolded before their very eyes. Mrs. Garfield **immediately** pointed toward the *eastern* sky. The sun, a *fiery* ball of *radiant* light, was just beginning to peek over the mountains in the distance. It was the *most beautiful* sight imaginable.

As the sun rose **higher**, *vibrant* colors—pink, gold, and blue—filled the sky and mesmerized the family. The scene looked like a famous painting! Emily's eyes widened at the sight of the colors, and Mr. Garfield watched **quietly** and smiled. What could be better than this *awe-inspiring* experience?

Together, they stood in the *morning* light and created a *special* memory that would **forever** remain in their hearts and minds.

"SUNRISE ADVENTURE" MENTOR TEXT REFERENCE GUIDE

Adjectives by Category

See Section 1 (Parts of Speech) of Part 4: Your Grammar Refresher for additional information about adjective types.

- **Descriptive Adjectives:** gentle, early, boundless, beautiful, towering, babbling, spacious, twinkling, crackling, joyous, comforting, peaceful, warm, tranquil, breathtaking, eastern, vibrant, famous
- **Comparative:** bigger, more curious
- **Superlative:** youngest, most beautiful
- **Compound**: long-awaited, awe-inspiring
- **Coordinate**:
  - "After the *lengthy, scenic* car ride"
- **Cumulative**:
  - *"Essential camping* supplies," *"Crisp night* air"

Adverbs by Category

See Section 1 (Parts of Speech) of Part 4: Your Grammar Refresher for additional information about adverbs and how they modify different parts of speech.

- **Modifying Verbs:** barely, finally, nearby, swiftly, meticulously, closely, gently, clearly, suddenly, immediately, higher, quietly, together, forever
- **Modifying Adjectives:** breathtakingly (beautiful), slightly (bigger), early (the *next* morning)

Other Grammar Topics Included

Nonrestrictive Phrases (nonessential information)

As a reminder, nonrestrictive phrases contain "bonus" descriptive information that, if removed, does not impact the meaning of the sentence.

- "Early the next morning, Emily—*the youngest in the family*—shook her parents **gently** . . . "

Grammar Nerd Alert!

Because a comma follows the introductory phrase ("early the next morning"), dashes are used to set off the adjective phrase ("the youngest in the family) to avoid confusion with punctuation.

- "The sun, a fiery ball of radiant light, was just beginning to peek . . . "
- As the sun rose **higher**, *vibrant* colors—pink, gold, and blue—filled the sky and mesmerized the family.
  - Because the appositive phrase (pink, gold, and blue) contains items separated by commas, use dashes to set off the phrase to avoid confusion with punctuation.

Prepositional Phrases (some–not all)

- "The long-awaited camping trip ***to*** *Maine*"
- *"**After** a lengthy, scenic car ride"*
- " . . . they arrived ***at*** *a breathtakingly beautiful forest* ***with*** *towering trees and a babbling stream*"
- *"**Under** the twinkling stars"*
- *"**around** a crackling campfire"*
- "comforting warmth ***of*** *the fire"*
- "shook her parents gently ***from*** *their peaceful slumber"*
- "a breathtaking sight unfolded ***before*** *their very eyes*."
- beginning to peek ***over*** *the mountains* ***in*** *the distance.*

Lesson 3: Pronouns

Type of Lesson: Immersion

Time: 15 Minutes

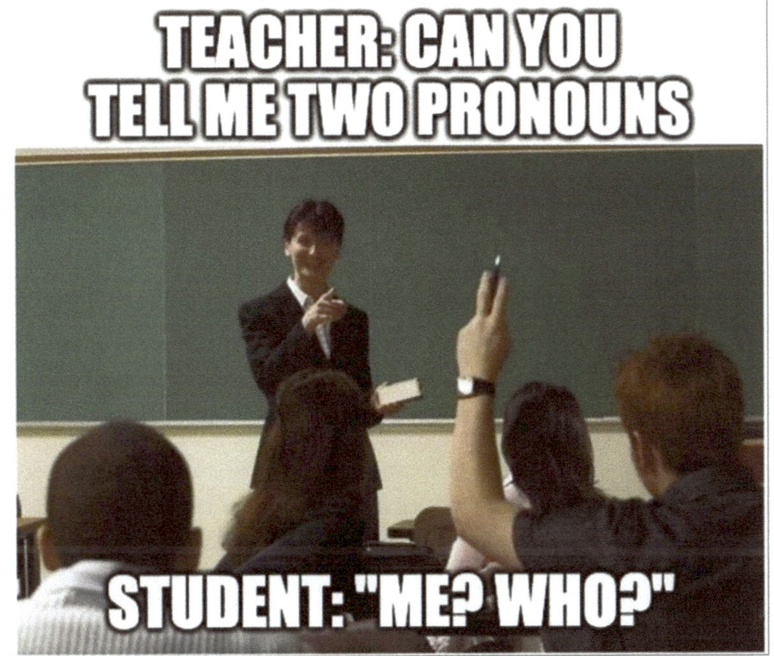

Author created using Imgflip AI tool

WHAT'S HAPPENING?

Students partner up and talk about either or both of the guiding questions:

- What do you notice about how pronouns are used?
- How are different pronouns used depending on where they are placed in a sentence?

YOU WILL NEED

- Long-term grammar partnerships
- Mentor text: "Acorns for You and Me" (Handout 4.3)
- Grammar notebooks

(Continued)

(Continued)

- *For the teacher's reference only:* "Acorns for You and Me" Mentor Text Reference Guide (see page 122). Use this to guide your prep and the class conversation.

Scan this QR code to access a printable version of Handout 4.3, the mentor text and reference guide for this lesson.

qrs.ly/l5ge0as

LESSON STEPS

1. Provide each partnership with one copy of the mentor text or project it for all to see. Read the mentor text aloud. Let the students know that pronouns are bolded in the story. If this is the students' first time examining pronouns, begin with a specific lens on personal pronouns (I, he, she, you, we, they, them, it, etc.).
2. Share something you notice about pronouns, such as, "Pronouns take the place of nouns and refer specifically to other nouns in the sentence (or a nearby sentence)."
3. Invite students to get curious about the sentences and the bolded pronouns in the mentor text. Share the guiding questions above. Ask them to jot down their thoughts in their grammar notebooks.
4. Visit around the room and listen to what students are saying.
5. Wrap up the lesson by sharing out some ideas that groups had. This may sound like, "Some groups noticed that: 'he' is used instead of Sammy and 'she' is used instead of Rosie; the pronoun 'it' connects back to the noun acorn. Pronouns like I, he, and she come at the beginning of the sentence and pronouns like me, him, and her come at the end of the sentence."

WHY THIS LESSON?

Pronouns are an essential component of grammar and establish clear and concise communication and help writers avoid repetition. As a starting point, students should know which personal pronouns to use with subjects of sentences and which to use with objects of sentences and how to choose between singular and plural pronouns. With this foundation in place, students can then work on identifying and implementing other types of pronouns, including possessive, reflexive, demonstrative, relative, and indefinite. You may choose to revisit this text again with an eye on one or more of the other pronoun types each time.

TIPS

- This immersion text contains all pronoun types included in the standards as outlined below.
- As a component of this lesson, review subject/verb pairs so that students can think in terms of subjective vs. objective case pronouns. As an entry point, lead students to the discovery that subjective case pronouns—I, he, she, we, they—take the place of the subject of the sentence. Objective case pronouns—me, him, her, us, them—take the place of words that are not subjects (objects). You may reference Section 10 (Pronouns Continued) of Part 4: Your Grammar Refresher for a detailed overview of each pronoun type.
- This text also includes examples of the following grammatical topics:
    - commas in a series
    - correlative conjunctions (not only/but also, either/or)
    - nonessential information
    - punctuating dialogue

HANDOUT 4.3: PRONOUNS IMMERSION TEXT

Acorns for You and Me

Sammy the squirrel, **who** was busy gathering acorns for the winter, scampered up and down the oak tree, **his** bushy tail twitching with excitement. **He** filled his cheeks with as many acorns as **they** could hold, and **he** scurried down the trunk to bury **them** in **his** secret hiding spot.

Most of the acorns were on the smaller side, except a **few**. "**This** is the biggest acorn I've ever found, and **it** is all **mine**!" Sammy exclaimed to **himself**, holding up a particularly plump one. **He** carefully dug a hole, placed the acorn inside, and covered **it** up with leaves. "**That** should keep **it** safe until winter," **he** thought with satisfaction.

Just then, Rosie the rabbit approached from **her** side of the forest. "Hello, Sammy!" **she** greeted **him** cheerfully. "What are **you** up to today?"

"**I** am collecting acorns for the winter," Sammy replied. "**It's** important to be prepared, **you** know."

Rosie nodded. "**That** is very wise of **you**," **she** said. "**I** am gathering berries, acorns, and nuts **myself**. Would **you** like to join **me**?" Either **you** or **I** can take the lead on our search."

Sammy hesitated. **He** still had many more acorns to collect. But then **he** thought about how much fun **it** would be to spend time with Rosie. "Sure, I'd love to!" he said with a smile. "**We** can prepare **ourselves** better if we work together."

Together, **they** hopped and scurried through the forest, collecting berries and acorns. **They** chatted and laughed, recognizing that teamwork makes the dream work. As the sun began to set, **they** said **their** goodbyes and headed back to **their** homes.

Sammy felt happy and content. He had not only gathered enough acorns for the winter but also made a new friend. Sammy knew that **he** and Rosie would have many more adventures together in the forest, **which** made **him** happy.

"ACORNS FOR YOU AND ME" MENTOR TEXT REFERENCE GUIDE

Types of Pronouns (with examples)

- **Personal:** I, he, she, you, it, we, they
- **Possessive**: his, her, their, mine
- **Reflexive**: himself, myself, ourselves
- **Demonstrative:** this, that
- **Relative**: who, which, that
- **Indefinite:** most, few, many

Other Grammar Topics Included

Commas in a series:

- He carefully dug a hole, placed the acorn inside, and covered it up with leaves.
- I am gathering berries, acorns, and nuts myself.

Correlative Conjunctions: (not only/but also, either/or)

- He had **not only** gathered enough acorns for the winter **but also** made a new friend.
- **Either** you **or** I can take the lead on our search.

Nonessential information:

- Sammy the squirrel, **who was busy gathering acorns for the winter**, scampered up and down the oak tree . . .
- Sammy knew that he and Rosie would have many more adventures together in the forest, **which made him happy**.

Punctuating Dialogue

- "This is the biggest acorn I've ever found, and it is all mine!" Sammy exclaimed to himself . . .
- "That is very wise of you," she said. "I am gathering berries, acorns, and nuts myself. Would you like to join me?"
- "Sure, I'd love to!" he said with a smile. "We can save time working together ourselves."

Lesson 4: Commas (and Other Punctuation)

Type of Lesson: Immersion

Time: 15 Minutes

WHAT'S HAPPENING?

Students will partner up and talk about either or both of the guiding questions:

- What do you notice about how commas are used?
- What words or phrases do you notice that come before or after a comma?

YOU WILL NEED

- Long-term grammar partnerships
- Mentor text: "Penguins: Amazing Birds of the Ice" (Handout 4.4)
- Grammar notebooks
- *For the teacher's reference only:* "Penguins: Amazing Birds of the Ice" Mentor Text Reference Guide (see page 128). Use this to guide your prep and the class conversation.

Scan this QR code to access a printable version of Handout 4.4, the mentor text and reference guide for this lesson.

qrs.ly/auge0b0

LESSON STEPS

1. Provide each partnership with one copy the mentor text or project it for all to see. Read the mentor text aloud.
2. Share something you notice about commas, such as, "Commas encourage us to slow down and pause as we're reading. Listen to how I pause at each comma while I read the story aloud."
3. Invite students to get curious about the sentences as they identify commas and other contextual information. Share the guiding questions above. Ask them to jot down their thoughts in their grammar notebooks.
4. Visit around the room and listen to what students are saying.
5. Wrap up the lesson by sharing out some ideas that groups had. This may sound like, "Some groups noticed that commas come after

some words and phrases that begin sentences; commas come before FANBOYS words (in compound sentences); commas are used to separate items in a list."

WHY THIS LESSON?

Commas are crucial tools for students to incorporate accurately and effectively in their writing. They help provide clarity within sentences and are used to separate words, phrases, and clauses. Some students have an ear for where commas should be placed, but most students need to learn the rules in the context of good writing. This mentor text includes examples of the major comma rules that students should learn through repetition, including the use of the Oxford comma.

Author created using Canva.com

TIPS

- As a class, review examples of phrases and clauses so students have a common language to use when discussing commas (they follow an introductory phrase, they combine independent clauses in a compound sentence, etc.).
- Emphasize the connection between reading (pausing at a comma) and writing with the intentional use of a comma for that effect on the reader.
- When adding information to a sentence, surround it with commas if it is not essential to the overall meaning of the sentence. If removing the information changes the meaning or intent of the sentence, then commas should not be used.

HANDOUT 4.4: COMMAS IMMERSION TEXT

Penguins: Amazing Birds of the Ice

Penguins are fascinating birds, aren't they? Living in some of the coldest places on Earth, these fluffy creatures are perfectly adapted to life in icy climates and have some cool features!

Appearance and Habitat

Penguins are easily recognizable by their black and white feathers, which help them blend in with the snow and water. They have a sleek, torpedo-shaped body that allows them to glide effortlessly through the water. Penguins live in Antarctica, as well as in other places like South America, Africa, and Australia. Did you know that a group of baby Emperor penguins in Antarctica dove off an ice cliff together on January 18, 2024? Yes, they really did!

Diet and Hunting

Penguins are expert hunters and primarily eat fish, squid, and krill. They use their strong flippers to propel themselves through the water at high speeds, and they catch their prey with their sharp beaks. Some species of penguins can dive to incredible depths in search of food and can hold their breath for several minutes at a time!

Behavior and Communication

Penguins are social birds and often gather in large colonies called rookeries. They use various sounds, like squawks and brays, to communicate with each other. Can you believe that penguins can recognize each other's calls in a noisy crowd? Because their calls are unique, they can easily find their mates and chicks even in a bustling colony.

Life Cycle

Penguins mate for life and typically lay two eggs at a time. Both parents take turns keeping the eggs warm and protected until they hatch. After the chicks are born, they rely on their parents' assistance for food and warmth. However, penguins grow up fast, and they can soon fend for themselves for food. Within a few years, they are ready to start a family of their own.

Conservation

Some studies, unfortunately, have shown that many species of penguins are facing threats due to climate change, habitat destruction, and pollution. It's important for humans to take action to protect penguins and their habitats. By reducing our carbon footprint, for example, we can help ensure a brighter future for these incredible birds.

Conclusion

Penguins are truly remarkable creatures that are able to thrive in some of the harshest environments on our planet. With their distinctive appearance and fascinating behaviors, there's so much to learn and appreciate about them. Indeed, a penguin's life is amazing!

"PENGUINS AMAZING BIRDS OF THE ICE" MENTOR TEXT REFERENCE GUIDE

The following is a breakdown of the topics addressed in the mentor text. For additional information about any topic, see Part 4: Your Grammar Refresher.

Commas

- compound sentence
- complex sentence
- tag questions and yes/no
- items in a series
- introductory words and phrases
- nonessential information
- appositive phrase
- interrupters
- dates

Marks of End Punctuation

- exclamation point
- question mark

Possessives

Contractions

CREATING MENTOR TEXTS

This chapter provides mentor texts to use in your classroom, but you can also create your own to continue to expand the items in your grammar immersion toolbox. To create your own mentor text, try out these steps:

1. The texts in this chapter are multi-use, though not all mentor texts need to be. In your planning, you should first determine whether you are designing your mentor text for a single topic/skill or for multiple purposes (again, think shared reading).
2. With a topic (or topics) in mind, work backward: Identify the specific areas of the skill that you want to include in the text by referencing the standards and your curriculum while also considering the needs of the students in front of you. For example, when thinking about nouns, you might choose—as a first step—to focus on singular, plural, and possessive nouns. If students have already mastered those components, you might design the text with a focus on abstract, irregular, and collective nouns.
3. Next, determine the type of text that you are going to create—narrative, informational, persuasive, etc.—and the topic for the text.
4. As you write the text, keep your students' grade level in mind and ensure that the text is accessible. You might consider using AI (ChatGPT, Gemini, etc.) to create an initial draft of the text that you can then go back and revise strategically. If you are using AI, be sure to make your prompt specific to the text type and topic, the specifics of the grammatical concept (e.g., singular, plural, and possessive nouns), and the grade level of the students.
5. Include multiple examples of the grammar concept(s) used in different ways, if possible. The examples should be easy for students to identify so that they can spend time hypothesizing about how the grammar concept works.

KNITTING THE CHAPTERS TOGETHER

We enjoy this process of creating immersion texts! AI makes it so quick, as well.

The next chapter will explore playful ways to learn grammar. Remember, Chapters 4, 5, 6, and 7 contain lessons that are designed for you to mix and match. Find mentor texts first, then choose some playful exploration experiences from Chapter 5. Follow up with some direct teaching lessons from Chapter 6. And finally, some reflection lessons from Chapter 7.

CHAPTER FIVE

Explore Lessons

Hypothesize and Play

What about experimentation? Play? Approximation? Grammar and mechanics shape meaning, and as in all language endeavors, we must make mistakes to move toward correctness. Where's the bridge between getting started and stretching with grammar and mechanics and being wrong?

—Jeff Anderson (2023, p. 3)

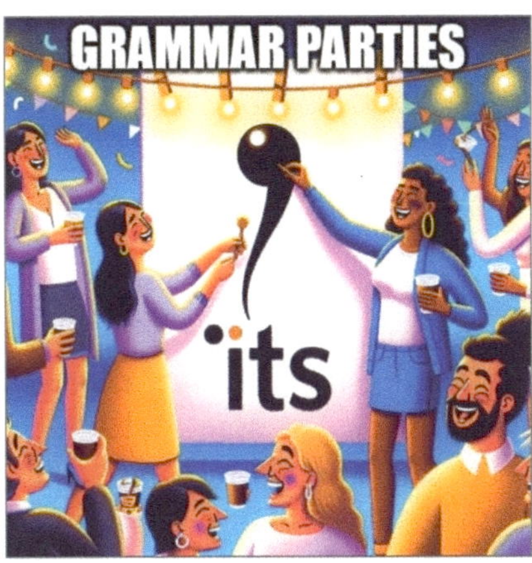

Author created using Imgflip AI tool

Oh, the cleverness of grammar nerds! Are you with us on Saturday night to play a little Pin the Apostrophe on the Contraction? Although that is not entirely what we mean by grammar play in Grammar Study, this chapter is. It is about opportunities to explore grammatical concepts both before and after explicit teaching days.

To the contrary of the exploratory approach to grammar is a baked-in belief that grammar learning must be about correctness 100% of the time. Your granny's grammar experiences have focused on accurate identification and then an expectation of immediate accurate usage. We teach, for example, what a subject and predicate is, ask students to identify them in a sentence, and then are confused when students are writing sentences that are fragments or run-ons. There must be an aspect of experimentation and play. I think Jeff Anderson (2023) said it best in the quote that opens this chapter, from the opening of *Mechanically Inclined*.

As a quick reminder, the Grammar Study unit phases are

Phase 1: Immersion

Phase 2: Focus Areas

- Explore
  - Explore and Hypothesize
  - Explore and Play
- Explicit Teaching
- Reflection

Phase 3: Transfer

Consider this chapter, along with Chapters 4 (Immersion), 6 (Explicit Teaching), and 7 (Transfer), a "choose your own adventure" experience. The guiding progressions in Chapter 3 act as a framework; refer to them as useful in your planning. For quick reference, once you have finished the Immersion phase of the unit, each Focus Area follows a "Explore and Hypothesize, Explicit Teaching, Explore and Play" pattern. This chapter is chock full of ideas for building play into grammar learning:

- Three "Explore and Hypothesize" lessons that are most suitable for the day before an explicit teaching day. These Explore and Hypothesize lessons are set up as provocation to invite students to create theories about a particular grammar concept. (See page 48 in Chapter 3 for suggested progressions.)
- Ten "Explore and Play" lessons that are best for the day(s) following an explicit teaching day. These allow for a deep exploration through experimentation, conversation, and feedback.

PLAY IS SERIOUSLY IMPORTANT

Play may sound frivolous and like something else to squeeze into an already packed daily schedule, but play is an essential part of learning for all ages. Recognized as essential by seminal child psychology researcher Lev Vygotsky (1967) back in the day and in the decades since, play has been deeply researched. Play for all, including adults, reaps huge benefits in life and learning, thus making this section of our book crucial to grammar learning (see National Institute for Play at https://nifplay.org).

THE GRAMMAR LOVERS' BOOK NOOK

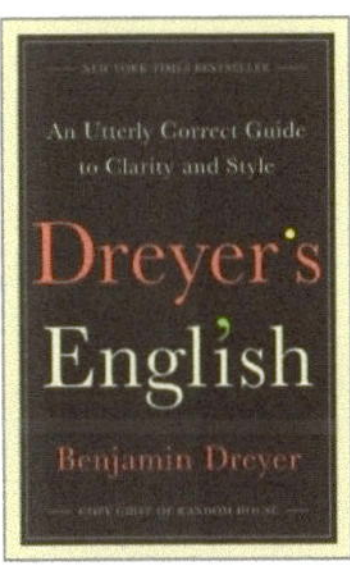

For Teachers: *Dreyer's English* by Benjamin Dreyer (2020)

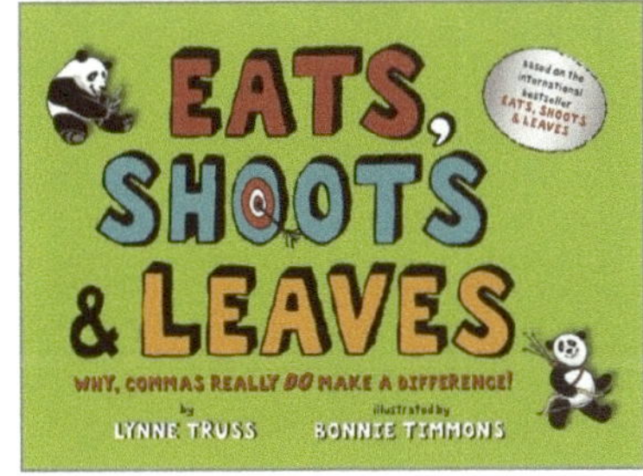

For Students: *Eats, Shoots & Leaves* by Lynn Truss (2006)

THE DIFFERENCE BETWEEN PLAY AND GAMES

Let's consider the difference between grammar play and grammar games. Grammar games have a winner and a loser, while play has an unpredictable outcome. An example of a grammar game is to see who can find the nouns in a sentence first. This sets up a tone of competition and, often, an emotionally charged outcome for the winner and the loser. Play is the opportunity to engage in a low-risk, high-reward experience in which the outcome is unique for each learner. We have avoided grammar games in the lessons that follow and opted for playful interactions with grammar instead.

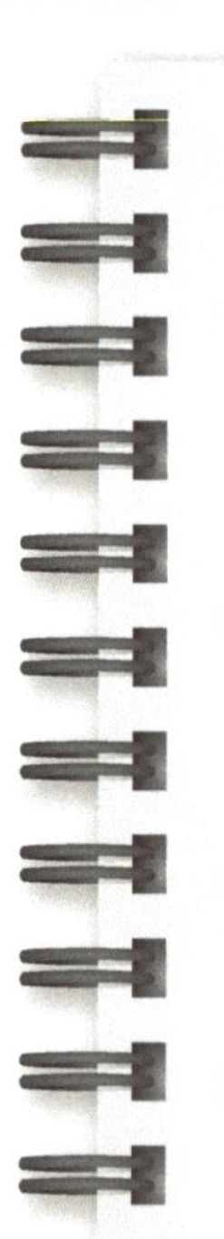

TIPS FOR INTERACTING WITH THIS CHAPTER

- Explore lessons ideally precede an Explicit Teaching day and follow an Explicit Teaching day. Why explore before explicit teaching? When students inquire and theorize about a certain concept, just like in a science experiment, they are more likely to engage in the explicit teaching days.
- Patty's dad once said, "I can't hear you with all of your talking." This is both a strange and wise comment. Take this advice to heart during these playful experiences, and let the students do most of the talking while you support the play. Encourage, challenge, remind, and support.
- If one of these experiences goes longer than the allotted grammar time, ask students to jot down where they left off. Pick up with the same lesson the next "grammar time."
- In lieu of correcting a mistake, challenge students to find what is awry. You might say, "It is almost a complete sentence. You are missing two things. See if you can find them." If students cannot, show them how to fix what they are doing and then ask them to try again.

EXPLORE AND HYPOTHESIZE LESSONS

There are three different approaches to the Explore and Hypothesize lessons. The first is a comparison: Students look at two to three related grammar concepts to theorize their similarities and differences. This may be comparing phrases and clauses, different verb tenses, or commonly confused words (their, they're, there). The second approach is a "before and after." Students study what it looks like before adding a grammatical technique and after. This may be showing a sentence without adjectives (before) and then a sentence with adjectives. This works particularly well with sentence expansion. The third approach is a mini-inquiry. Students are given a question to explore such as, "Where are commas used in writing?" or "What are the indicators of the beginning of a sentence? The end of a sentence?" Students study a piece of text, from a book or one of the immersion texts we have provided, to theorize answers to these questions.

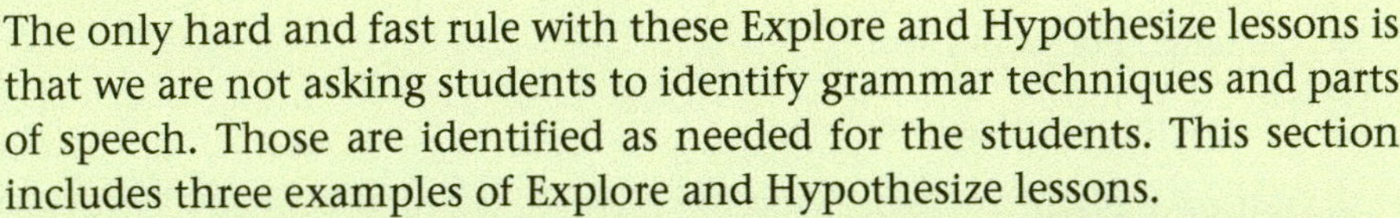

The only hard and fast rule with these Explore and Hypothesize lessons is that we are not asking students to identify grammar techniques and parts of speech. Those are identified as needed for the students. This section includes three examples of Explore and Hypothesize lessons.

LESSON NUMBER	TITLE OF LESSON	PAGE NUMBER
1	Who Are You Calling a Phrase?	136
2	Before and After: Prepositional Impact	139
3	Mini Inquiry	142

Lesson 1: Who Are You Calling a Phrase?

Type of Lesson: Explore and Hypothesize

Time: 10 minutes

WHAT'S HAPPENING?

Long-term partnerships will discuss the differences between phrases and clauses. They will jot down their theories.

YOU WILL NEED

- Who Are You Calling a Phrase? either projected or printed for each partnership (Handout 5.1)
- Grammar notebooks
- Long-term grammar partnerships
- Pencils or pens

Scan this QR code to access a printable version of Handout 5.1, Who Are You Calling a Phrase?

qrs.ly/cnge0b4

LESSON STEPS

1. Share or project the Who Are You Calling a Phrase? handout.
2. Ask students to talk with each other about what they think the differences are between phrases and clauses.
3. Encourage partners to write down their hypotheses.
4. Listen in to some conversations to gather information that will help you introduce the Explicit Teaching of phrases and clauses.

WHY THIS LESSON?

Phrases and clauses are two important parts of sentences. Sometimes people use these synonymously, but they are very different. Clauses (either independent or dependent) have a subject and predicate, while phrases are parts of sentences without a subject and predicate.

TIPS AND ALTERNATIVE USES

- It is important to give students the time to grapple with the differences between phrases and clauses. Give them encouragement, but try not to give them the answer. You may prompt them with words like, "What else do you notice? You are on the right track. Maybe consider . . . ?"
- Use this example, and the others from Chapter 3 on pages 73–75, as templates for any future grammar concepts that you would like students to compare.
- You may want to recreate this handout by including clauses from books you are reading together. Take some of the sentences in that text and turn them into phrases. This can draw upon the background knowledge of a text, making this resource more user friendly by becoming more or less sophisticated.

HANDOUT 5.1: WHO ARE YOU CALLING A PHRASE?

CLAUSES	PHRASES
A dragon with a rainbow umbrella smiled at me.	A dragon with a rainbow umbrella
Before the dragon smiled at me	Hopped over the puddle
The rainbow umbrella is his favorite.	Sang a song about pickles
The unicorn, on the other hand, loved glitter.	A sneaky unicorn with glitter
Although the juggler loved jellybeans	Is juggling jellybeans
	In a castle made of candy

Guiding Questions:

Make your own discoveries, of course. But if you are not sure where to start, these questions may inspire you.

Compare the phrases and clauses. What are you noticing?

Is there anything missing in the phrases that is found in the clauses? Or the other way around?

Lesson 2: Before and After: Prepositional Impact

Type of Lesson: Explore and Hypothesize

Time: 10 minutes

WHAT'S HAPPENING?

Long-term partnerships will be looking at a "before and after" set of sentences. They will theorize what a preposition and prepositional phrase does to a sentence.

YOU WILL NEED

- Before and After: Prepositional Impact, projected or printed for each partnership (Handout 5.2)
- Long-term grammar partnerships
- Grammar notebooks
- Pencils or pens

Scan this QR code to access a printable version of Handout 5.2, Before and After: Prepositional Impact.

qrs.ly/3pge0bh

LESSON STEPS

1. Share or project the Before and After: Prepositional Impact handout.
2. Ask students to talk with each other about what they think the impact is on sentences when using prepositions and prepositional phrases.
3. Encourage partners to write down their hypotheses.
4. Listen in to some conversations to gather information that will help you introduce the "explicit teaching" of phrases and clauses.

WHY THIS LESSON?

One of the most common ways of teaching your granny how to use prepositions and prepositional phrases was to memorize as many prepositions as

(Continued)

(Continued)

possible. Although knowing which words act as prepositions is good, it is much more important to learn how they function in a sentence.

TIPS AND ALTERNATIVE USES

- Even though prepositions and prepositional phrases may be found in the standards in a grade before or after yours, they are super easy to use and highly effective in sentence expansion. Just having a bank of prepositions for students to use as possible ways to expand a sentence helps.
- Use this "before and after" as a template for future grammar studies. Simply choose a grammar concept and show what it looks like when it is not used and then when it is used.
- A great way to trim down sentence length is to notice whether we have included too many prepositional phrases, making it awkward to read. When revising, students can hunt for prepositions (using a bank of prepositions) to see how many they may be using in a single sentence. This exercise helps students look closely at their sentences.

HANDOUT 5.2: BEFORE AND AFTER: PREPOSITIONAL IMPACT

Prepositions! Such a helpful part of speech to expand sentences. Look at the collection of "before and after" sentences below. Look even more closely at the underlined preposition and the prepositional phrase.

Hypothesize (make your best guesses) with your partner answers to these questions:

1. What is the impact of prepositions and prepositional phrases on a sentence? In other words, what happens to a sentence when a prepositional phrase is added?
2. How do prepositions make sentences better? Worse?
3. Come up with as many ideas as you can. Jot your hypotheses (best guesses) in your grammar notebook.

SENTENCE WITHOUT PREPOSITIONS AND PREPOSITIONAL PHRASES	SENTENCE WITH PREPOSITIONS AND PREPOSITIONAL PHRASES
Take deep breaths.	Take deep breaths into your nose and out of your mouth.
Practice patience.	Practice patience with yourself and others.
I felt strongly.	I felt strongly about my decision.
Celebrate small wins.	Celebrate small wins at every chance.
Welcome mistakes.	Welcome mistakes during times of learning.

Some cool prepositions to know and use:

USE TO SHOW A PLACE	USE TO SHOW TIME	USE TO SHOW DIRECTION
above	after	into
below	before	out of
between	during	through
behind	until	across
under		around

Lesson 3: Mini Inquiry

Type of Lesson: Explore and Hypothesize, Explore and Play, or Both

Time: 10–15 minutes

WHAT'S HAPPENING?

Partnerships begin with a question that guides the participants' exploration of a chosen text. The question will also guide them as they theorize the expectations or rules of a particular area of grammar.

YOU WILL NEED

- An inquiry question
- A text that includes grammatical elements specific to that question
- Grammar notebooks
- Long-term grammar partnerships

LESSON STEPS

1. Choose an inquiry question. For example, *When does an author use a comma before a closing quotation mark?*
2. Choose a text that includes those grammatical elements frequently. Provide each partnership with a copy of that text. For the inquiry question above, we chose a passage from *Pie*, a middle-grade novel by Sarah Weeks.
3. Ask partners to read the text and write down answers to the question and/or mark up the text.
4. Discuss as a class some of the answers students discovered.

WHY THIS LESSON?

When exploring how grammar is used by authors, students can extract valuable information about grammar. This discovery sets them up for deeper understanding of grammar usage. Basically, inquiry is not just for immersion.

TIPS AND ALTERNATIVE USES

- These mini inquiries are useful for both types of Explore lessons. They can be held before or after an Explicit Teaching day.
- On days that you reflect on grammar, questions often arise. Sometimes, a mini inquiry is a way to find answers or, at the very least, theories.
- After partners study the text for a bit, match them up with another partnership to share their discoveries.

SAMPLE INQUIRY AND PASSAGE

When does an author use a comma before a closing quotation mark?

> "And one more thing," Alice said. "I have a hunch it's the same person who broke into the pie shop."
>
> "Enough!" barked Alice's mother. "If I hear one more word about keys or cats or cockamamie ideas about people climbing through windows, wearing gold earrings, I promise you my head is going to jump right off my neck and fly around this room like a bald eagle."
>
> Alice's father arrived with the aspirin and shooed Alice and Charlie out of the room. Charlie seemed relieved.
>
> "I'd better get going," he told Alice again. "Thanks for lunch. And good luck finding Lardo."
>
> "What do you mean, 'good luck'?" Alice asked. "I thought you were going to help me."
>
> Charlie began shifting his weight from one foot to the other.
>
> "I'm awful busy," he said, looking down at his shoes. "And, like I said, Miss Gurke is waiting. . . ."

Grammar Nerd Alert!

Use an exclamation point or question mark instead of a comma before a dialogue tag when the quoted dialogue expresses strong emotion or poses a direct question.

(Continued)

(Continued)

> "Did anyone ever tell you that you're a terrible liar, Charlie Erdling?"
>
> "I'm not lying," he said. "I really do have a delivery to make. I'll show you the shopping list if you don't believe me."
>
> "Don't bother. I get the message," Alice said. "You don't think Lardo's been catnapped, do you?"
>
> Charlie looked down at the ground.
>
> "Probably not," he said softly.
>
> "Fine. Then I don't want your help anyway," Alice told her. (Weeks, 2013, p. 83)

Photos 5.1 and 5.2. Partnerships engage in inquiry

EXPLORE AND PLAY LESSONS

Explore and Play lessons invite students to grapple with grammatical concepts in a playful way. This play, as discussed earlier in the chapter, is essential and the heart of a true Grammar Study. Including the mini-inquiry lesson from the Explore and Hypothesize section, there are 10 lessons that can be used as templates for future grammar studies. In the Explore and Play lessons in this section, we encourage you to allow students to invent additional ways of playing with grammar concepts. In fact, a few of these ideas came straight from students taking part in a Grammar Study. The only hard and fast rule with Explore and Play lessons is that they do not become a game where there is a winner and loser.

LESSON NUMBER	TITLE OF LESSON	PAGE NUMBER
4	Sentences From Sentences	146
5	Word Cards	148
6	Presto Change-o!	151
7	Mimic Sentences	154
8	A Sort of Discovery	156
9	Construction Kits	159
10	Fill in the Blanks	162
11	Grammar Scavenger Hunts	165
12	Co-Authoring	168

Lesson 4: Sentences From Sentences

Type of Lesson: Explore and Play

Time: 10 minutes

WHAT'S HAPPENING?

Long-term partnerships will take the words of a sentence and create multiple sentences with them.

YOU WILL NEED

- A sentence or a few sentences you really like
- Scissors
- Long-term grammar partnerships
- Grammar notebooks

LESSON STEPS

1. In advance of the lesson, choose a sentence in a text that the class is reading or choose one from mentor text set from Chapter 4. Write the sentence on paper or on sentence strips. Cut out each word and punctuation of the sentence and scramble the words up.
2. Display the cut-up words and punctuation under a document camera or secured to the board for the class to see.
3. At the top of a page in the grammar notebook, invite partners to begin by writing the shortest sentence they can make.
4. Then invite the partners to look at the words that they didn't use in their short sentence and add a word (or more than one word) to lengthen the sentence or create new sentences.
5. Prompt the pairs to make as many sentences as possible in five minutes.
6. Combine grammar partnerships so there are two sets of long-term partners meeting with each other. Ask them to compare sentences with other grammar partners and challenge each other to prove how they know each one is a sentence.

WHY THIS LESSON?

First of all, it is playful! It's also a challenge, and it gives more practice in sentence construction.

TIPS AND ALTERNATIVE USES

1. The goal is not to find the original sentence, but if students do, that's swell, too.
2. The last five minutes, when partners prove to other partners why the sentences they wrote are actually sentences, is a crucial part of this lesson. If you need more time for this, stretch this lesson to two grammar sessions.
3. The example sentence used in Photo 5.3 is quite sophisticated. Gauge the sentence you choose by what your students know and have studied.
4. An extension to this lesson is studying a few sentences that were created and identifying why those parts fit together or create agreement.

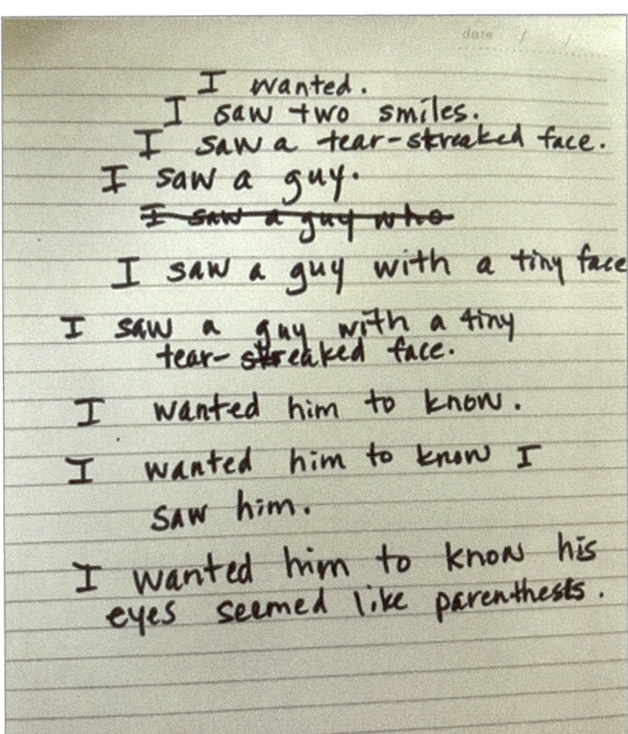

Photo 5.3. Student-created sentences using the words and punctuation in the cut-up sample sentence: "I wanted him to know that I saw him, a guy who, even with a tear-streaked face, seemed to have two tiny smiles framing his eyes like parentheses" (Reynolds & Kiely, 2015).

Lesson 5: Word Cards

Type of Lesson: Explore and Play

Time: 10–15 minutes

WHAT'S HAPPENING?

Students work with a collection that includes words from all parts of speech, endings, and punctuation. They will create sentences and sort words using anything you may be focusing on in grammar. The word cards can be used if you are studying writing sentences, sentence agreement, using different parts of speech, or punctuation.

YOU WILL NEED

- Word cards (see Handout 3.7 in Chapter 3) and envelopes or Ziplock bags to store them in (if you followed the lesson progression from Chapter 3, you already have these ready to go)
- Long-term grammar partnerships
- Grammar notebooks

LESSON STEPS

1. Ask the students to prepare their word cards. (More on that in the Tips below.)
2. Choose a focus or challenge for the lesson. For example, Write a sentence that includes a preposition.
3. Partners work together to select words, endings, and punctuation from their cards to create something that matches the focus or challenge.
4. Partners write what they have designed in their grammar notebooks and label the important parts. If students are writing sentences that include prepositions, they will label the prepositions.

WHY THIS LESSON?

This lesson can be used repeatedly throughout the year to provide scaffolding for grammar usage. It is a playful interaction that can grow in complexity and creativity throughout the year.

TIPS AND ALTERNATIVE USES

- Try out different challenges and even ask students to submit some challenge ideas for consideration.
- The first time you use word cards, spend one grammar session devoted to cutting out the words as a class. This is a bit of a pain but worth the investment because they will be used over and over again.
- Before cutting out the words, quickly color the back of each page in a unique color combination. For example, one partnership may use a blue marker with a red crayon, and another just an orange crayon. When (not if) the word cards end up on the floor, it will be easy to find the baggie to which they belong.
- There are a good number of word cards. You may want to start with fewer cards and then introduce more as the year progresses. This way, students will not be overwhelmed by the number of cards.

Examples of challenges for word cards: Start with a simple sentence and add a preposition. Write a sentence with three commas. Write a sentence that shows agreement. Write a sentence with a compound predicate. Write the sentence with the words in alphabetical order.

Photo 5.4.
Partnerships spreading out word cards for the first time and just getting to know them

(Continued)

(Continued)

Photo 5.5. Challenge complete! Students add the sentence to their grammar notebook with some commentary about the grammar concept.

Photo 5.6. Students working with the word cards after a few experiences with them. They remember many of the cards and often jump right into the challenge searching for particular parts of speech.

Lesson 6: Presto Change-o!

Type of Lesson: Explore and Play

Time: 10–15 minutes

WHAT'S HAPPENING?

Students work with sentence strips of prewritten sentences or other grammatical concepts. They will take these sentences and, in some way, combine them to create new sentences or use specific parts of speech to expand the sentences.

YOU WILL NEED

- Sentences typed up and printed out (or the Presto Change-o Handout 5.3)
- Any parts of speech that you want students to work with, either to be cut out or on a chart
- Long-term grammar partnerships
- Grammar notebooks

Scan this QR code to access a printable version of Handout 5.3, Presto Change-o.
qrs.ly/o7ge0bi

LESSON STEPS

1. Print out a few sentences. You can make your own or choose sentences (preferably brief ones) from some favorite books. If they are appropriate for your learners, use the sentences in Handout 5.3.
2. Ask students to cut out the sentences and any parts of speech you want them to practice with.
3. Invite students, with their partners, to combine or expand sentences. They will jot down these sentences in their grammar notebooks.
4. Partners label the sentences they wrote with reminders or explanations of what they did to create this new sentence. Writing the "before and after" sentence is also a helpful option. So is color coding with highlighters or colored pencils.

(Continued)

(Continued)

WHY THIS LESSON?

When students construct, combine, or redesign sentences that are prewritten, they engage in a scaffolded experience that will lead to greater understanding. Eventually, students will use this process with sentences they have written themselves.

TIPS AND ALTERNATIVE USES

- The example in Handout 5.3 uses prepositions to expand sentences with prepositional phrases. You can work with this same document when you want students to combine sentences, add adjectives or adverbs, change verb tenses, or any other grammar skill this fits with.
- Save the base sentences in an envelope to come back to and use in different ways.
- Coach students throughout this experience by supporting approximations and encouraging play.

Photo 5.7. A long-term partnership using Presto Change-o! with some teacher coaching

HANDOUT 5.3: PRESTO CHANGE-O! USING PREPOSITIONS TO EXPAND SENTENCES

Cut out the sentence strips and the prepositions. Begin with one sentence you have cut out, choose a preposition, and finish the sentence with your own words. Jot them in your grammar notebook and label what you did to expand the sentences using prepositions. (Extra challenge: See if you can find when prepositions turn simple sentences into complex sentences!)

Example: Take deep breaths *between lessons.*

Take deep breaths.
Remind yourself you can do hard things.
Stay calm and carry on.
Keep going.
Writers love to write.
They found their strength.
Friends support each other.
Write your own simple sentence:
Write your own simple sentence:
Prepositions to choose from: above, across, after, against, along, around, at, before, behind, below, between, despite, during, except, inside, like, near, of, off, on, outside, over, past, than, toward, under, until, up, within

Lesson 7: Mimic Sentences

Type of Lesson: Explore and Play

Time: 10–15 minutes, two to three sessions

WHAT'S HAPPENING?

You will study one sentence to see how it is constructed and write additional sentences that mimic that construction.

YOU WILL NEED

- A sentence that you love that includes grammatical concepts that align to the unit
- Chart paper, whiteboard, or other way to display the sentence
- Grammar notebooks
- Long-term grammar partnerships

LESSON STEPS

1. Choose a sentence you like, preferably from a book the class is reading. For example,

   "I would make a great assistant knight because I am smart, I work hard, and whatever I don't know, I promise to learn." (Rothman & Oswald, 2020)

2. Write the sentence on the board or chart paper.
3. Examine the sentence: Read it with the students. Ask them, "What do you notice about this sentence?" Ask partners to identify craft or conventions used by the author (punctuation marks, rhymes, similes, sentence structure, parts of speech, etc.). Circle and label each item on the original text. Add any that you want to draw to their attention. List them on the board.
4. Mimic the sentence: Tell the class, "I think I could write a sentence just like (author's name)!" Model a sentence of your own on the board that matches the pattern of the original sentence.
5. Write together (this might be the next day): Compose a few sentences as a class and list them with the mentor sentence. You may start with a few words and then ask partnerships to finish by following a similar sentence structure.

6. Write in partnerships: Invite the students to work in pairs to create sentences of their own, first orally and then in writing. Join with another partnership and share and compare sentences, giving feedback.

TIPS AND ALTERNATIVE USES

- If you love the idea of mimicking sentences, check out *Patterns of Power* by Jeff Anderson and Whitney LaRocca (2023). They have paved this road for grammar learning for all ages.
- When students are writing, give them time to revise sentences so that one or more of them uses the model sentence.
- Collect model sentences throughout the year. Vary how sophisticated they are by the readiness of students.

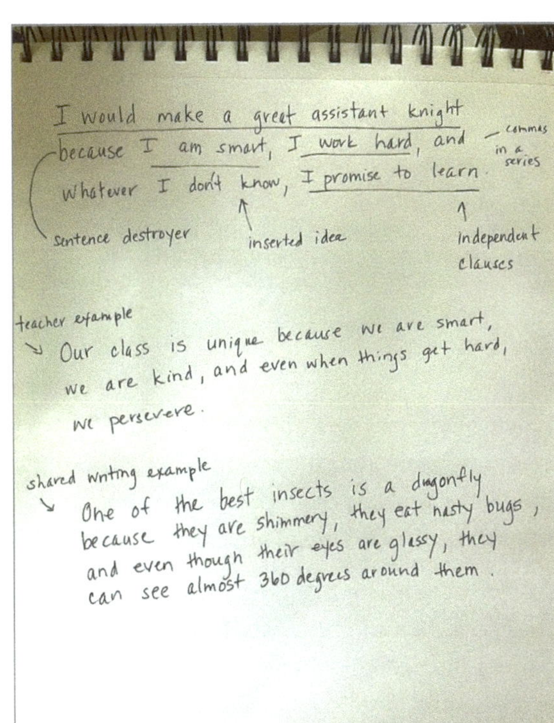

Photo 5.8.
One chart showing the progression of the steps of this lesson

Lesson 8: A Sort of Discovery

Type of Lesson: Explore and Play

Time: 10 minutes, two sessions

WHAT'S HAPPENING?

Partners sort grammatical concepts (both sentences and parts of speech) into categories. When sorting, partners build knowledge of grammar rules (especially the strange ones).

YOU WILL NEED

- Words or sentences that will be cut out (see Handout 5.4, Sort of Discovery, for an example)
- Predetermined categories
- Scissors
- Envelopes or baggies
- Long-term grammar partnerships
- Grammar notebooks

Scan this QR code to access a printable version of Handout 5.4, Sort of Discovery. qrs.ly/29ge0bm

LESSON STEPS

Day 1:

1. Provide each partnership with Handout 5.4. You may create your own handout by choosing different parts of speech (proper and common nouns, regular and irregular verbs, etc.).
2. Ask partnerships to color the back of the paper in their own color combinations. For example, one partnership may color in red and blue crayon, while another colors in yellow marker and green crayon. This helps identify which group these cards shall be returned to when they fall to the floor.
3. In one minute, ask partnerships to cut out the words by following Pam Koutrakos's (2020) PCS (perimeter, column, single) method of first cutting the picture frame, then cutting the columns, then cutting the single words.
4. Invite partners to read over the words and create their own categories, sorting the words into piles based on the categories chosen.
5. Ask them to put the word cards into an envelope or baggie.

Day 2:

1. Share categories that you have selected based on your grammar focus. In Handout 5.4, the categories are words that would be only nouns, only verbs, or words that can act as both.
2. Ask partnerships to categorize the words together.
3. Then invite partners to compare with other partners.
4. Reveal the correct sort. Ask students to jot down in their notebooks what they discovered from the sort.

WHY THIS LESSON?

Our minds hold onto information in categories. When students have the opportunity to compare, converse, and sort, the learning is more likely to stick.

TIPS AND ALTERNATIVE USES

- When students create their own categories, they get to know the words on the cards first. When choosing categories for students, think of grammatical concepts you would like them to know, such as phrases and clauses, nouns and adjectives, independent and dependent clauses, or adjectives and adverbs.

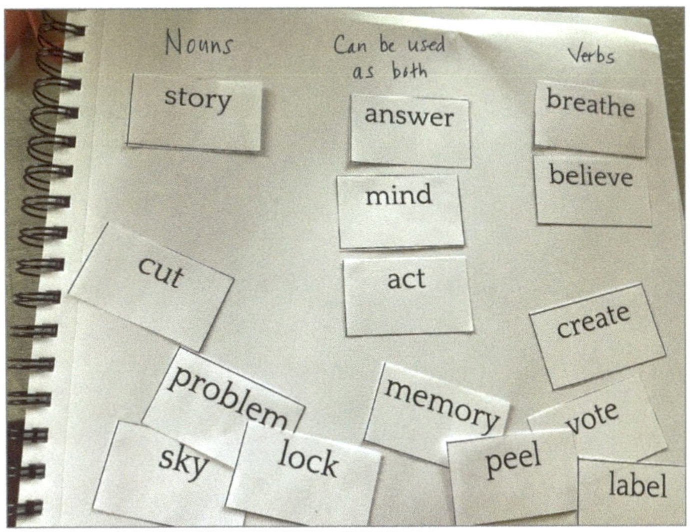

Photo 5.9.
A grammar sort in progress

HANDOUT 5.4: SORT OF DISCOVERY

First, color the back of this paper. Cut the words out using the PCS method: cut the picture frame, then columns, and then singles. Then, sort the words into categories. You will make these categories up to get to know the words.

breathe	story	answer
act	memory	cut
sky	lock	problem
peel	believe	label
mind	vote	create

Lesson 9: Construction Kits

Type of Lesson: Explore and Play

Time: Two 10-minute sessions

WHAT'S HAPPENING?

Students will use objects of different shapes and/or colors to create a model of how to write sentences of different designs. You can use anything you have in collections. The example here uses Unifix cubes (Photo 5.10).

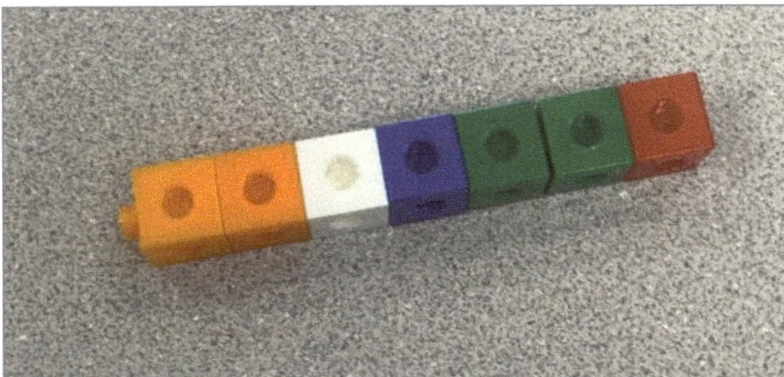

Photo 5.10 Unifix cubes

YOU WILL NEED

- Unifix cubes or other objects of different sizes and shapes
- Sticky notes or labels
- Paper
- Tape or staplers
- Grammar notebooks
- Long-term grammar partnerships

LESSON STEPS

1. After having explicitly taught a grammatical concept (e.g., complex sentences, adverbs and verbs), pass out the objects (e.g., Unifix cubes), sticky notes/labels, and tape/staplers to the student partnerships.
2. Ask grammar partnerships to
    a. Create a model to show how and when the concept is used. Choose different colors or shapes for the different parts of speech, clauses, phrases, and/or punctuation. See Photo 5.11 for an example.

(Continued)

(Continued)

b. Label the objects using the sticky notes/labels to indicate different parts of speech, clauses, phrases, and/or punctuation.

c. On paper, write a step-by-step set of instructions to show how to use the model.

3. Ask partnerships to share with each other. Listen to conversations to be sure there is accuracy in their model.

WHY THIS LESSON?

Suspending the use of actual words and thinking about parts of speech and how they work together builds an understanding of grammar. When partners deliberate on what to include in their model, they build syntactical knowledge.

TIPS AND ALTERNATIVE USES

- We must acknowledge the second graders of Kim Clancey's class who came up with this idea! They wanted a way to create a model of how to construct a sentence and brilliantly thought up this clever approach.
- If you do not have Unifix cubes or similar manipulatives, connect with lower-grade teachers or teachers of math. They will likely have some you can borrow.
- Come back to the models as you dig into other parts of speech. For example, use a compound sentence model and add a new color to show where the adjective or preposition might go.

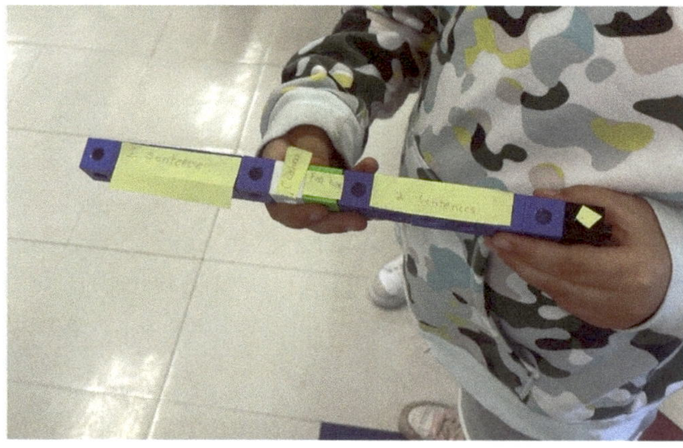

Photo 5.11.
Students created a model of a compound sentence. The blue cubes stand for simple sentences or independent clauses, the white cube is the comma, the green cube is the FANBOYS, and the black cube represents the end punctuation.

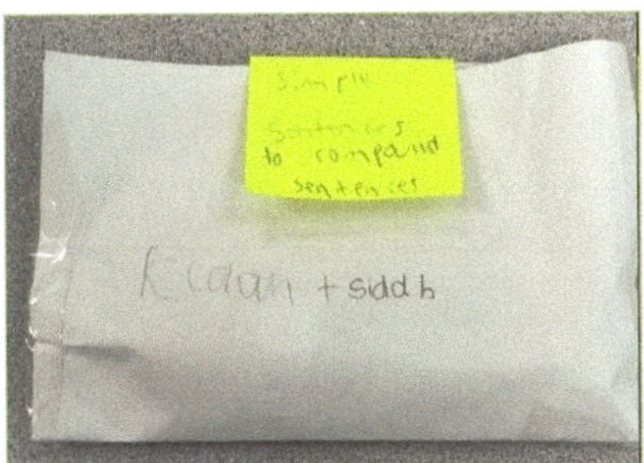

Photo 5.12.
After students made a model, they packaged it in an envelope.

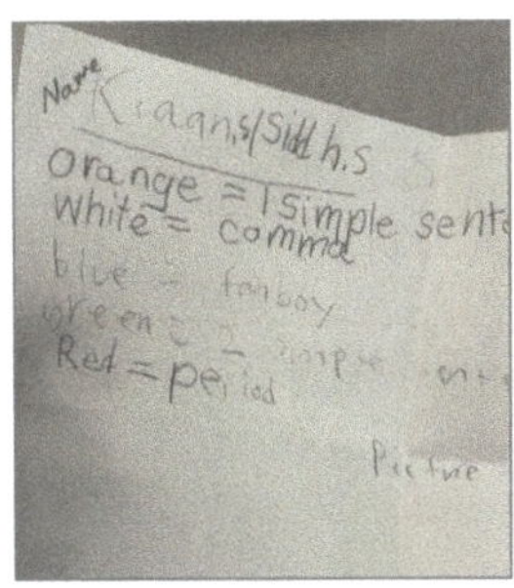

Photo 5.13.
In the envelope they included a key to identify what each color represented.

Photo 5.14.
Many students also included a sketch with steps to follow.

Lesson 10: Fill in the Blanks

Type of Lesson: Explore and Play

WHAT'S HAPPENING?

Similar to *Mad Libs* or the 19th-century parlor game *Consequences,* in this lesson you will take a piece of text and remove certain parts of speech. In its place, identify the part of speech that is needed to complete the sentences. Partners will ask for parts of speech, fill the words in, and then read out the passage, often making each other chuckle. After reading the nonsense version, partners will replace the misfit words with a more correct option.

YOU WILL NEED

- A few pieces of text that are missing certain parts of speech but indicate what part of speech needs to be added in their place. (See Handout 5.5, Fill in the Blanks, for an example.)
- Long-term grammar partnerships
- Pencils or pens
- Clipboards

Scan this QR code to access a printable version of Handout 5.5, Fill in the Blanks.

qrs.ly/aoge0bp

LESSON STEPS

1. Pass out a copy of the fill-in-the-blank text to each partnership, along with a clipboard. (See Handout 5.5 for an example.)
2. Provide the following directions to the pairs:
   a. Partner 1 holds the passage on the clipboard, while Partner 2 looks in a different direction.
   b. Partner 1 asks for parts of speech to fill in the blanks indicated in the passage.
   c. Partner 2 provides words that correspond to the parts of speech.
   d. When all the blanks are filled in, the partnership reads the text aloud together.
   e. Chuckle at the strange sentences that are designed.
3. Pair up partnerships to share what they created.

WHY THIS LESSON?

Aside from being good fun, this is the experience most adults say taught them parts of speech. Hearing how different words create an entirely different meaning also helps with word selection.

TIPS AND ALTERNATIVE USES

- To give students extra practice, use AI to create texts that zoom in on certain grammatical concepts. For example, ask AI to write you a paragraph about a particular topic and to use the simple past tense. With the right AI tool, you can even specify the grade level; this is such a time saver! Make the text simple enough for students to read with understanding.
- As an alternative, first try this as a whole class, and then, on another day, have students partner up with each other.
- Students can also take a piece they have written and remove parts of speech for this experience.

Go to an AI tool and try the following prompt to see what it generates: "Write a piece of nonfiction text about unlikely animal friendships using prepositional phrases and commas in a series."

Hummingbirds

Hummingbirds are (adj) happy creatures that can be found in (place) Clearwater Marine Aquarium. These (adj) silly birds are known for their vibrant colors and their ability to (action verb) throw in mid-air. They have long, slender (noun) dogs that are perfectly adapted for sipping (noun) dolphins from flowers. Did you know that hummingbirds can (action verb) muck up to 80 times per second? That's incredibly (adjective) melted! They are the only birds that can (action verb) ride a horse backwards and even upside down. Hummingbirds are also known for their incredible (noun) pool. They can (action verb) Cooking at speeds of up to 60 miles per hour! These (adjective) bad birds are a joy to watch as they (action verb) act, bringing beauty and energy to our gardens.

Photo 5.15. Student work using the hummingbird fill-in-the-blank text

HANDOUT 5.5: FILL IN THE BLANKS

Hummingbirds

Hummingbirds are (adjective) _____________ creatures that can be found in (place) _____________. These (adjective) _____________ birds are known for their vibrant colors and their ability to (action verb) _____________ in mid-air. They have long, slender (plural noun) _____________ that are perfectly adapted for sipping (noun) _____________from flowers. Did you know that hummingbirds can (action verb) _____________ up to 80 times per second? That's incredibly (adjective) _____________! They are the only birds that can (action verb) _____________ backward and even upside down. Hummingbirds are also known for their incredible (noun)_____________. They can (action verb) _____________ at speeds of up to 60 miles per hour! These (adjective) _____________ birds are a joy to watch as they (action verb) _____________, bringing beauty and energy to our gardens.

Lesson 11: Grammar Scavenger Hunts

Type of Lesson: Explore and Play

Time: 10 minutes

WHAT'S HAPPENING?

Partners read a passage or a few pages from a book. When they find something on the scavenger hunt list, they jot it down.

YOU WILL NEED

- A list of what to hunt for (choose concepts that have been taught)
- A photocopied passage, a book, a magazine, or any type of writing that uses sentences. (Poems and songs break so many rules that we do not want to include them here.) See the Handout 5.6 for a sample list and passage for this lesson.
- Pens or pencils
- Grammar notebooks
- Long-term grammar partnerships

Scan this QR code to access a printable version of Handout 5.6, Scavenger Hunt.

qrs.ly/lsge0by

LESSON STEPS

1. Give students a passage or ask them to go into any text they are reading in class.
2. Give students a list of what to try to find in the passage.
3. Partners read together and hunt for the grammatical items on the list.
4. Students write down what they find.

WHY THIS LESSON?

This type of discovery happens naturally in a Grammar Study approach. When students find what they are learning in grammar in the texts they read (or find that an author chose not to use grammar accurately), they are eager to share.

(Continued)

(Continued)

TIPS AND ALTERNATIVE USES

- Adjust the different scavenger hunts across the year to both practice and review the grammatical concepts you have taught.
- If there is a doozy of a grammatical faux pas, you may want to keep that as something to go back to for a laugh. After all, *Eats, Shoots & Leaves* by Lynn Truss (2006) is now a classic set of books for adults and kids alike.

Photo 5.16. The student used a page from *The Maze Runner* by James Dasher for his scavenger hunt.

Photo 5.17. A page from *Hatchet* by Gary Paulsen had lots to find on the scavenger hunt!

HANDOUT 5.6: SCAVENGER HUNT

With your partner, read the text below. Together go on a hunt to see if you can find:

1. Prepositions and prepositional phrases
2. Verbs of being (am, is, are, was, were, be, being, been)
3. Sentence destroyers (also called subordinating conjunctions)

Sample Passage From *Remember Us* by Jacqueline Woodson, Chapter 1

The moon is bright tonight. And full. Hanging low above the house across the street where an orange curtain blows in and out of my neighbors' window. Out and in. And past the curtain there's the golden light of their living room lamps. Beyond that, there is the pulsing blue of their television screen. I see this all now. I see a world continuing.

And in the orange and gold and blue I'm reminded again of the year when sirens screamed through my old neighborhood and smoke always seemed to be billowing. Somewhere.

That year, from the moment we stepped out of our houses in the morning till late into the night, we heard the sirens. Down Knickerbocker. Up Madison. Across Cornelia. Both ways on Gates Avenue. Down Ridgewood Place. Rounding the corners of Putnam, Wilson, Evergreen . . .

Evergreen. Sometimes a word comes to you after time has passed. And it catches you off guard. Evergreen. The name of a family of trees. And the name of a block in Brooklyn. Evergreen. Another way of saying forever.

That year, nothing felt evergreen.

Palmetto. A word that has never left me. A word that in my mind is evergreen. Palmetto. The name for both a stunning tree and an oversize cockroach. Palmetto was also the name of a street in my old neighborhood. And that year, Palmetto Street was burning.

Lesson 12: Co-Authoring

Type of Lesson: Explore and Play

Time: 10 minutes

WHAT'S HAPPENING?

Co-authoring is an experience in which the teacher writes collaboratively with students. This enables students to practice grammar skills aloud without having to be concerned about encoding. When composing aloud, with partners, students can also easily revise their ideas without much fuss (like erasing and starting over). Co-authoring can occur in both whole groups and small groups. You can practice single sentences or write a portion of a text together. In this sample, we have shared how to do this by composing one sentence.

YOU WILL NEED

- Chart paper or a notebook (if you have a document camera)
- Marker or pen
- A focus on what you want to write and practice
- Any anchor charts or resources that will help students practice the chosen grammar skill
- Long-term grammar partnerships

LESSON STEPS

1. Pick a grammatical focus, such as appositives.
2. Share the focus with students. "Today, we will be co-authoring a few sentences that include appositives. I will start us off."
3. Write the first bit for students to see. Notice in Photo 5.18 the teacher wrote a sentence that included an appositive about her pets.
4. Ask students to compose the next part aloud with their long-term partners. Give a grammatical focus, such as "Compose a sentence together that includes an appositive. When you compose this sentence aloud, say where you would also add punctuation."
5. While students are composing aloud, write down another sentence based on what you are hearing from a conversation. As you write

down the next sentence, ensure accurate use of grammar (even if the students themselves were inaccurate).

6. Gather students back together to share what you wrote down. Point out something grammatical to pay attention to. In Photo 5.18, the teacher pointed out the commas.

7. Repeat steps 4 through 6 as many times as you wish.

WHY THIS LESSON?

Composing a text together allows for scaffolded practice of grammatical skills. Because you are making the final decision about what is written down, students will see accurate use of grammar. Composing aloud, also called oral rehearsal, is quite beneficial for writers.

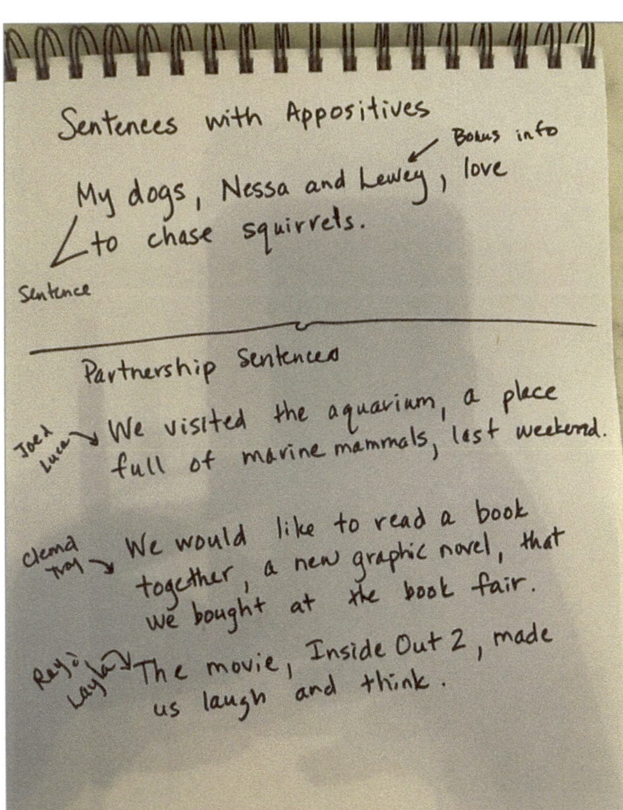

Photo 5.18. One example of co-authoring practicing appositives

TIPS AND ALTERNATIVE USES

- Co-authoring is a bounty of oral composition, so be sure students are sharing in partnerships and that you are listening in to select the words

(Continued)

(Continued)

and sentences you will write. It is not a time for students to watch you write for 10 minutes. It is also not one student raising their hand and one student getting the chance to give an idea.

- You can write a collection of sentences, as Photo 5.18 has shown. Or you may want to compose a written piece together. This can be a paragraph, a story, an informational piece, an opinion text, or another type of writing.
- You can give them a topic or focus if it is needed. This can be anything from a topic everyone knows about, like the classroom or school, SEL, a shared story, a response to a book, and so on.

KNITTING THE CHAPTERS TOGETHER

This chapter provided a collection of Explore lessons. Two of these lessons are used to hypothesize before an Explicit Teaching day; nine lessons are used to play with grammatical concepts to build know-how; and one (Lesson 3) can be used for both. For a moment, think about traditional grammar instruction of identification, fill-in-the-blank worksheets, and memorization of parts of speech. These lessons shake up instruction so that students can roll up their sleeves, so to speak, and build grammar understanding.

Perhaps you have already chosen an immersion text from Chapter 4 and paired it with some Explore days.

In the next chapter, you will find a collection of Explicit Lessons that show the how-to of grammar concepts. This collection will be an indispensable resource for Grammar Study and continues to build units for your students to study.

CHAPTER SIX

Explicit Lessons

Anchor Charts and How-Tos

Teaching tools create an impact on students' learning. They help students hold onto our teaching and become changed by the work in the classroom.

—Kate Roberts and Maggie Beattie Roberts (2016)

In Grammar Study, students have plenty of opportunities during the Immersion phase of each unit to generate ideas, questions, and hypotheses as they study mentor texts, leaning into inquiry both individually and in partnerships. Following Immersion, students will explore and play with the topics in greater depth, guided periodically by teacher-led explicit instruction. We have been calling these days "Explicit Teaching days." That's when you address conundrums and confusions you've seen students having. These lessons are designed to turn these tripping points into tipping points for students, giving them the clarity they need for steadier understanding of a concept.

This chapter provides a series of lessons that you can implement during the Explicit Teaching days of a unit of study. We have selected topics that are relevant to a wide range of students and provide a springboard to other grammatical concepts. These lessons follow the same structure as those from Chapters 3 and 4, though here we also add specific tips for connecting the area of focus of each lesson to other grammar topics. The lessons addressed in this chapter are listed in Table 6.1.

Table 6.1 • Lesson Progression in This Chapter

LESSON NUMBER	TITLE OF LESSON	PAGE NUMBER
1	Capitalization and End Punctuation	175
2	Items in a Series	178
3	Prepositions	181
4	Introductory Phrases	185
5	Quotations and Punctuation	189
6	Conjunctive Adverbs	193

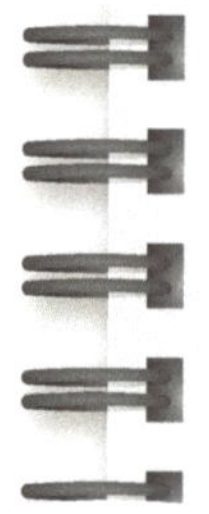

TIPS FOR INTERACTING WITH THIS CHAPTER

- Use the lessons and anchor charts as ready-to-go teaching tools.
- Use the "pairs well with" descriptions in the lesson tips to identify other topics to teach alongside, or in addition to, the lesson topic.

At the end of the chapter, we provide four additional anchor charts that you can use or modify. Our hope is that you will find inspiration in and use the structure from the Essential Sentences unit in Chapter 3 and that you will mix and match the lessons in Chapters 4 through 7.

THE GRAMMAR LOVERS' BOOK NOOK

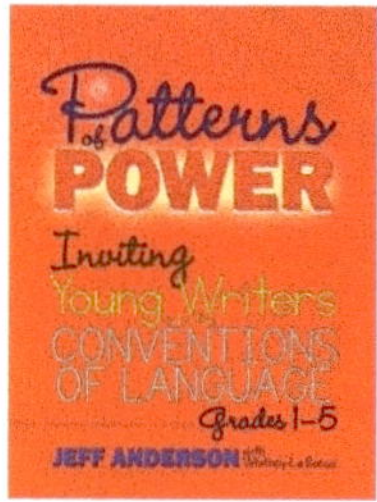

For Teachers: *Patterns of Power* by Jeff Anderson and Whitney LaRocca (2023)

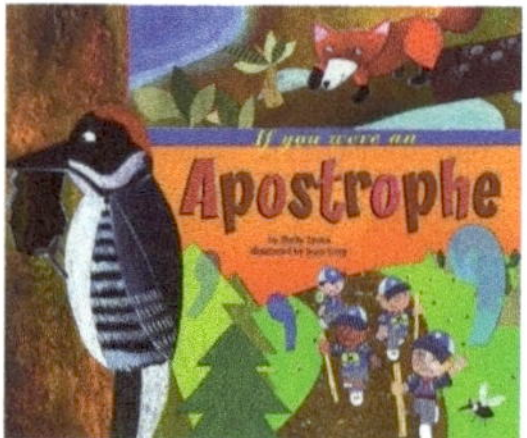

For Students: *If You Were an Apostrophe* (and the whole Word Fun Collection) by Shelly Lyons (2009)

Lesson 1: Capitalization and End Punctuation

Type of Lesson: Explicit Teaching

Time: 10–15 minutes

YOU WILL NEED

- An anchor chart on capitalization and marks of end punctuation (see Figure 6.1 for an example)
- The mentor sentences without punctuation listed in Step 3 below; see the punctuated versions here:
  - Are we playing soccer during recess?
  - Recess is the best!
  - The students played soccer during recess.
- Grammar notebooks
- Long-term grammar partnerships

LESSON STEPS

1. Begin by telling students that all sentences begin with a capital letter and end with a mark of punctuation. Name and review the three marks of end punctuation.
   - Period: Comes at the end of a sentence; it marks the end of a complete thought.
   - Question mark: Used to show that a question is being asked.
   - Exclamation point: Used to show emotion or excitement.
2. Show students an example of each sentence type, noting the initial capital letter and the mark of end punctuation. For example:
   - The students learned about punctuation.
   - What types of punctuation did the students learn?
   - Using punctuation is so fun!
3. Read aloud the following sentence (or create your own) and show students how meaning changes depending on the punctuation used.

(Continued)

(Continued)

- The game is canceled?
- The game is canceled.

4. Ask students to work in their partnerships to add capitalization and punctuation to the following sentences. You can create your own if you'd prefer.
   - are we playing soccer during recess
   - recess is the best
   - the students played soccer during recess
5. With students still in pairs, provide words and have students create sentences to demonstrate their understanding of capitalizing and end punctuation. Have them record additional examples of each sentence type in their grammar notebooks, labeling the capital letters and end punctuation.

WHY THIS LESSON?

Capitalization and punctuation errors may be the most frustrating thing teachers see in students' writing. Teachers of all grades are confounded by students' lack of capitals and punctuation. Capitalization and punctuation are an essential foundation of writing because they provide clarity for readers. Marks of end punctuation help a reader understand how to read a sentence (e.g., as a question, with an excited tone), and they mark a clear end to a sentence. Likewise, capitalized words at the beginning of a sentence tell the reader that a new sentence is beginning. These are fundamental components of writing that will help students to communicate their ideas clearly and accurately.

TIPS

- While modeling for students, read the sentences aloud and use your voice intonation to emphasize how a sentence should be read; have students practice chorally.
- Mention that the personal pronoun "I" is always capitalized, whether it begins a sentence or falls within a sentence.
  - **I** bought new sneakers.
  - The sneakers that **I** bought are blue.
- This lesson pairs well with instruction on naming specific sentence types for each mark of end punctuation (i.e., declarative = period, interrogative = question mark, exclamatory = exclamation point).

Figure 6.1 • Sample Anchor Chart

Capitalization + Punctuation

— Capitalize the first letter of a sentence.

The students played kickball.

Can we play kickball?

— Capitalize the pronoun "I".

Tell him that I am home.

I love reading mystery books.

— Add end punctuation to all sentences.

. A **period** ends a statement.

The game is cancelled.

? A **question mark** asks a question.

Is the game really cancelled?

! An **exclamation point** shows excitement or emotion.

I can't believe the game is cancelled!

Lesson 2: Items in a Series

Type of Lesson: Explicit Teaching

Time: 10–15 minutes

YOU WILL NEED

- An anchor chart on listing items in a series (see Figure 6.2 below for an example)
- The mentor sentences listed in lesson Step 3 below; see the punctuated versions here:
  - I like **to run**, **to swim**, and **to bike**.
    - List of infinitives
  - I will buy **apples**, **oranges**, or **bananas.**
    - List of nouns
  - Sienna **walked** to the movies, **bought** popcorn, and **met** her friend Mary.
    - List of verbs
- Grammar notebooks
- Long-term grammar partnerships

LESSON STEPS

1. Begin by telling students that one of the specific ways that writers use commas is to separate items in a list. The commas help the reader slow down and understand clearly what is being listed. Any time three or more items are listed, commas are needed to separate them. A FANBOYS word (usually "and" or "or") is added before the final item in the list. See the FANBOYS lesson in Chapter 3 for more on this acronym.
2. Using the following two sentences or creating your own, model the process for using commas to separate items in a series:
   a. My favorite animals are **frogs, snakes,** and **kangaroos**!
      i. This sentence lists nouns in a series.
   b. The squirrel ran **over the fence**, **between the cars**, and **up the tree**.
      i. This sentence lists prepositional phrases in a series.

3. Ask students to work in their partnerships to add commas to the following sentences and explain their thinking; as always, you can create your own sentences.
    a. I like to run to swim and to bike.
    b. I will buy apples oranges or bananas.
    c. Sienna walked to the movies bought popcorn and met her friend Mary.
4. Consider one of the following extension activities:
    a. Create sentence strips that contain items in a series. Cut up the sentences and have students work in groups to put them together, adding commas in the appropriate place.
    b. Have students use word cards to create and punctuate sentences of their own that contain different types of listed items.

WHY THIS LESSON?

Students must know how to separate items in a list to ensure that their writing communicates clear and accurate information. If a comma is missing, the meaning of the information can change. Students can start small by listing single words in a series and build in complexity to phrases and clauses.

TIPS

- Be sure to explain that the items listed in a series need to be equal grammatically (nouns, adjectives, phrases, clauses, etc.).
    - You can't say, "I will buy apples, oranges, or eat bananas."
- There is much debate about whether the comma before the FANBOYS word is necessary. Known as the Oxford comma, it adds clarity to what is being listed, and we recommend that you teach students to use it.
- When items in a series themselves contain commas, use semicolons to separate them to avoid confusion with too many commas.
    - I visited Bar Harbor, Maine; Salem, Massachusetts; and Portsmouth, New Hampshire.
- This lesson pairs well with instruction on parts of speech (prepositions, adjectives, nouns, verbs) and parallel structure.

(Continued)

(Continued)

Grammar Nerd Alert!

Once students have mastered listing items in a series, there are two grammatical structures that bend the rules described above that you might consider teaching to more advanced writers as a form of differentiation.

- **Asyndeton**: The elimination of FANBOYS from a list. This is an intentional move by the writer to create a sense of urgency or a fast pace. Here is an example used by A.P. Language and Composition teachers everywhere:
  - "It was the best of times, it was the worst of times, it was the age of wisdom, it was the age of foolishness." (*A Tale of Two Cities* by Charles Dickens)
- **Polysyndeton:** The inclusion of additional FANBOYS words in a list, which creates an added sense of emphasis to each item in the list.
  - At the barbecue, I ate hot dogs and ribs and chicken and corn and watermelon. I'm stuffed!

Figure 6.2 • Sample Anchor Chart

Items in a Series

When listing 3 or more items:

1. Separate each item with a comma.
2. Add a FANBOYS word before the last item.

→ My favorite animals are frogs, snakes, and bats!

→ The squirrel ran over the fence, between the cars, and up the tree.

Lesson 3: Prepositions

Type of Lesson: Explicit Teaching

Time: 10–15 minutes

YOU WILL NEED

- An anchor chart on how to create prepositional phrases (see Figure 6.3 for an example)
- Table 6.2, the companion chart that lists commonly used prepositions
- Grammar notebooks
- Long-term grammar partnerships

LESSON STEPS

1. As context for the lesson, remind students that adjectives modify nouns and adverbs modify verbs. Begin by explaining that prepositions are words that relate or connect a noun or pronoun to another word in the sentence, providing description and detail. Prepositions include words such as in, on, above, below, between, before, after, and so on. Display Table 6.2, the chart of commonly used prepositions.
2. Explain to students that prepositions are most commonly used within prepositional phrases, which include a preposition and a noun (to + the store; in + the car). When prepositional phrases add information about a verb, they act as adverbs. When they add information about a noun, they act as adjectives. Students should practice writing both types of prepositional phrases, though most students will write adverbial prepositional phrases early on, which answer questions such as where, when, and how. These types of phrases typically provide information about location and time.
3. Using an anchor chart like the one in Figure 6.3, show students how to create prepositional phrases. You may use common examples such as: over the fence, into the house, before the game, and so on.
4. Model for students how to create prepositional phrases.
    a. To add information about a verb: Start with a subject and verb and then ask where, when, how about the verb. For example,
        i. The student tripped
            - **in** the hallway (where)

(Continued)

(Continued)

- **after** lunch (when)
- **on** a banana peel (how)

b. To add information about a noun: Start with a noun and ask the questions which one? or what kind?

i. The books **on** the shelf are mine.

ii. The car **in** my spot is parked illegally.

iii. The man **with** two children is next in line.

5. Give students a chance to practice writing sentences that include prepositional phrases. Have students talk in their partnerships about their sentences.

Table 6.2 • Commonly Used Prepositions

COMMONLY USED PREPOSITIONS	
about	above
across	after
against	along
among	around
at	before
behind	between
beyond	by
down	during
except	from
in	into
near	of
off	on
onto	out
over	past
to	toward
under	until
up	upon
with	within

Scan this QR code to access a printable version of Table 6.2.

qrs.ly/3zge0c0

WHY THIS LESSON?

Prepositional phrases provide detail and description in student writing and can be incorporated with a focus on elaboration. As a cautionary note, too many prepositional phrases can make writing overly repetitive. However, after completing this lesson you and the students will have a common language to use about prepositional phrases, which is great for providing targeted feedback (include a prepositional phrase here; eliminate a few prepositional phrases from this paragraph, etc.).

TIPS

- Have students practice with one preposition and see how many nouns they can add to it to create different phrases.
  - **In** the car, **in** my house, **in** the book, **in** her jacket, and so on.
- Show students that multiple prepositional phrases can be joined with FANBOYS words
  - He jumped **over** *the fence* and **into** *the pool.*
- Descriptive words can be added to prepositional phrases.
  - **into** the freezing *pool*
  - **under** the filthy *bridge*
- Prepositional phrases can also contain pronouns (to + pronoun) and must use the correct type of pronoun. See Section 10 (Pronouns Continued) of Part 4: Your Grammar Refresher.
  - We went to dinner **with** *them.*
  - Keep this **between** *you and me.*
  - I gave the letter **to** Angela and *her.*
- Instruction on prepositional phrases pairs well with the following topics:
  - Introductory phrases
  - Subject/Verb agreement (ignore prepositional phrases)
  - Indefinite pronouns (pay attention to prepositional phrases)
  - Pronoun case (I vs. me)
  - Parallel structure
  - Misplaced modifiers

(Continued)

(Continued)

Figure 6.3 • Sample Anchor Chart

Prepositions

above, below, around, between, in, on,
into, onto, near, among, to, over, with . . .

Create Propositional Phrases

- Preposition + Noun ...to the park ...in the house

OR

- Preposition + Pronoun(s) ...between you and me ...to her

Add Prepositional Phrases to Verbs

- The student tripped in the hallway.
- Let's keep this between you and me.

Add Prepositional Phrases to Nouns

- The books on the shelf are mine.
- The girl in the window is happy.

Lesson 4: Introductory Phrases

Type of Lesson: Explicit Teaching

Time: 10–15 minutes

YOU WILL NEED

- An anchor chart on how to create introductory phrases (see Figure 6.4 for an example)
- Multiple simple sentences for practice adding introductory phrases; sample sentences are listed below. Feel free to remove the introductory phrases for practice or use them as constructed for modeling.
  - In the middle of the night, the sound of thunder woke me up.
  - With a confident smile, the speaker began her presentation.
  - At the top of the mountain, the climbers celebrated their accomplishment.
  - Before the long day at school, the children played outside.
- Grammar notebooks
- Long-term grammar partnerships

LESSON STEPS

1. Begin by reminding students that a phrase is a group of words that does not have a subject/verb pair and cannot stand alone. Introductory phrases begin sentences and are followed by a comma and a main clause (main idea of the sentence). Think of an introductory phrase as the initial setup for the main clause(s) of the sentence; it sets the scene and provides background information/context before the subject and verb arrive in the sentence.
2. Show students how sentences they've written with prepositional phrases can be restructured to put the prepositional phrase at the beginning. Use the following examples to model or create your own.
   a. Justin went for ice cream *after the game.*
      i. After the game, Justin went for ice cream.

(Continued)

(Continued)

b. The kids played in the woods *near the school.*

i. Near the school, the kids played in the woods.

3. Ask students to write a sentence with a prepositional phrase that comes after the verb. Then, have them flip the prepositional phrase from the end of the sentence to the beginning. Remind them that a comma follows the introductory phrase.

4. Have students talk in pairs about the sentences they wrote. Partnerships can continue writing sentences together. Ensure that students have models in their grammar notebooks.

5. *Optional:* Structure #2: Introductory Participle Phrase. For students who are ready for a more complex structure, model the introductory phrase that begins with verb + ing. As described in Section 4 (Phrases) of Part 4: Your Grammar Refresher, participle phrases act as adjectives and describe the subject (noun or pronoun) that they precede. Use the following sentences or create your own.

   a. Running to the mall, Suzette found 10 dollars on the ground.

      i. *Ask:* Who or what was running to the mall? (Suzette)

   b. Hoping to win the lottery, Maureen bought 100 tickets.

      i. *Ask:* Who or what was hoping? (Maureen)

6. For more information about potential issues with introductory participle phrases, see Section 12 of Part 4: Your Grammar Refresher on dangling modifiers.

7. *Optional:* Structure #3: Introductory Infinitive Phrase. Tell students that an infinitive phrase takes the form of "to" + verb and any other descriptive information. Use the following sentences or create your own.

   a. **To find** the treasure, they used a map.

   b. **To lower** the gate, she plays the organ.

WHY THIS LESSON?

Introductory phrases provide another way for students to vary their sentence structure, moving away from beginning sentences with the standard subject/verb pair. Students can start with prepositional phrases and move on to more complex structures like participle phrases; both types are included on the anchor chart above as a reference, but you should determine your entry point based on the students in front of you.

TIPS

- In addition to providing students with feedback about the sentence types that they're using, you can also reference introductory phrases as a specific way for students to vary their sentence structure.
- When a sentence with an introductory phrase is read aloud, the comma provides a break for the reader between the introductory idea and the rest of the sentence.
- Introductory phrases are different from dependent clauses that begin complex sentences. As a reminder, though a dependent clause cannot stand alone, it does contain a subject/verb pair whereas a phrase does not. For further clarification, review the phrases/clause comparison in Part 4: Your Grammar Refresher.
- This lesson pairs well with instruction on prepositional phrases and dangling modifiers.

Grammar Nerd Alert!

All of the sample sentences in this lesson, despite their length or seeming complexity, are simple sentences because they have only one subject/verb pair.

(Continued)

(Continued)

Figure 6.4 • Sample Anchor Chart

Introductory Phrases

Set the scene for the sentence.

1. Write the introductory phrase.

2. Add a comma.

3. Write the main part of the sentence.

→ Begin with a prepositional phrase:

- After the game, Justin got ice cream.
- Near the school, the kids played in the woods.

→ Begin with a verb + "ing" phrase:

- Running to the mall, Sophia found 10 dollars.
- Hoping to win the raffle, Dorothy bought 100 tickets.

→ Begin with "to" + verb:

- To find the treasure, they used a map.
- To catch the fish, he used a net.

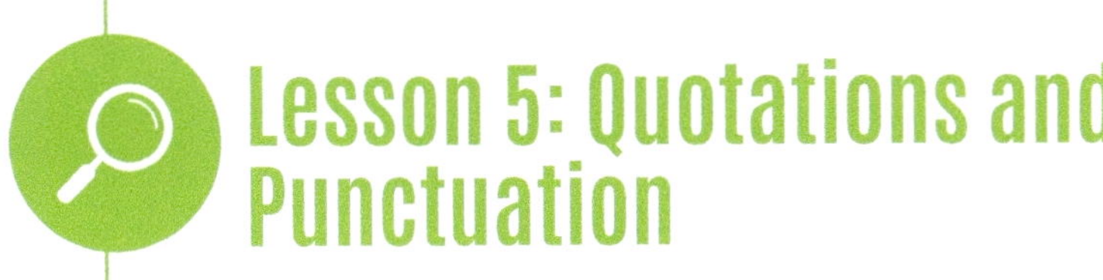

Lesson 5: Quotations and Punctuation

Type of Lesson: Explicit Teaching

Time: 10–15 minutes

YOU WILL NEED

- An anchor chart on how to use and punctuate quotation marks (see Figure 6.5 for an example)
- For immersion purposes, you might use an immersion mentor text from Chapter 4 (such as the "Sunrise Adventure" Mentor Text, page 116), that includes quotation marks and punctuation.
- Punctuated sample sentences from Lesson Steps 4:
  - "Don't forget to shut off the lights," said Elizabeth.
  - Mahatma Gandhi said, "You must be the change you wish to see in the world."
  - John Lennon wrote, "You say I am a dreamer, but I'm not the only one."
  - "There's nothing like a good book in bringing folks together," remarked Coyote Sunrise.
- Long-term grammar partnerships

LESSON STEPS

1. Begin by telling students that quotation marks are used to create dialogue in stories and also to directly quote the words of other people. There are specific rules that apply to using quotation marks, including where punctuation (commas, periods, question marks, etc.) are placed.
2. Provide an overview of the following process that students should use when including quotes:
   a. Figure out which words in the sentence need to be quoted.

(Continued)

(Continued)

   b. Surround or "hug" the words with quotation marks.
   c. Give credit to who said the words (dialogue tag).

3. Use the following two sentences—or create your own—to model the process for students:
   a. "Don't forget to shut off the lights," said Elizabeth.
   b. Mahatma Gandhi said, "You must be the change you wish to see in the world."
4. Provide an opportunity for practice. Use the following unpunctuated sentences and have students add punctuation: quotation marks, commas, and end punctuation.
   a. Don't forget to shut off the lights said Elizabeth
   b. Mahatma Gandhi said You must be the change you wish to see in the world
   c. John Lennon wrote You say I am a dreamer, but I'm not the only one
   d. There's nothing like a good book in bringing folks together remarked Coyote Sunrise

WHY THIS LESSON?

Utilizing and correctly punctuating quotation marks is an important skill for students in narrative, informational, and opinion/argument writing. It takes lots and lots of practice. This lesson provides a foundation for students that they can refer to during subsequent units that involve quotations. In addition, as readers, students will be more aware of how dialogue and quoted source materials function, which can aid in comprehension.

TIPS

- Before the quote or dialogue, add a comma after the word *said* (or any other descriptive word (exclaimed, questioned, shouted, etc.) used as a tag.
- Periods and commas always go inside the closing quotation mark, whereas colons and semicolons go outside the closing quotation mark;

(Continued)

question marks and exclamation points fall either inside or outside the closing quotation mark depending on the structure of the sentence.

- As an extension of this lesson, provide information about rules related to using question marks and exclamation points with quotes. See Section 14 (Punctuation) of Part 4: Your Grammar Refresher for rules and sample sentences.

- More advanced writers may choose to break up the quoted material and reference the speaker (and perhaps additional information about the speaker) in the middle of the quote.
    - "The result of the game," the exhausted referee said, "is a tie."
    - Be sure that when the speaker attribution is removed, the sentence is properly structured and makes sense:
        - The result of the game is a tie.

- This lesson also pairs well with using quotation marks to punctuate the titles of short texts (e.g., "Ozymandias" is both the name of a poem by Percy Shelley and an episode title in the TV show *Breaking Bad*). Longer works, like TV shows, books, and movies, are italicized or underlined. Finally, quotation marks can be used to emphasize a sarcastic or ironic tone.
    - Though John was "working late" yesterday, I saw him at the concert.

(Continued)

Figure 6.5 • Sample Anchor Chart

Quotes and Punctuation

Adding quotes and dialogue:

1. **Figure out which words in the sentence need to be quoted.**
2. **Surround or "hug" the words with quotation marks.**
3. **Give credit to who said the words.**

Use commas and end punctuation:

A) Before the quote or dialogue

→ John Lennon wrote, "You say I'm a dreamer, but I'm not the only one."

→ Hailey asked, "Can you hear me?"

B) After the quote or dialogue

→ "Don't forget to turn off the lights," said Elizabeth.

→ "This is the best trip ever!" exclaimed the child.

Lesson 6: Conjunctive Adverbs

Type of Lesson: Explicit Teaching

Time: 10–15 minutes

YOU WILL NEED

- An anchor chart on how to use conjunctive adverbs (see an example in Figure 6.6)
- Two sets of simple sentences (We love to use sentence strips for this!)
- Grammar notebooks
- Long-term grammar partnerships

LESSON STEPS

1. Begin by reviewing compound sentences and the fact that there must be a complete sentence on either side of the FANBOYS conjunction.
2. Using an anchor chart like the one illustrated in Figure 6.6, show how to take two simple sentences, choose a conjunctive adverb (see page 232 in Part 4: Your Grammar Refresher for a complete list by category), and connect the sentences. You may use the following simple sentences or choose your own: *I wanted to sleep. The dog kept me awake.*
3. Model for students the two ways to use conjunctive adverbs.
    a. To begin the second sentence
        i. *Example:* I wanted to sleep. However, the dog kept me awake.
        ii. *Rule*: Capitalize the conjunctive adverb and add a comma.
    b. To combine the two sentences using a semicolon
        i. *Example*: I wanted to sleep; however, the dog kept me awake.
        ii. *Rule*: Following the semicolon, do not capitalize the conjunctive adverb. Add a comma.
4. Give students a chance, in partnerships, to try connecting predetermined simple sentences. You may use the following simple sentences or write your own for students to try: *John forgot to study for the test. He received a poor grade.*
5. Ask students to jot down the two sentences that they combined using a conjunctive adverb and explain their process.

(Continued)

(Continued)

WHY THIS LESSON?

Conjunctive adverbs offer another option for students to create compound sentences or to establish a clear transition between two sentences or ideas. Although technically adverbs, conjunctive adverbs function much like coordinating conjunctions and act as transitions in connecting two independent clauses. In this lesson, you can help students understand the level of nuance that conjunctive adverbs offer. For example, instead of saying "but" to show contrast, a student might select *conversely, however, on the other hand, nevertheless,* and so on. Incorporating conjunctive adverbs strategically will provide students with another layer of depth in their writing.

Students and adults alike often misuse conjunctive adverbs in a manner that results in a run-on sentence. There are two types of errors that we often see:

1. When a comma instead of a semicolon is used to connect independent clauses with a conjunctive adverb. This results in a comma splice (see the run-on sentence anchor chart in Figure 6.7 below).
   a. **Incorrect:** I wanted to sleep, however the dog kept me awake.
      i. To correct, use either a period or semicolon in place of the comma (as modeled above).
2. When the information that follows the conjunctive adverb is a phrase (not a complete sentence), a comma (not a semicolon) should be used.
   b. **Incorrect:** The villain made too many mistakes; thus *leading to his inevitable capture.*
      i. The participle phrase "leading to his inevitable capture" cannot stand alone, so a semicolon cannot be used.
      ii. The correct punctuation with this type of structure is a comma.
      iii. *The villain made too many mistakes, thus leading to his inevitable capture.*

Grammar Nerd Alert!

When a participle phrase follows the main clause, the structure is called a loose sentence. Writers use this structure to present the main idea of the sentence and then elaborate on it.

TIPS

- Make sure that students double check that they have complete simple sentences (subject/verb pair) on either side of the conjunctive adverb.
- As an extension lesson, show students how conjunctive adverbs can be used as interrupters:

(Continued)

- *Example:* She wanted to buy new shoes. The store, however, was sold out.
  - The conjunctive adverb is surrounded by commas.
  - If the conjunctive adverb is removed, the sentence must still make sense (e.g., The store was sold out).
- This lesson pairs well with instruction on semicolons, transition words and phrases, extension lessons on adverbs, and compound sentences.

Figure 6.6 • Sample Anchor Chart

Conjunctive Adverbs

1. To begin a sentence:

[Sentence #1 + C.A. + Comma + Sentence #2]

→ I wanted to sleep. However, the dog kept me awake.

1. To combine two sentences

[Sentence #1 + Semicolon + C.A. + Comma + Sentence #2]

→ I wanted to sleep; however, the dog kept me awake.

ADDITIONAL ANCHOR CHARTS

In addition to the six lessons and corresponding anchor charts detailed above, we have created four additional anchor charts for you to use or adapt. Though these charts do not contain detailed lesson plans, our hope is that the six lessons above have provided a template for you to use to develop your own lessons. We've also included these charts to further model our approach to making learning visible and to encourage you to create your own charts for any topic. For each anchor chart that follows, we provide a brief overview of the grammatical topic/skill. You may also read further about each topic in Part 4: Your Grammar Refresher.

Correcting Run-On Sentences

A run-on sentence occurs when the incorrect type of punctuation—or no punctuation at all—is used to combine two simple sentences. When only a comma is used to combine two simple sentences, it's called a *comma splice*. Use the following strategies to correct a run-on sentence. In the following example, no punctuation is used between the two sentences; the same corrections would apply, as well, if there were only a comma between the two sentences.

Figure 6.7 • Run-On Sentences Anchor Chart

Correct a Run-On Sentence

Example: My neighbor's dog is barking I can't sleep.

1. **Add a semicolon.**

   → My neighbor's dog is barking; I can't sleep.

2. **Add a period.**

   → My neighbor's dog is barking. I can't sleep.

3. **Add a comma + FANBOYS.**

   → My neighbor's dog is barking, so I can't sleep.

4. **Add a Sentence Destroyer and a comma.**

   → Because my neighbor's dog is barking, I can't sleep.

Nonrestrictive/Parenthetical Information

To enhance writing through description, writers add nonrestrictive/parenthetical phrases and clauses that are nonessential to the overall meaning of the sentence. In fact, if the information is removed, the sentence must still make sense. Nonessential elements are set off by commas, dashes, or parentheses. The following examples provide steps that students can utilize to make their writing more descriptive with nonessential information.

Figure 6.8 • Nonessential Information Anchor Chart

Add Nonessential Information

Process:

1. Find a noun to describe.
2. Place the descriptive information after the noun.
3. Surround the information with commas.
4. Make sure as you complete the sentence that it still makes sense without the extra information.

Examples:

- Betty, the fastest player on the team, is a forward.
- My cousin, who owns a restaurant, loves to cook!
- The Statue of Liberty, a New York landmark, is made of copper.
- Soo's new television, which she bought yesterday, works beautifully.

Add Details With Adjectives

The following chart contains examples of individual adjectives (yellow, hot, flat, etc.) as well as coordinate (bright, sunny), cumulative (expensive diamond), and compound adjectives (brown-eyed)—all of which are explained in detail in Section 1 (Parts of Speech) of Part 4: Your Grammar Refresher.

Figure 6.9 • Detail With Adjectives Anchor Chart

Add Detail With Adjectives

Process:

1. Find a noun to describe.
2. Ask "What kind?" or "How many?" about the noun.
3. Add the adjective(s) before the noun.

- the yellow bus
- the hot coffee
- the flat tire
- several students

- Julio lives in a blue house.
- She pulled up in her fancy car.
- The bright, sunny sky made me happy.
- He bought her an expensive diamond ring.
- The brown-eyed girl smiled warmly.

Energize Verbs With Adverbs

This chart is designed to introduce students to the basics of using adverbs (often ending in -ly) to describe verbs. As we know, adverbs also describe adjectives and other adverbs. Section 1 (Parts of Speech) of Part 4: Your Grammar Refresher contains examples of the types of adverbs that could be used to develop a separate chart for more advanced writers.

Figure 6.10 • Energize Verbs With Adverbs Anchor Chart

Energize Verbs With Adverbs

Process:

1. Find a verb that you want to describe.
2. Ask: When, where, how, or how often?
3. Pick an adverb.
4. Try adding it **before** and also **after** the verb to see which way sounds better.

Examples:

- Nestor ran **quickly** up the stairs.
- The students participated **actively**.
- My parents **always** arrive on time.
- I **rarely** practice the piano.
- They live **nearby**.

KNITTING THE CHAPTERS TOGETHER

So far, we have examined how students can learn through inquiry, exploration, and explicit instruction with the assistance of mentor texts, games, and anchor charts to reinforce learning. The next step in the process is to ensure that students not only retain the grammatical concepts and skills that they have learned but also transfer them effectively to their own writing. Chapter 7 provides a clear framework for ensuring that the critical step of transfer takes place for students.

CHAPTER SEVEN

Transfer Lessons

Tools and Schedules

Grammar is my enemy.

—William Stafford

Arguably, the most frustrating experience when teaching grammar is not seeing it applied in writing. This brief but essential chapter will create a bridge from Grammar Study to writing, ensuring greater (not always perfect) grammatical command.

This chapter suggests a few tried-and-tested transfer experiences. You will likely use only some of them in a unit, and we built this chapter so it unfolds in a progression that we have found most useful for students. Transfer experiences described in this chapter are the following:

- Co-creating tools for transfer
- Practicing using the tool
- Weaving grammar skills into current and future writing lessons
- Transferring into other content areas
- Transferring to a test-like prompt

Because the transfer lessons are set up as experiences in a progression, they are a different format from earlier lessons in this book. But you can still spot them with the red-orange headings and pencil-to-notebook icon.

Before we dive into the experiences, let's first explore the concept of transfer. As Grant Wiggins (2012) stated, "Transfer is the goal of education." When students apply what they have been studying to a novel setting or situation where not everything is predictable, we create the conditions for transfer. These conditions alone do not guarantee that students will adopt grammatical skills in that novel experience, but by coaching, we can increase the likelihood that grammar will stick. And, with repeated, well-designed opportunities for transfer, students will deepen their knowledge and use of language.

TIPS FOR INTERACTING WITH THIS CHAPTER

It is vital for teachers, as we support the transfer of grammar into writing, to keep a few expectations in mind:

1. **Expect approximations:** In every grade and at every age, when we try something new, we attempt to use it the best we can. Students may fall short of mastery, but with continued practice and opportunities for transfer, they will refine their skills.
2. **Expect some forgetting:** When using new grammatical skills, it is common for students to forget what they have previously learned. "One of the 'important peculiarities' of human learning is that certain conditions that produce forgetting—that is, decrease our ability to access what we have stored in our memories—actually create opportunities to enhance our level of learning" (Bjork & Bjork, 2019). So you may see more sophisticated usage of prepositions, while simultaneously seeing clunky sentence structure or missing punctuation. Take a deep breath. This is part of the process.
3. **Expect surprises:** Look for the gems of learning that bubble up in the transfer experience. There are moments of unexpected, uniquely crafted pieces. Photo 7.1 shows one of our favorite gems!

Grammar Nerd Alert!

There is wonderful complexity in this passage. Of note, the final sentence contains two dependent clauses ("why I want to be an engineer" and "because I could program robots to do things for me." The student could have simply said, "The last reason is because . . . " but the student added the dependent clause "why I want to be an electrical engineer" to include clarifying detail, which adds a layer of sophistication to the writing.

Photo 7.1
One student using sentence structure intentionally in a quick response

When I get older, I would love to specialize being an electrical engineer/computer engineer. I would want to be this be-cause my dad is one, and because I am good with computers. The last reason why I want to become an electrical engineer/computer engineer is because I could program robots to do things for me.

THE GRAMMAR LOVERS' BOOK NOOK

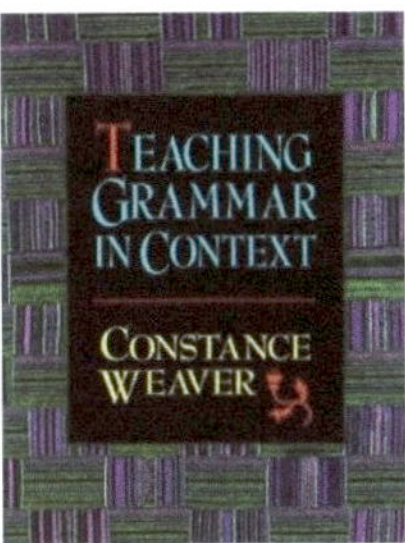

For Teachers: *Teaching Grammar in Context* by Constance Weaver (1996)

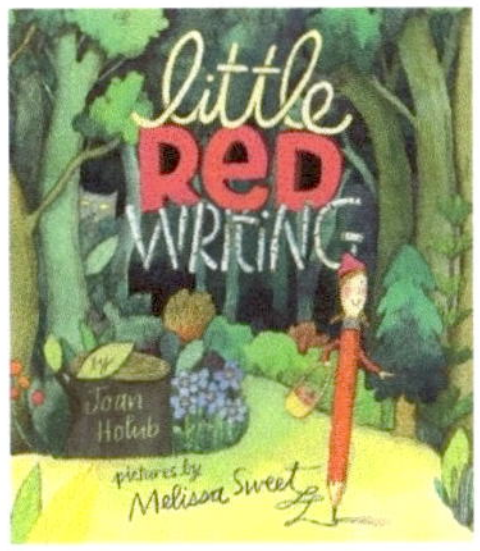

For Students: *Little Red Writing* by Joan Holub (2013)

FIRST, CO-CREATE TOOLS FOR TRANSFER

Perhaps this is teacher intuition, but co-creating tools is also backed by research. As noted in *How People Learn: Brain, Mind, Experience, and School*, "A key finding in the learning and transfer literature is that organizing information into a conceptual framework allows for greater 'transfer'; that is, it allows the student to apply what was learned in new situations and to learn related information more quickly" (Bransford, 2000).

When you and your students co-create a tool that students can use in all sorts of writing, there will be greater ownership and, therefore, likelihood that this tool will support students as they write. Once that tool has been created, we suggest sharing it with any of the classes in which students will be writing. For instance, if students leave for science or social studies, they can use their tool for writing in those settings as well.

You'll want these tools to become permanent fixtures in your class. They are meant to be referred to repeatedly so that students can practice their grammar skills in many different types of writing. This consistent practice proves incredibly useful for internalizing grammar skills and using them to craft writing to communicate.

We are intentionally keeping this tool co-creation broad and flexible. We want you and your students to make what you need at the end of a Grammar Study. It will be unique to you and your learners. Because of this, the tools will be personalized and, therefore, more effectively used.

Steps to Co-Create a Tool

1. Choose the focus.
2. Ask partners to browse their notes in their grammar notebooks, the charts that were created from the direct teaching days, and the reflections gathered as a class. Highlight or name what is most important to remember.
3. Either on chart paper or digitally, write down what is most helpful to remember. This may look like one or more of the following:
    a. A "how-to" with steps as reminders for when students are writing
    b. Reminders or tips on using a grammar concept in writing
    c. An "If . . . Then . . . " to give examples of scenarios in which students may take action (e.g., If you are listing items in a series, then add commas after each item.)
    d. Writing to teach younger students about a grammatical topic
    e. What you and your students imagine will be most useful
4. Once the tool is complete, give students a chance to use it to revise a piece of writing that has already been completed.

See Photos 7.2 and 7.3 for sample tools that other classes have created.

Photo 7.2. Partnerships made their own tools to share with the entire class

Complex Sentences

We can use this when:

- We want to provide multiple details in one sentence.
- We want to explain our thinking.
- We want to compare/contrast and explain ("although, while...")
- We want to show cause and effect ("because...")

A complex sentence:

- Combines one independent clause and one dependent clause (a phrase/group of words that doesn't make sense on its own)
- Has a sentence destroyer (After, Although, As, When, While, Until, Because, Before, Since) either at the beginning of the sentence or in between the two clauses.
- May or may not have a comma depending on the order of the clauses
    - Independent + Dependent = No comma
    - Dependent + Independent = Comma

  *If there is a comma, it goes after the dependent clause and before the independent clause.

Photo 7.3
One part of a class resource on using different types of sentences

SECOND, PRACTICE USING THE TRANSFER TOOL

Before bringing the tool you create into the designated writing time, give students a chance to practice using it with their partner. Choose a piece of writing that students have already completed. Ask them to revise their writing. Photos 7.4 and 7.5 show what this may look like.

Photo 7.4
Students refer to the transfer tool as they review their writing on the computer.

One teacher's observation when students first used their co-created tool:

> This activity was great for students to reflect and look back on their writing.
>
> It was interesting to notice that some students were focused on whether their sentences made sense or not, some were taking stock of what kind of sentences they had and tried to diversify, and some were focused on whether their punctuation was correct.

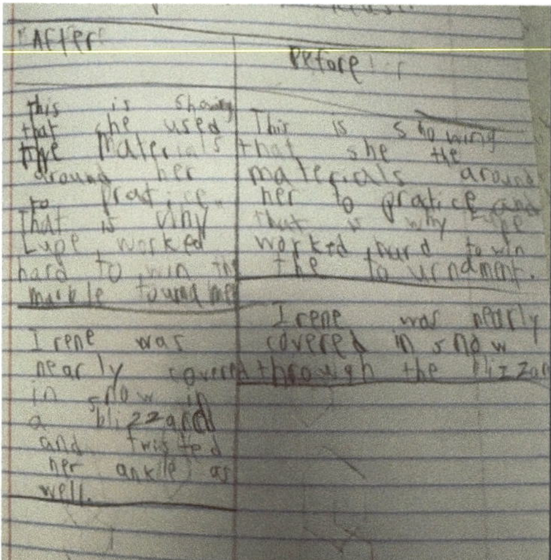

Photo 7.5
One student created a before and after showing how their sentences evolved.

THIRD, BRING INTO CURRENT AND FUTURE WRITING LESSONS

Throughout this book, we have kept in mind that grammar learning is deep and nuanced. There is a process of approximating, leading toward mastery. As such, the grammar we teach in each unit will cycle through the entire writing curriculum at different times in the writing process. Each unit of Grammar Study will be integrated into writing throughout the school year. See Table 7.1, which shows how grammar across the writing curriculum could look.

In Table 7.1, the row headings indicate the stages of the writing process, and the column headings are the different writing assignments or units that students will engage with. We recommend using the co-created tool in explicit writing lessons at different stages of the writing process. We then recommend spiraling those tools and lessons throughout the year, moving them earlier and earlier in the writing process. This will give ample opportunity to revisit and craft writing with greater grammatical fluency.

In other words, the grammatical focus of Unit 1 (Sentences) will be taught during the editing stage of the first writing unit. Then, in Writing Unit 2, Sentences will be taught during revision and Grammar Unit 2 (Agreement) is focused on during the editing phase. And so on throughout the scope and sequence of the entire year.

Table 7.1 • One Suggestion for Building Grammar Learning Into Writing Units

	WRITING UNIT 1	WRITING UNIT 2	WRITING UNIT 3	WRITING UNIT 4	WRITING UNIT 5
Drafting			Grammar Unit 1: Sentences	Grammar Unit 2: Agreement	Grammar Unit 3: Describing Words and the Words They Describe
Revising		Grammar Unit 1: Sentences	Grammar Unit 2: Agreement	Grammar Unit 3: Describing Words and the Words They Describe	Grammar Unit 4: Punctuation Exploration
Editing	Grammar Unit 1: Sentences	Grammar Unit 2: Agreement	Grammar Unit 3: Describing Words and the Words They Describe	Grammar Unit 4: Punctuation Exploration	Grammar Unit 5: Nibs and Knobs (the rest of the random standards)

Adapted from *The Power of Grammar* **by Mary Ehrenworth and Vicki Vinton (2005).**

FOURTH, TRANSFER TO OTHER AREAS

It is never too early (or late) to bring grammar knowledge into writing in any situation. Consider the following ideas to bring grammar into other subjects.

Share the Wealth

If you work in a departmentalized setting where students have multiple teachers of different content areas, we can assure you that the other teachers wish for stronger grammar fluency. They have much to teach in their content area, and adding grammar lessons is usually too much. However, if you share the co-created tools with the content area teachers, they can use them as simple reminders as students write. What we have found is that students often end up surprised that they are also meant to use grammar effectively in areas aside from English Language Arts.

Easy Opportunities to Respond in Writing

When students are writing in any subject area, we can ask them to use a particular grammar concept to answer with a clear and meaningful response.

For example, we may ask for a response using compound or complex sentences, such as,

- Because the colonists were taxed by Great Britain, they decided to ban British imports.
- When the water reached 32 degrees Fahrenheit, it turned to ice.
- After dividing by two, I came up with the answer.

FINALLY, TRANSFER TO TEST-LIKE PROMPT

Scan this QR code to access a printable version of the question set.

qrs.ly/3nge0c5

We know that there is always some sort of state assessment that will test students on their grammar knowledge. As such, we recommend finding test samples or released items to take a few minutes to transfer grammar knowledge to this unique setting.

On the following page (Handout 7.1) is a fourth grade test-like question set. Each state differs in how it evaluates grammar usage. Check out the released items from your state that sample the types of questions they will encounter.

KNITTING THE CHAPTERS TOGETHER

Together we have traversed the wonderful world of Grammar Study. We have introduced the concept and the layout of units. We have shared resources to use when studying grammar to keep it collaborative, playful, and sticky. And now, we move to a chapter on assessment.

HANDOUT 7.1: SAMPLE QUESTION SET

Instructions for students: Read the passage carefully and choose the best answer for each question. Good luck!

(1) Once upon a time, in a small village, there lived a kind old woman named Mrs. Thompson. (2) She had a beautiful garden filled with colorful flowers and delicious vegetables. (3) Every morning, Mrs. Thompson would water her plants and sing cheerful songs. (4) The children in the village loved to visit her garden because they could play and help her pick ripe tomatoes and sweet strawberries. (5) Mrs. Thompson always had a big smile on her face, and she shared her harvest with everyone.

1. **Which of the following sentences is a simple sentence?**
   A. Mrs. Thompson watered her plants and sang cheerful songs.
   B. The children loved to visit her garden because it was fun.
   C. Mrs. Thompson had a beautiful garden.
   D. Although it was sunny, they decided to stay inside.
2. **Identify the compound sentence from the options below.**
   A. Mrs. Thompson had colorful flowers in her garden.
   B. The children played in the garden, and they helped pick strawberries.
   C. Because it was morning, she watered her plants.
   D. She smiled at the children who were visiting.
3. **Which sentence is an example of a complex sentence?**
   A. The garden was beautiful, and the vegetables were delicious.
   B. Mrs. Thompson sang while she watered her plants.

C. The children played and laughed in the garden.

D. She shared her harvest with everyone.

4. **What type of sentence is sentence (5)?**

A. Simple sentence

B. Compound sentence

C. Complex sentence

D. None of the above

5. **Which of the following sentences combines two ideas using a conjunction, making it a complex sentence?**

A. Sentence (1)

B. Sentence (2)

C. Sentence (3)

D. Sentence (4)

CHAPTER EIGHT

Assessment

For Learning and *of* Learning

Author created using OpenAI

This chapter on assessment is late in the book for a reason. As teachers, we often think of assessment first, especially in a setting where grades are a hefty focus. However, in order to assess with accuracy, we must first decide on what experiences we are going to give students in their learning process. Once we have established and strengthened those practices, we can then assess where students are on their journey to mastery. Heads up: This chapter has a little bit on assessment for grading but a whole lot more on assessment for *learning*.

What do we mean? Although assessment is a deep and broad topic, we will focus on two types: assessment *of* learning and assessment *for* learning. Both serve various purposes in the teaching and learning process. The subsections that follow give a brief overview of how each of these types of assessment can (and ought to be) used in classrooms. For more, see James Popham's (2014) book *Transformative Assessment*. Popham is one of the most trustworthy experts on assessment and his book does a deep dive on the types of assessments and their uses.

THE GRAMMAR LOVERS' BOOK NOOK

For Teachers: *Getting It Right* by Michael W. Smith and Jeffrey D. Wilhelm (2007)

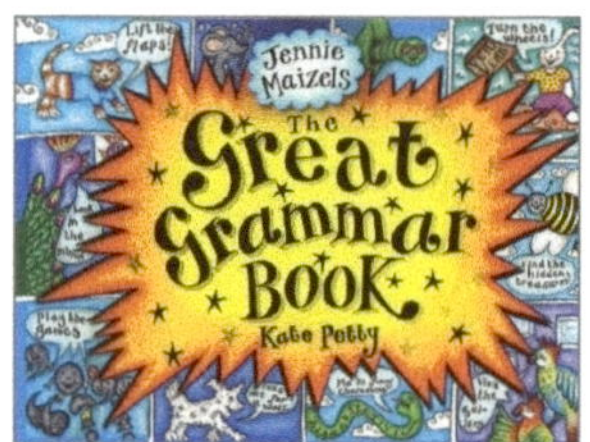

For Students: *The Great Grammar Book* by Jennie Maizels and Kate Petty (1996)

ASSESSMENT *OF* LEARNING

Assessment of learning is also known as summative assessment. Educators tend to use such assessments for grading purposes. These assessments

- can give information about what a student has learned after a period of time.
- are usually high stakes because they most often impact students' grades and, eventually, their academic record.
- often rank students or make decisions about their progress in comparison to others in the class.

Scan the QR code to read more about Black & Wiliam's formative assessment study.

qrs.ly/tnge0c9

ASSESSMENT *FOR* LEARNING

Assessment for learning is also known as formative assessment. In a pivotal study by Black and Wiliam (1998), formative assessment has the potential to double the rate of student learning. These assessments

- happen in between summative assessments in order for the teacher to provide ongoing feedback.
- are primarily meant to help make instructional choices based on what students know, almost know, and do not yet know.

- give information to students about their progress.
- are usually low stakes and not counted toward a final grade.

To use a (kind of off-putting) metaphor, assessments *for* learning are like going for a check-up at the doctor, and assessments *of* learning are akin to an autopsy. One informs of progress, and the other tells us the end results. Both assessments are essential and must be used selectively. When assessments of learning and for learning are used incorrectly, there can be a significant negative impact on student learning, especially as they proceed through the three phases of learning (see Chapter 3).

Remember, when learning grammar, there is a lot of forgetting, relearning, approximations, and experimentation. We are not solely focused on rules and correctness 100% of the time because we want to expand the space for students to grapple with grammar. We use each grammar moment as a stepping stone to mastery. When using formative assessment, we guide students along this pathway, making even more intentional instructional choices, resulting in expedited learning.

This chapter

- begins with suggestions for assessment *for* learning. We have suggestions for all of the different parts of a Grammar Study, including immersion, grammar play, explicit teaching, reflection, and transfer.
- shares ideas for assessment *of* learning.

TIPS FOR INTERACTING WITH THIS CHAPTER

- ☐ Remember, assessment is meant to measure the impact of instruction. Hold tight to the approach from this book as you consider how and when you will assess.
- ☐ Assessment can sometimes become long and dragged out. We don't want students to feel over-assessed as they study grammar. Choose what to assess, when, and how. The assessment matrix at the end of the chapter (Table 8.1) will be very helpful.
- ☐ Students can also suggest additional ways that they can show you their grammar knowledge. Once they feel what Grammar Study is, they will hold a bigger stake in sharing their knowledge and wanting to track it themselves.

ASSESSMENT *FOR* LEARNING: EXAMPLES AND USES

As a teacher you are already assessing for learning in virtually every bit of instructional time. You are always on the lookout for what students can do, almost do, and not yet do. And you are adjusting your teaching accordingly. Capitalize on that spidey sense of yours and use that to make instructional choices such as the following:

- revisiting a lesson you already taught
- referring to charts that have been created
- allowing queries to guide you on, perhaps, unexpected avenues of learning grammar
- extending one session into another because students just need more time
- challenging students to find what may be an incorrect usage of grammar
- partnering students to teach one another
- creating small groups for targeted support
- anything else that you think your students would benefit from

Next, we'll begin thinking about assessment throughout a grammar unit. We highlight many opportunities for all of the phases of the unit: Immersion, Focus Areas, and Transfer.

Assessment During the Immersion Phase: Look for Broad Strokes

Photo 8.1 Looking over the shoulders of students gives us lots of information about their learning.

As you know from earlier chapters, the purpose of Immersion time is to work through the surface learning phase. This is a prime opportunity to see what students already know. You can look at pre-assessments and pinpoint the big commonalities found within the class. Michelle Philippin (personal communication, August 9, 2024), one of the most intuitive teachers we know, gathered information about her students while they were taking the pre-assessment, and then she categorized their responses:

> It was fascinating to see what the students came up with here in the fall of 5th grade.
>
> In reviewing student responses, they overwhelmingly fell into three buckets:
>
> - Noticing punctuation: identification of periods, commas, capitalization
> - Noticing length (i.e., word count, remarking that sentences were "short" or "long")
> - Comments on content (i.e., "nonfiction," reiteration of facts, evaluation of vocabulary, attempt to determine/analyze meaning)

Photos 8.2 and 8.3 show sample assessments that Ms. Philippin's students completed.

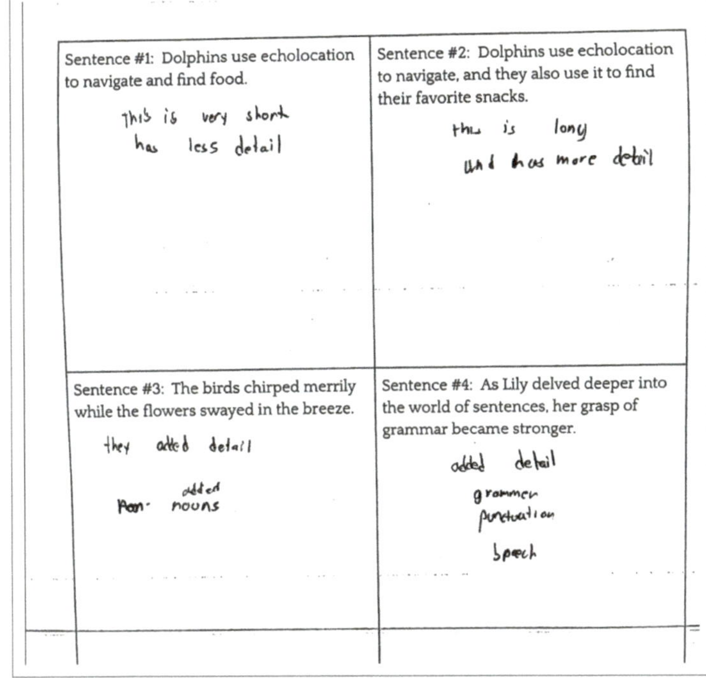

Sentence #1: Dolphins use echolocation to navigate and find food. This is very short has less detail	Sentence #2: Dolphins use echolocation to navigate, and they also use it to find their favorite snacks. thu is long and has more detil
Sentence #3: The birds chirped merrily while the flowers swayed in the breeze. they added detail Pron- added nouns	Sentence #4: As Lily delved deeper into the world of sentences, her grasp of grammar became stronger. added detail grammer punctuation speech

Photo 8.2
One pre-assessment in Ms. Philippin's class

Photo 8.3
Another pre-assessment from Ms. Philippin's class

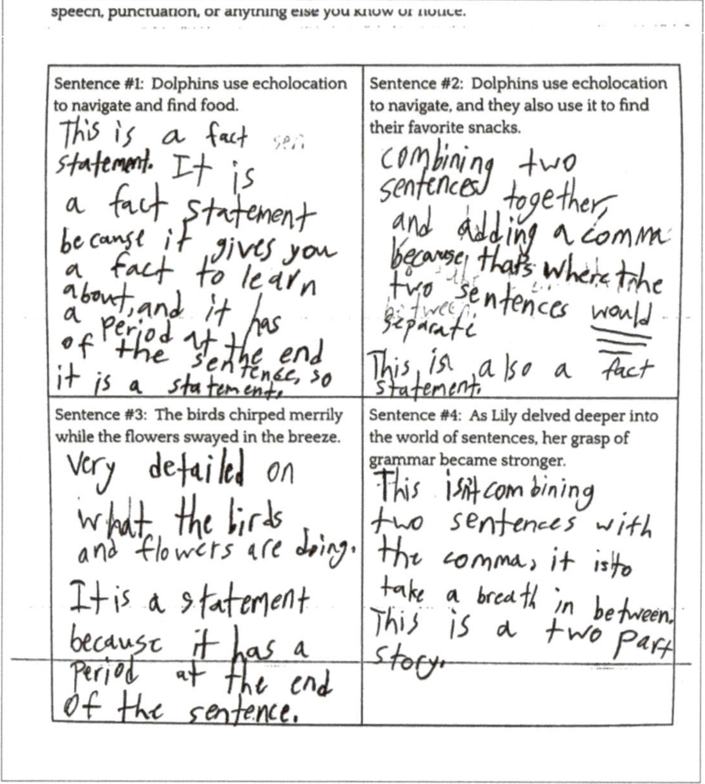

speech, punctuation, or anything else you know or notice.

Sentence #1: Dolphins use echolocation to navigate and find food.	Sentence #2: Dolphins use echolocation to navigate, and they also use it to find their favorite snacks.
This is a fact statement. It is a fact statement becanse it gives you a fact to learn about, and it has a period at the end of the sentence, so it is a statement.	combining two sentences together, and adding a comma because that's where the two sentences would separate. This is also a fact statement.
Sentence #3: The birds chirped merrily while the flowers swayed in the breeze.	**Sentence #4: As Lily delved deeper into the world of sentences, her grasp of grammar became stronger.**
Very detailed on what the birds and flowers are doing. It is a statement because it has a period at the end of the sentence.	This is combining two sentences with the comma, it is to take a breath in between. This is a two part story.

Ms. Philippin also had a few students who stood out in their grammar knowledge, identifying subjects, verbs, and parts of speech. But most came with little knowledge of sentences.

Based on this information, Michelle adjusted the following Immersion lessons to include students studying a mentor text and comparing sentences. She suggested teachers "encourage kids to put on 'special grammar glasses' as we do this work that help us examine the structure separate from, or perhaps *while,* holding the meaning. Perhaps the 'glasses' offer a split screen. We see *what* this sentence is saying, but the 'grammar glasses' invite us to think about *how* it is being said" (M. Philippin, personal communication, August 9, 2024).

Notice this slight shift in Michelle's wording? We bless you to do the same at any point in grammar instruction. Adjust for what feels right for you and your students. Use your innate cleverness to try out different phrasing or experiences suitable to your learners. Responsive grammar instruction is key.

Assessment in the Explore, Hypothesize, and Play Focus Area: Record Misconceptions

Scan this QR code to download a blank version of the Anecdotal Notes template.

qrs.ly/g4ge0ch

During grammar play, assessment should occur through teacher observations. The easiest way to keep track of student learning is to have a place to jot down what you are noticing. This can be in a notebook or in a more structured template, like a grid where you write down what you are observing for each student. Photo 8.4 shows an example of one day visiting a classroom during grammar instruction on a "play day." Patty simply walked around from partnership to partnership, listened to their conversation, and jotted down her observations. We recommend that you keep a record-keeping tool nearby for all formative assessments. It is just so handy.

Anecdotal Notes

Date: 9/22

Lens: Sentences: Pre-assessment and Immersion—Explore Days, too

Duncan need end punctuation	Brianna Q: How many indep clause can you have?	Shay using some grammar lingo	Ruth I+I ✓ FANBOYS ✓
Ahmed Q: can you turn simple sent to comp. sent?	Roger FANBOYS mix up	Shaun independent clause ✓	Cam Q: other conjunctions?
Chadwick caps needed compound sent ✓	Tiana simple & compound sentence ✓	Izzy independent clause needed after FAN	Liz using phrases not clauses
Jack simple sentence noun & verb ✓	Denny Compound Sentence ✓	Brixton sitting & listening mostly	Yanira indep. clause ✓ cap & periods
Abby needs more background	Shantel I+I ✓ FANBOYS ✓ caps & periods	Nat content of sentences rather than design	Pedro translating—cross linguistic transfer?

Photo 8.4.
One teacher's notes that she gathered when listening to partnership conversations

Assessment During the Explicit Teaching Focus Area: Capitalize on the Moments Students Practice

In every Explicit Teaching lesson, there is a time when you model and a time when the students try out what you model. Capitalize on the moments when students try what you are teaching. Because they are trying this very briefly, it is a quick but helpful opportunity to continue to observe, listen, and note any new learning and any misconceptions in your record-keeping tool.

At some points, we may even take a look at grammar notebooks for more insight into grammar learning. Photo 8.5 shows what a student jotted down in their notebook after a direct teaching lesson.

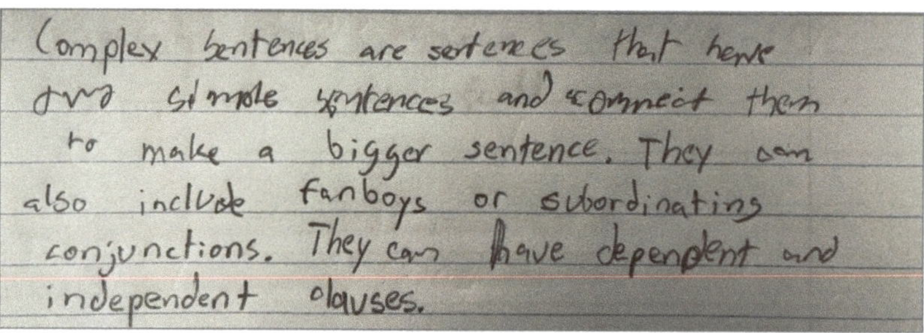

Photo 8.5 Student notes after direct instruction

Looking at this, we see some mastery and some confusion—just what we expect to see in Grammar Study. This learner is somewhat accurate about how complex sentences are designed. They know clauses can be independent and dependent, and they are aware of subordinating conjunctions. However, they are mixing up FANBOYS with "sentence destroyers." Such helpful information!

Assessment During the Reflect Focus Area: Gather Queries, Understandings, and Misunderstandings

Reflection days are a wonderful opportunity to come together as a whole class and ask students to share what they know and are still curious about. This whole-class discussion will reveal a lot to you, including what most of the class understands. Misconceptions may arise, but students can build conversation around this. Photo 8.6 is an example of a chart that came from a day of reflection. Ms. Cho would chart only what was accurate, culling out some of the misconceptions students may have had.

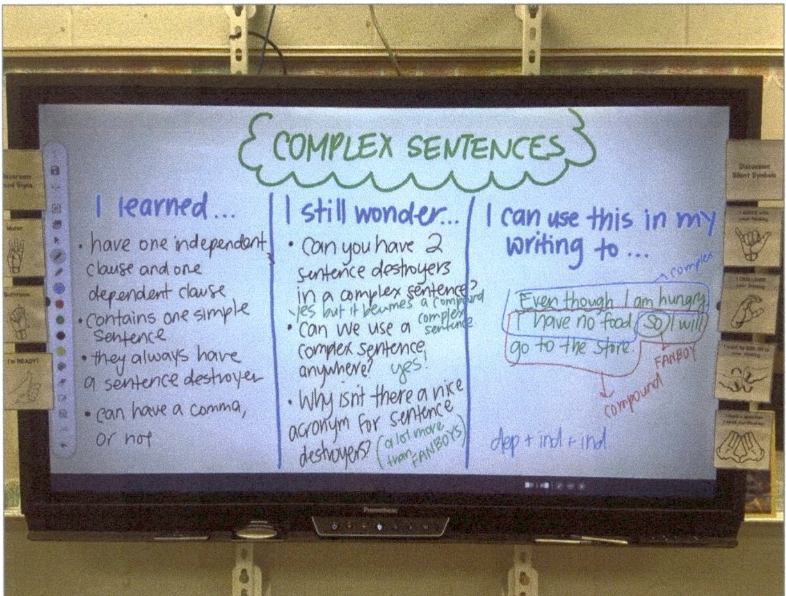

Photo 8.6
One collection of reflections that also give Ms. Cho a lot of data to work with. You can see that on the spot, in some, cases she changed colors and clarified some things

ASSESSMENT *OF* LEARNING: EXAMPLES AND USES

> **Grammar Nerd Alert!**
>
> For the "I still wonder" question in Photo 8.6 about having two sentence destroyers in one sentence, the structure can be Dependent + Independent + Dependent:
>
> **After** we left the movie theater, we stopped for ice cream **because** we were hungry.

You are now at the juncture where you have spent a lot of time supporting students through formative assessment (assessment *for* learning) and need to get some grades in your gradebook. You likely also want to see where students stand with their learning and application of grammar know-how. Following are three suggestions for the types of assessments you may want to consider using.

Pre- and Post-Assessment

This one may be our favorite because students see the vast difference between what they knew just a few short weeks ago and what they know now. Ask students to go back to the pre-assessment that you gave. Whatever they have done with the pre-assessment, now ask them to take a sticky note, a utensil of a different color, or write on a blank version of the pre-assessment. Ask students to write what they know now. Photos 8.7 and 8.8 offer a few examples.

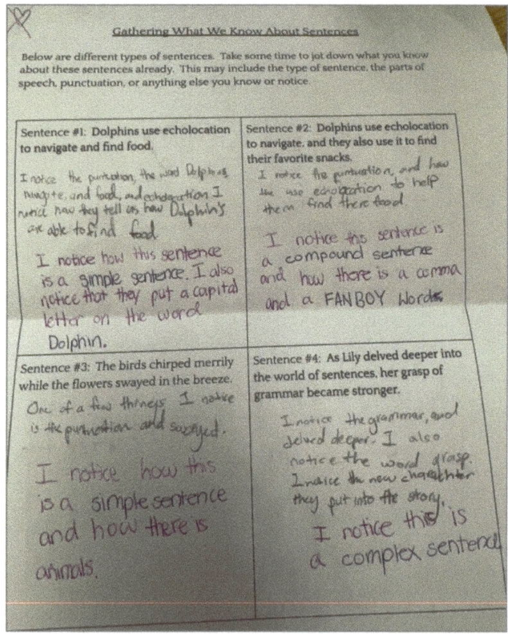

Gathering What We Know About Sentences

Below are different types of sentences. Take some time to jot down what you know about these sentences already. This may include the type of sentence, the parts of speech, punctuation, or anything else you know or notice.

Sentence #1: Dolphins use echolocation to navigate and find food.	Sentence #2: Dolphins use echolocation to navigate, and they also use it to find their favorite snacks.
I notice how this sentence is a simple sentence. I also notice that they put a capital letter on the word Dolphin.	I notice this sentence is a compound sentence and how there is a comma and a FANBOY word.
Sentence #3: The birds chirped merrily while the flowers swayed in the breeze.	Sentence #4: As Lily delved deeper into the world of sentences, her grasp of grammar became stronger.
I notice how this is a simple sentence and how there is animals.	I notice this is a complex sentence

Photo 8.7. One example of a pre-assessment turned post-assessment

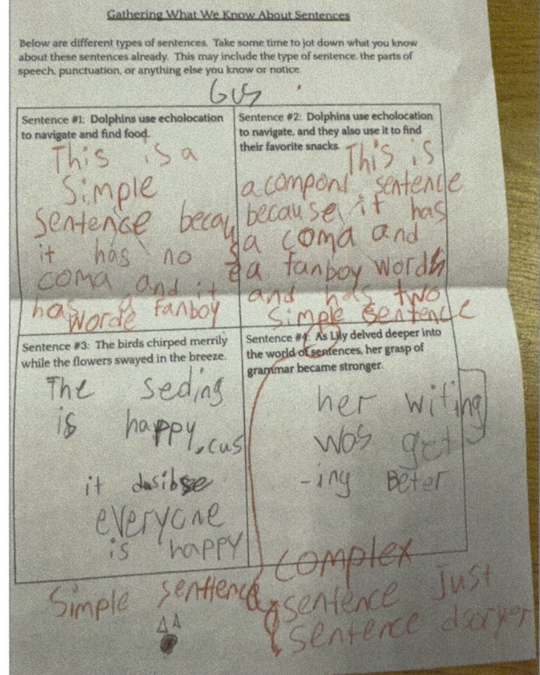

Gathering What We Know About Sentences

Below are different types of sentences. Take some time to jot down what you know about these sentences already. This may include the type of sentence, the parts of speech, punctuation, or anything else you know or notice.

Sentence #1: Dolphins use echolocation to navigate and find food.	Sentence #2: Dolphins use echolocation to navigate, and they also use it to find their favorite snacks.
This is a simple sentence because it has no coma and it has words fanboy	This is a compond sentence because it has a coma and a fanboy words and has two simple sentence
Sentence #3: The birds chirped merrily while the flowers swayed in the breeze.	Sentence #4: As Lily delved deeper into the world of sentences, her grasp of grammar became stronger.
The seding is happy cus it dusibse everyone is happy	her witing was get-ing beter

Simple sentence complex sentence Just sentence deeper

Photo 8.8 It may not be impeccable handwriting, but it sure does show some evidence of learning!

Yes, in some of these examples, there are still some misconceptions. That is information for us as we support grammar application in writing. But, wow, what a difference a few weeks make when students engage with grammar in ways different from our grandparents!

Show What You Know

In the "show what you know" assessment, we ask students to do a little bit of writing and then label their writing with the selected grammar concepts. It may sound something like this:

It is time to show off what you know about sentences. You will do this by writing four sentences or more.

Here's what you need to do:

- Don't be too picky about your topic. If you are stuck, write about a favorite place.
- Make sure you have one simple sentence, one compound sentence, and one complex sentence.
- Include one or more prepositional phrases.
- Label your writing to show where each type of sentence is and the prepositional phrases.

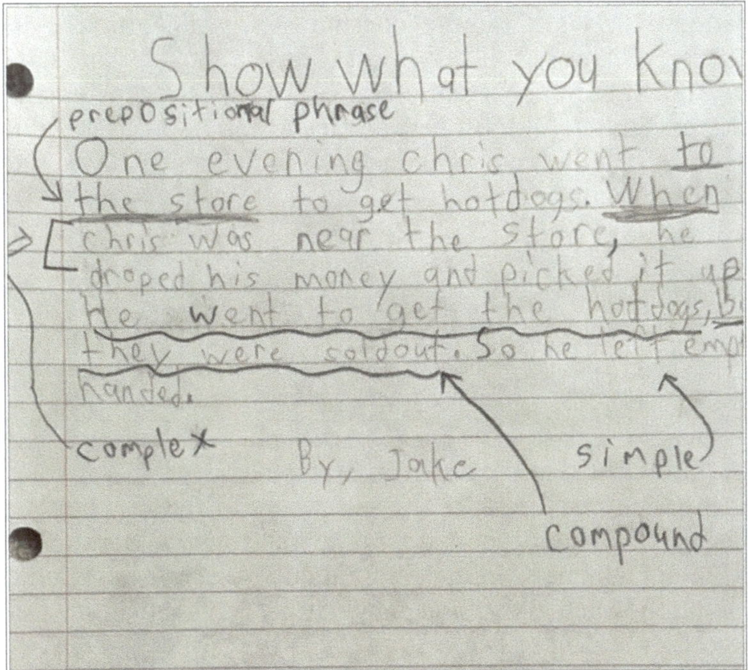

Photo 8.9
One example from a fifth grader showing what he knows

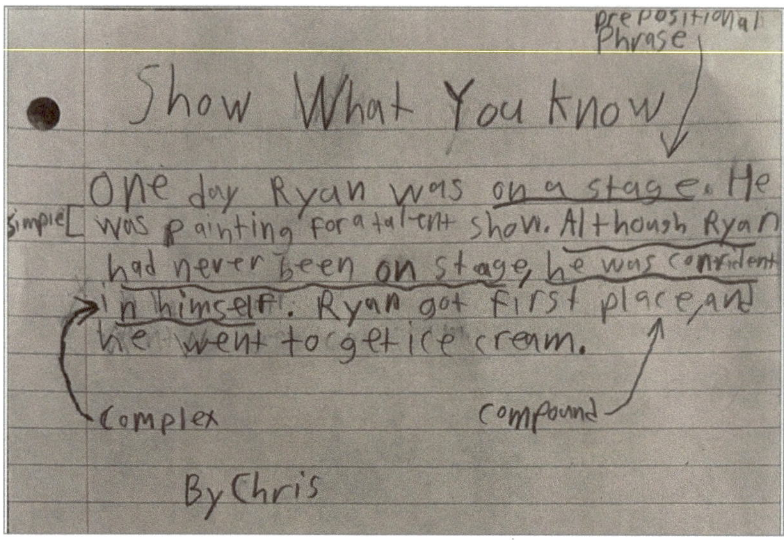

Photo 8.10. A seventh grader with the same "show what you know" criteria.

Standardized Test-Like Questions

Scan this QR code to access a printable version of Handout 8.1.

qrs.ly/67ge0cj

In a world of standardized testing, it helps to expose students to the type of grammar questions that they may encounter. Please only use these sorts of assessments periodically. They really don't do the job of teaching grammar, though they resemble the worksheets and workbooks of our past. Remember, this is not your granny's grammar!

Handout 8.1 is a sample question set. As mentioned in Chapters 3 and 7, you may want to take a look at your state assessment to find a better resemblance to what your students may encounter. And just between us, AI can be a very helpful tool to create these assessments in a snap. That's what we used with this example.

HANDOUT 8.1: TARDIGRADES: THE AMAZING MICROSCOPIC CREATURES

(1) Tardigrades, also known as water bears, are fascinating microscopic creatures. (2) They are found in various environments, from the deepest oceans to the highest mountains. (3) Tardigrades have an incredible ability to survive in extreme conditions, such as extreme temperatures, high radiation, and even the vacuum of space.

(4) Tardigrades are tiny animals that can live in very tough places. (5) Tardigrades can survive in extreme temperatures, and they can also survive without water for a long time. (6) Although tardigrades are very small, they have a special protein that protects their cells from damage.

(7) Tardigrades are incredible creatures that can survive in extreme conditions. (8) They adapt and thrive in environments where most other organisms cannot. (9) Tardigrades continue to amaze scientists and researchers with their resilience and adaptability.

Which of these is a compound sentence?

A. Sentence 1

B. Sentence 7

C. Sentence 5

D. Sentence 9

How do you know it is a compound sentence?

A. It has two independent clauses

B. It has a subordinating conjunction

C. It has a dependent clause

D. It has a preposition

Which of these sentences is a complex sentence?

A. Sentence 3

B. Sentence 4

C. Sentence 5

D. Sentence 6

How do you know it is a complex sentence?

A. It has a subordinating conjunction

B. It has one independent clause and one dependent clause

C. It has a comma connecting the dependent clause to the independent clause

D. All of the above

What is the correct way to combine sentences 7 and 8 into a complex sentence?

A. Tardigrades are incredible creatures that can survive in extreme conditions, they adapt and thrive in environments where most other organisms cannot.

B. Because tardigrades are incredible creatures that can survive in extreme conditions, they adapt and thrive in environments where most other organisms cannot.

C. Tardigrades are incredible creatures that can survive in extreme conditions, so they adapt and thrive in environments where most other organisms cannot.

D. Tardigrades are incredible creatures that can survive in extreme conditions; They adapt and thrive in environments where most other organisms cannot.

To wrap up this chapter on assessment, we want to share a matrix with you (see Table 8.1). This assessment matrix is inspired by Pam Koutrakos (2018) and her work in word study. Pam showed us that there are multiple entry points for gathering information about student learning. We took a page from her book *Word Study That Sticks* and adapted this concept for grammar learning. Remember, we are not always assessing for correctness. More often, we are assessing for growth.

Scan the QR code to access a printable version of the assessment matrix.

qrs.ly/bxge0cn

In the matrix, the areas to assess are listed across the top. Listed down the left column are different times that students can be assessed. The X indicates when the two meet. As you can see, there are ample opportunities for, let's say, assessing whether or not students are using the language of grammar. What's more, these include both formative and summative assessments.

KNITTING THE CHAPTERS TOGETHER

As we send you into Your Grammar Refresher (if you have not explored it yet), we want to leave you with a few parting words of inspiration.

By taking on this approach you are breaking the mold of traditional grammar instruction. You're taking a stand and saying, "My students are not going to be taught grammar in

Table 8.1 • Assessment Matrix: Different Opportunities to Assess Grammar Learning

AREAS OF ASSESSMENT	USING THE LANGUAGE OF GRAMMAR (E.G., PARTS OF SPEECH, SENTENCE TYPES)	APPLYING GRAMMAR IN GRAMMAR STUDY EXPERIENCES (IMMERSION, FOCUS AREAS, TRANSFER)	USING LEARNED GRAMMAR IN WRITING	SYNTHESIZING GRAMMAR SKILLS
Partnership conversations	x	x		x
Play experiences	x	x		x
Pre- and post-assessments	x		x	x
Quick writes		x	x	
Show What You Know	x		x	
Revising and editing a piece of their own writing			x	x
Grammar notebooks	x	x		x
Standardized test-like assessments	x			x

the same way their grannies (and grandpops) and their great-grannies were taught. Grammar deserves so much more than that. Students deserve so much more than that."

Grammar "the forgotten foundational skill" is no more. Bit by bit, you will weave together experiences that build actionable and detailed grammar knowledge and skills.

When engaging in a Grammar Study, remember to

- allow grammar learning to unfold across time.
- keep in mind that immediate correctness is not the aim of grammar learning.

- encourage curiosity and play with grammar.
- make grammar learning the most FUNdamental part of your classroom.

You've got this!

PART FOUR

Your Grammar Refresher

iStock.com/Alona Horkova

Your Grammar Refresher: All You Need to Know About Grammar and Standards

Take a moment and reflect on your experiences as a student learning grammar. Were those experiences playful and fun? Was grammar something you talked about with your friends at lunch or on the playground because you were so excited by it? Chances are that you, like so many of us, learned grammar in a more dry, mechanical way. Maybe you were asked to define a participle or gerund, explain the dangers of a split infinitive, or provide reasons why modifiers should never dangle. Whatever the case, our overall focus with grammar instruction is not to memorize or define, but to examine how grammatical concepts function in the context of writing and how students can leverage grammar to enhance their writing and communicate complex ideas thoughtfully and purposefully.

For additional grammar resources, scan this QR code to watch Tim break down some of the most important grammar concepts in this refresher.

qrs.ly/pbgkpra

This grammar refresher is an invitation for you to join us on a tour of grammatical concepts and skills that are essential for student writers. As throughout this book, we believe that Grammar Study works best when beginning at the sentence level and building from there. This refresher is structured in a similar manner, starting small at the word/phrase level and layering on concepts that build upon each other. With that in mind, you may choose to read the refresher straight through, getting the full scope in the process. Or, if you are looking to review certain concepts immediately, you can jump ahead straight to them. I know I would jump straight to dangling modifiers too, if I were you!

The following is a breakdown of the refresher sections and the specific topics included within each section, as well as the pages that those sections appear on in this refresher.

Now, let us go then, you and I . . .*

**A nod to the late great T.S. Eliot and the ellipsis*

SECTION 1: PARTS OF SPEECH

Before looking at how words are strung together to form phrases and clauses, let's first review the essential parts of speech so that we have a shared vocabulary for subsequent sections. Students, too, must have a clear understanding of parts of speech and how to use them, but that comes in the context of studying mentor sentences—as we'll see below—and not merely memorizing definitions. However, it is critical that you and your students share a common grammar language so that they can comprehend and effectively apply your feedback related to their writing.

Nouns

Nouns refer to people, places, and things (see Table P4.1).

There are multiple categories to consider when it comes to nouns.

- Singular: boat, car, dog, lady, river, love, equality, freedom, family
- Plural: apples, chairs, cities, doctors, dresses, watches
    - Reminder: add "es" to singular nouns that end in sh, ch, x, z, s, or ss.
        - wishes, watches, boxes, kisses, etc.
- Irregular Plurals: woman/women; mouse/mice; goose/geese
- Proper Nouns (capitalize them): William Shakespeare, New York City, the White House, Wednesday, January.
- Collective Nouns: group, crew, pack, flock, pile, etc.
- Abstract Nouns: love, sadness, freedom, knowledge, intelligence, kindness, etc.

Table P4.1 • Singular and Plural Nouns

SINGULAR NOUN	PLURAL NOUN
child	children
foot	feet
goose	geese

SINGULAR NOUN	PLURAL NOUN
man	men
mouse	mice
ox	oxen
person	people
tooth	teeth
woman	women

Pronouns

Pronouns take the place of nouns and most often refer to an antecedent (the noun that the pronoun refers to in the sentence).

Among other things, pronouns help the writer avoid repeating the same noun(s) over and over in sentences. We will go into great detail with pronouns below, but here is a general overview.

- Commonly used pronouns:
    - I, you, he, she, we, they, us, them, his, her, our, your, etc.
        - Annabel rode **her** horse yesterday. **She** had so much fun!
        - *Her* is a pronoun (possessive pronoun, to be exact) referring to the antecedent **Annabel.**
        - *She* replaces Annabel to avoid repeating the name again in the second sentence.
- Indefinite pronouns, a separate category from those above, do not have an antecedent. There are specific rules for subject/verb agreement with these pronouns that we'll get into below.
    - Someone, anyone, everyone, nobody, all, some, few, most, etc.
        - *Someone* is waiting outside my house.
        - *Most* of the players scored goals.
        - *Some* of the money is missing.

Verbs

Verbs come in a variety of forms and are the motor within a sentence; they create the action (in most cases).

- He **runs** quickly
- The student **finished** her homework.
- Isabel **is** a student.
- The band **sounds** amazing!

Irregular verbs don't follow the standard pattern of adding "ed" to form the simple past tense. Instead, they have forms that must be memorized. Table P4.2 lists some common examples.

Table P4.2 • Irregular Verbs—Root Form and Past Tense

ROOT FORM OF VERB	PAST TENSE
be	was/were
bring	brought
do	did
fly	flew
go	went
have	had
keep	kept
make	made
pay	paid
ring	rang
say	said
sell	sold
sit	sat
sleep	slept
steal	stole
swim	swam
tell	told

The following aspects of verbs will all be discussed below:

- Subject/verb agreement
- Types of verbs
- Tense

- Active/passive voice
- Mood

Adjectives

Adjectives provide description and detail as they describe (modify) nouns and pronouns.

There are different categories/groups of adjectives to consider such as size, shape, age, color, etc. In the following examples, the adjective is in bold and the noun or pronoun it describes is italicized.

- He bought the **red** *house.*
- She pulled up in her **fancy** *car.*
- **These** *shoes* no longer fit me.
- I love **Spanish** *food.*
- *Everyone* **available** must set the table.

Adjectives and Commas

When two or more adjectives (known as coordinate adjectives) are listed consecutively, it can be challenging to decide whether or not a comma is needed. Sometimes our grammar ear can work it out, but here's the rule:

- A comma is needed when both adjectives are part of the same group and are of equal importance in their description of the noun. If you can swap the order of the adjectives and the sentence still makes sense, then you have coordinate adjectives, which must be separated by a comma.
  - The cloudy, dark sky filled me with awe.
  - Her loyal, caring friends stood by her during challenging times.
- Do not use a comma if adjectives come from different groups and one adjective is stronger in weight than another. These are cumulative adjectives that function as one unit to modify the noun. Use the same test to check with your ear.
  - He bought her an *expensive diamond* ring.
    - You can't say "a diamond expensive ring."
  - The *silly blue* hat made her costume complete.
    - "A blue silly hat" just doesn't sound right.

Comparative and Superlative Adjectives

Comparative adjectives are used to compare two people or things.

- One syllable words: add "er"
  - Faster, stronger, quicker
- Two syllable words: add "er" or "more"
  - Busier, quieter, more boring
- Three or more syllables: add "more"
  - More expensive, more beautiful

Superlative adjectives compare three or more people or things.

- One syllable words: add "est"
  - Fastest, strongest, quickest
- Two syllable words: add "est" or "most"
  - Busiest, quietest, most boring
- Three or more syllables: add "most"
  - Most expensive, most beautiful

Adverbs

Adverbs are modifiers that are used to describe verbs, adjectives, and other adverbs.

In many cases, adverbs will end in "ly," but it's important to understand how they function in a sentence in relation to the other parts of speech.

Modifying a Verb

- Nestor *ran* **quickly.**
- I **rarely** *practice* the piano.

Modifying an Adjective

- The couple *enjoyed* a **very** <u>long</u> meal.
  - The adverb "very" describes the adjective "long," which is describing the noun "meal."
- The book *is* **too** <u>challenging</u> to read.
  - The adverb "too" describes the adjective "challenging," which is describing the noun phrase "the book."

Modifying an Adverb

- Chris **almost** never *forgets* to practice his saxophone.
  - The adverb "almost" modifies the adverb "never"
- The kid *rode* his bike **dangerously** fast after the ice cream truck.
  - The adverb "dangerously" modifies the adverb "fast"

Prepositions

Prepositions are words that relate or connect a noun or pronoun to another word in the sentence, providing description and detail. Table P4.3 lists commonly used prepositions.

Table P4.3 • Commonly Used Prepositions

COMMONLY USED PREPOSITIONS	
about	above
across	after
against	along
among	around
at	before
behind	between
beyond	by
down	during
except	from
in	into
near	of
off	on
onto	out
over	past
to	toward
under	until
up	upon
with	within

Prepositions are most commonly used within prepositional phrases, which include a preposition and a noun or a pronoun.

- Prepositions with nouns: to the store; in the car; over the fence; beyond the wall; among the ferns
- Prepositions with pronouns: to him; with us; for them; between you and me

When prepositional phrases add information about a verb, they act as adverbs. When they add information about a noun, they act as adjectives.

- Adverbs
    - I **went** *to the mall.*
    - She **jumped** *over the fence.*
    - Can you **send** the email *to me?*
- Adjectives
    - **The books** *on the shelf* are mine.
    - **The kid** *over there* is shouting.
    - **The girl** *in the window* is happy.

Conjunctions

Conjunctions are used to combine words, phrases, and clauses.

After we cover phrases and clauses in depth below, we will explore conjunctions thoroughly. Conjunctions are critical for students to utilize to provide detail and expand their sentence complexity. Without getting into the types specifically, the following are common conjunctions:

- For, and, nor, but, or, yet, so
- Because, while, since, though, although, even though, as, until, where
- Not only/but also; either/or; neither/nor
- Furthermore, moreover, hence, indeed, consequently, nevertheless, thus*

*These are technically adverbs (conjunctive adverbs, to be precise), but they nevertheless function like conjunctions—as we'll see below.

Grammar Nerd Alert!

When a pronoun follows a preposition it must be in the objective case. See more on pronouns below in Section 10. Consider:

- Ask her to bring the cookies *to* **me**.
- Will they go to dinner *with* **us**?
- Let's keep this *between* **you and me.**

Sorry, but you will now notice the incorrect "between you and I" in conversation, in songs, etc.

Interjections

Interjections are words or phrases that insert intense emotion or a quick change in feeling.

They are not part of a sentence, though they naturally connect to the idea of the sentence that they precede or follow. Interjections are punctuated with a comma or an exclamation point—and sometimes a period. Though effective in small doses, they should not be overused!

- Yikes! Can you believe the size of that fish?
- Hooray, we won the game!
- Yuck! You used cayenne instead of chili powder.
- What? You must be kidding me with that joke!

SECTION 2: SUBJECTS AND VERBS

The subject/verb pair lies at the heart of understanding how sentences and many grammatical concepts operate. A sentence consists of a subject and a predicate. The way to make this more student-friendly is to describe the subject as the person or thing doing the action of the verb and the predicate as what the subject is doing in the sentence; the predicate will always contain the verb. Consider the following examples:

Identifying Subject/Verb Pairs

Example 1:

- Elizabeth swims three days a week.
    - To identify the subject/verb pair, look first for the verb (usually an action, with the exception of "to be" and a few other auxiliary verbs, as described below) and ask, "Who or what is doing the verb?"
    - In the sentence above, the verb is "swims" (clear visual of action). Who or what swims? Elizabeth. We know that Elizabeth is the subject of the verb swims.
    - **Note:** The sentence would be grammatically correct if it were written "Elizabeth swims." The fact that she swims three days a week provides additional information within the predicate of the sentence.

Example 2:

- Wolfgang, the smartest child in the class, received a perfect score on the quiz.
    - In this example, when the verb "received" is separated from its subject "Wolfgang" by a modifying phrase, it's helpful to ask who or what received to be sure that we identify the correct subject—Wolfgang.
    - Also, "the smartest child in the class" is a modifying phrase because it describes (or modifies) Wolfgang; see more information below on nonessential information.

Example 3:

- Following the torrential downpour that lasted 10 minutes, Suzanne realized her car windows were open.
    - Subject/verb pairs do not always appear at the beginning of a sentence. The verb "realized" does not come until after the comma. Who or what realized? Suzanne (the subject).

Finding verbs and their subjects is particularly useful for understanding subject/verb and pronoun/antecedent agreement. More on this later. It's also helpful when thinking about different sentence structures (compound, complex, compound/complex), which all have multiple clauses. See Section 7 for more information on sentence types.

Linking, Auxiliary, and Modal Verbs

Do not be afraid of these seemingly intense verb forms. You use them all the time intuitively, but let's put a face to the name.

Linking Verbs

When a verb is not a clear action, students may have a more challenging time finding the verb(s) in a sentence. This is often the case with "is" and "are" and "was"—forms of the verb *to be*. They are considered linking verbs when used in the following way because they *link* the subject with the predicate. Consider the following examples:

- Alexandra **was** a student.
    - In this sentence, "a student" is considered a predicate noun because it gives information about Alexandra—the subject.

Author created using Imgflip AI tool

- Alexandra **is** tall.
    - In this sentence, "tall" is considered a predicate adjective because it describes the subject—Alexandra.

Students do not need to necessarily know the terms *predicate noun* or *predicate adjective,* but they should be able to identify "was" and "is" as the verb in each sentence, respectively.

When used in this manner, other linking verbs include *seem, become, look, feel, taste, smell, sound.*

- The shoes **smell** awful!
- I **feel** tired.
- Those cupcakes **look** delicious.

As a reminder, linking verbs "link" the subject to the predicate. Notice, however, what happens here: He **looked** at the delicious cupcakes. "Look" is now an action verb and no longer a linking verb. Isn't the English language grand?

Auxiliary Verbs

Also known as helping verbs, auxiliary verbs "help" in communicating verb tense, mood, and voice—each of which is covered in the next section. The primary verbs to know are *be* and *have*:

- **to be**: am, is, are, was, were, be, been, being
- **to have:** have, has, had, having

Without going too much into verb tense here, forms of "to be" create progressive tenses and forms of "to have" create perfect tenses. Both will be explained in detail below. The following are examples of how auxiliary verbs connect to other verbs as helpers:

- I **am eating** chocolate cake.
- The cat **was chased** by the dog. (example of passive voice)
- They **were singing** through the windows.
- She **had dreamed** of being a lawyer.
- I **will have paid** off my car before the term ends.

Grammar Nerd Alert!

The verb forms that follow the auxiliary verbs are called present ("ing") and past ("ed") participles and are explained further below. Note that *paid*, in the last example, is an irregular verb, so the past participle form does not end in "ed."

Modal Auxiliary Verbs

Known simply as "modals" to those within the grammar community, these verb forms consist of different types of helping verbs that establish what someone could do, might do, should do, etc. Modals include *can, could, may, might, must, shall, should, will, would.*

Rather than connecting to the participle form like the previous auxiliary verbs, modals attach themselves to the root form of the verb.

- He **can** *eat* 10 cookies in one sitting.
- She **may** *want* to study a little harder before the test.
- I **shall** *open* the door for you, my lady.
- The parents **will** *find* the mess eventually.

SECTION 3: MORE ON VERBS: TENSE AND MOOD

Author created using Imgflip AI tool

Verb Tenses

The following is a brief overview of verb tenses, including when and how they should be used. When we think about tense, the most important aspect is time: present, past, and future. For each tense explained below, the bullets include examples related to time.

Simple Tense

Simple tenses provide a description without referencing any other type of action that might be ongoing or already completed.

- He *rides* his bike to school. (Present)
- He *rode* his bike to school yesterday. (Past)
- He *will ride* his bike to school on Friday. (Future)

Progressive Tense

Progressive tenses describe an activity that is taking place at some specific time—it is in progress.

Here are the auxiliary verbs described in the previous section in action.

Present Progressive (am/is/are + "ing")

- Something that's in progress.
  - I *am playing* soccer.
  - They *are sleeping* now.

Past Progressive (was/were + "ing")

- Something that was occurring at a particular time.
  - I *was playing* soccer yesterday.
  - They *were sleeping* during the game.

Future Progressive (will be + "ing")

- Something that will be in progress in the future.
  - I *will be playing* soccer tomorrow.
  - She *will be sleeping* after the game.

Perfect Tense

Perfect tenses refer to actions that are completed relative to some other point in time and use the auxiliary verb "have" in the form outlined below.

Present Perfect (have/has + past participle)

- An action that happened at an indefinite time in the past or an action that is still ongoing.
  - I have driven the same car for almost 10 years.
  - She has ridden six different horses in her life.

Past Perfect (had + past participle)

- An action in the past that occurred before a different action (also in the past).
  - I had driven my car for a month before I received my license plates.
  - She had ridden six horses before she turned 10.

Future Perfect (will have + past participle)

- An action in the future that will happen prior to a different action.
  - I will have driven my car 100,000 miles by the end of the year.
  - She will have ridden her horse twice today before her parents get home.

Active and Passive Voice

In terms of verb voicing, *active* refers to the subject doing the action of the verb while *passive* refers to the subject being on the receiving end of the action (verb). Consider the impact on the subject in the following two examples, which were always my favorite models for high school students who could relate.

- I broke the lamp.
    - Active Voice: I, the subject, completed the action (broke). It's clearly my fault.
- The lamp was broken [by me].
    - Passive Voice: If we leave out the "by me" phrase, it's not clear who actually broke the lamp.

Consider the difference between a child selecting active or passive voice in this scenario while explaining the broken lamp to a parent. Although the majority of writing (particularly academic writing) should utilize active voice, passive voice can be used strategically to emphasize the subject as the receiver of the action (among other reasons).

- The trophy was given to *the best player on the team.*

Verb Moods

When we talk about mood in relation to verbs, we're talking about the intent of the speaker of the sentence. Is the speaker stating a fact, raising a question, giving a command, posing a condition, or expressing doubt or uncertainty? The following is a brief overview of each mood:

Indicative

Statement of a fact or opinion; the majority of sentences that you read and write fall within the indicative mood

- She is the best player on the team.
- We found 20 dollars in the street.

Interrogative

Statement of a question (interrogative is often lumped within the indicative mood, but the standards separate them out)

Grammar Nerd Alert!

With commands, the implicit (yet invisible) subject of the sentence is "you" (e.g., [You] Give me 20 dollars before the end of the day.)

- Is she the best player on the team?
- Where did they find 20 dollars?

Imperative

Statement of command

- Give me 20 dollars before the end of the day.
- Stop driving so fast on the highway!

Conditional

Situations that contain conditions (if-then), often introduced with an "if" clause

- If I owned a car, then I wouldn't ride the bus.
- If she had studied more, she would have passed the exam.

Subjunctive

An expression of doubt/uncertainty, a wish, or an implied command. The subjunctive most often utilizes "were" and "be" as the verb form.

- I wish I were taller.
- It is critical that you be on time for the meeting.
- If I were you, I would buy a boat.

After learning about the subjunctive, you will never be able to unhear when someone says, "If I was you . . ." Sorry.

SECTION 4: PHRASES

Now that we know that a sentence must have a subject/verb pair—at a minimum—let's look at the phrase, which plays a critical role in sentence development. A *phrase* is a group of words that does not contain a subject/verb pair and cannot stand alone:

- the bouncing ball
- her fancy car
- our fire pit

To take these groups of words and make them complete sentences, we need to add a **subject**/verb pair:

- **Melanie** caught the bouncing ball.
- **She** drove her fancy car.
- **We** roasted marshmallows in our fire pit.

There are five types of phrases that students will need to incorporate into their writing at varying levels of sophistication: prepositional, infinitive, appositive, participle, and gerund.

Prepositional Phrase

As discussed above, a preposition locates or directs items in a sentence. The prepositional phrase is made up of a preposition and a noun or pronoun (to + the store; by + my house; in + the game):

- He went *to the store.*
- They drove *by my house.*
- She stayed *in the game.*

See Figure P4.3 for a list of frequently used prepositions.

Appositive Phrase

An appositive phrase renames or provides additional information about a noun. It is typically offset by commas or dashes when the information it contains is not essential to the meaning of the sentence:

- Mateo, a good student, studies every night.
- My son, Ryan, is an excellent artist.

Essential vs. Nonessential Information

Consider the difference between nonessential versus essential information in the following sentences:

- Dave Matthews, a famous musician, is an excellent guitar player.
    - The appositive (a famous musician) is surrounded by commas because it can be removed from the sentence without changing the meaning of the sentence—we will still know that Dave Matthews is an excellent guitar player.

- The famous musician Dave Matthews is an excellent guitar player.
  - In this sentence, if the name "Dave Matthews" were removed, it would be unclear who the famous musician is. His name is essential to the meaning of the sentence; therefore, there are no commas around it.

Punctuating Lists

When an appositive (or other nonessential information) contains items listed in a series that are separated by commas, use dashes to surround the bonus information to avoid confusion with the commas. For more information on dashes, see Section 14: Punctuation below.

Consider the difference between the two sentences below. In the second sentence, the dashes help to clarify the meaning.

- The sunset, pink, yellow, and orange, filled the sky with beautiful colors.
- The sunset—pink, yellow, and orange—filled the sky with beautiful colors.

The following phrases—participle, gerund, and infinitive—are considered verbal phrases, which means that they look like verbs, sound like verbs, and might be confused with verbs, but they function in sentences as parts of speech other than verbs—either as nouns, adjectives, or adverbs. You may recall these phrases from your studies of a world language.

Participle Phrase

A present participle takes the form of [verb + ing] and a past participle takes the form of [verb + ed]—with the exception of irregular verbs. Participles function as adjectives. A participle phrase is the participle plus the noun or noun phrase being described.

- *The* ***singing*** *child* performed well in the concert.
- *The* ***falling*** *leaves* created a colorful pattern on my lawn.
- *The* ***parked*** *car* remained on my block for a week.
- *The* ***painted*** *wall* turned out to be the wrong color.
- The building, ***damaged*** *by the storm*, lost power.

Beginning a Sentence With a Participle Phrase

In both examples below, the introductory participle phrase functions as an adjective, describing the subject that follows—Matthew and the family, respectively.

- ***Hoping*** *to buy new shoes,* Matthew went to the mall.
- ***Traveling*** *home from the beach,* the family stopped for a snack.

See Section 12 below for information about dangling modifiers.

Gerund Phrase

A gerund, like a participle, takes the form of [verb + ing] but functions as a noun in the sentence.

- Swimming is fun.

As mentioned in Section 2, it's helpful to first identify the verb and then find its subject. Although "swimming" might appear to be a verb, we can recognize the "working" verb: is. When we ask "who or what" is, we determine that the subject is "swimming." Since we already know that subjects are either nouns or pronouns, we can see that "swimming" is a noun in this sentence.

- Sarah passed the test by *memorizing* facts.
- Michelle's newest hobby, *organizing,* became a successful job.
- Chris enjoys *reading* beside the pool at night.

Infinitive Phrase

An infinitive phrase is a verb form made up of "to" + verb (to run, to sing, to dance) that functions as a noun or a modifier (adjective or adverb) in a sentence.

- He wanted *to run* home in the rain.
  - The subject/verb pair is "he wanted"; as such, *wanted* is the "working" verb and *to run* is the infinitive.
  - "To run home in the rain" is the full infinitive phrase.

- *To learn* the guitar takes time.
  - In this case, the infinitive phrase "to learn the guitar" functions as the subject of the verb *takes.*
- Dave continued *to sing, to jump,* and *to dance* while on stage.

Infinitives vs. Prepositions

Students may initially confuse the "to" in an infinitive phrase with the preposition "to." Having them check for a verb or a noun/pronoun within the phrase can help clear up the confusion. For example,

- Dave started *to sing* to the crowd.
  - to sing = infinitive (to + verb)
  - to the crowd = prepositional phrase (to + noun)

Verbal Summary

Recognizing that verbals are not "working" verbs can help students understand how to read and analyze complex sentence structures and how to create a variety of sentence types, manipulating grammatical structures in the process.

Participle

- *Swimming in the ocean,* Clara discovered a starfish.

Gerund

- *Swimming in the ocean* is my favorite activity.

Infinitive

- Clara wanted *to swim* in the ocean until sunset.

SECTION 5: CLAUSES

As noted above, a phrase—a group of words without a subject/verb pair—cannot stand alone as a complete sentence; instead, phrases must be part of, or connect to, a clause—a group of words that does contain a subject/verb pair.

Independent Clause

The first clause that all students learn is the independent clause, which—as described in Section 1 above—must contain at a minimum a subject/verb pair.

- *Alfred* reads.
  - Subject + verb
- *Alfred* reads outside.
  - Subject + verb + adverb

When students are learning to write independent clauses—also known as simple sentences (see Section 7 below)—they will practice including adjectives, adverbs, prepositions, and so on to make their writing more detailed and developed.

- *The man* jumped over the bench **to save** time.
  - Flashback to above: This is an independent clause because it only has one subject/verb pair: the man (s)/ jumped (v); **to save**, as we now know, is an infinitive and not a "working" verb in the sentence.
- *The extremely athletic and physically fit man* jumped over the bench **to save** time.
  - The description of the man—extremely athletic and physically fit—is part of the subject.
  - Who or what jumped? The extremely athletic and physically fit man (subject)
  - Even though this is a longer sentence, it still contains only one independent clause.

Dependent Clause

The second type of clause—and, I would argue, the key component to varied and complex writing—is the dependent (or subordinate) clause.

These clauses contain a subject and a verb but cannot stand alone as a complete sentence; instead, they depend on independent clauses to make them complete. Dependent clauses are formed by attaching a subordinating conjunction

Author created using Imgflip AI tool

(also known in student-friendly language as a "sentence destroyer") to a subject/verb pair. Although subordinate means "lesser in rank" (think elves), dependent clauses are critical in establishing the type of relationship (time, cause/effect, contrast, etc.) that will follow with the independent clause. Table P4.4 is a list of subordinating conjunctions organized by relationship category:

Table P4.4 • Subordinating Conjunctions Organized by Relationship Category

RELATIONSHIP	SUBORDINATING CONJUNCTIONS (*SENTENCE DESTROYER*)
Time	after, as, as long as, as soon as, before, once, since, until, when, whenever, while
Cause and Effect	because, since, so that, in order that, now that
Contrast/ Concession	although, though, even though, whereas, while, even if
Condition	if, unless, only if, provided that, in case, as long as
Comparison	as, as much as, whereas
Place	where, wherever
Purpose	in order to, so that

Creating Dependent Clauses

To create a dependent clause, follow this formula: **subordinating conjunction** + *independent clause.*

- **Even though** the man jumped over the bench
  - *The man jumped over the bench* is a complete sentence, but by adding "even though" to the beginning of the sentence, we create a dependent clause. The

independent clause "the man jumped over the bench" has been "destroyed" by the subordinating conjunction *even though*. Although this sounds scary, destroying the independent clause allows for more complex writing.

Creating Complex Sentences

To make a dependent clause complete, add a comma and an *independent clause*. This is called a complex sentence and will be elaborated on in the next section.

- **Even though** the man jumped over the bench, *he still lost the race.*
- **Before** the game started, *the team warmed up.*
- **Because** the game was tied at the end of the second half, *the game went to overtime.*

Relative Pronouns in Dependent Clauses

Relative pronouns (who, whom, which, that, whose) also begin dependent clauses. See additional information on relative pronouns in Section 7: Sentence Types and Section 10: Pronouns Continued.

- Listen to the coach **whom** *we trust.*
- Sally is our friend **who** *reads the most.*
- The book **that** *I just finished reading* was exciting!
- The beautiful sunset, **which** *I can see right now*, is painting the sky with vibrant colors.

Grammar Nerd Alert!

"That" is used to introduce essential information while "which" is used to introduce nonessential information. Use a comma before *which* and no comma before *that*.

SECTION 6: CONJUNCTIONS

Conjunctions are used to combine words, phrases, and clauses and show relationships between ideas.

Coordinating Conjunctions

Coordinating conjunctions are used to combine words, phrases, and clauses.

The acronym FANBOYS (for, and, nor, but, or, yet, so) is an easy way for students to remember these conjunctions, which they will use frequently—and in different ways—in their writing.

- I like *apples* **and** *oranges.* (words)
- I like *to eat apples* **and** *to eat oranges.* (phrases)
- *I like apples*, but *I like oranges more.* (clauses)

Use coordinating conjunctions to combine independent clauses (comma + FANBOYS) in compound sentences. See Section 7: Sentence Types for more information.

Subordinating Conjunctions

Subordinating conjunctions begin dependent (subordinate) clauses (as described above).

They are also known as "sentence destroyers" because they turn independent clauses into dependent clauses when they are added.

There is no nifty acronym like FANBOYS, but a clearly displayed anchor chart will help students access the power of these conjunctions in their writing. As a reminder, the following are commonly used subordinating conjunctions, with examples of how they can be used to create complex sentences:

- because, while, despite, if, even though, although, though, since, before, after, during, when, as, until, whoever, whenever
  - *Because he likes apples and oranges*, he bought a fruit salad.
  - *Even though he likes apples*, he prefers oranges.
  - *After he ate all of the apples*, he started to eat the oranges.

Conjunctive Adverbs

Conjunctive adverbs, though technically adverbs, function much like coordinating conjunctions and act as transitions in connecting two independent clauses. They provide levels of nuance in showing relationships. Conjunctive adverbs can also be used as interrupters within sentences to connect two thoughts or ideas.

Table P4.5 provides a list of commonly used conjunctive adverbs organized by relationship category.

Table P4.5 • Conjunctive Adverbs Organized by Relationship Category

RELATIONSHIP	CONJUNCTIVE ADVERB
Addition	additionally
	also
	furthermore
	in addition
	moreover
Comparison	in the same way
	just as
	likewise
	similarly
Conclusion	all in all
	in conclusion
	in summary
	overall
	therefore
	to sum up
Contrast	conversely
	however
	in contrast
	instead
	nevertheless
	nonetheless
	on the other hand
	still
Emphasis	certainly
	indeed
	naturally
	notably
	obviously
	surely
Example	for example
	for instance
	in particular
	namely
	specifically

(Continued)

(Continued)

RELATIONSHIP	CONJUNCTIVE ADVERB
Result/Outcome	accordingly
	as a result
	consequently
	hence
	therefore
	thus
Time	afterward
	finally
	in the meantime
	meanwhile
	next
	subsequently
	then

Conjunctive adverbs are used in three ways:

1. To interrupt a sentence
    - Examples:
        - I was, **indeed**, unable to sleep because the dog kept me awake.
        - I wanted ice cream. There were, **however**, no Dairy Queen stores around.
    - Rules:
        - The conjunctive adverb, *as an interrupter*, is offset by commas.
        - The conjunctive adverb can be removed from the sentence without changing the meaning of the sentence.
2. To begin a sentence
    - Examples:
        - I wanted to sleep. **However**, the dog kept me awake.
        - I finally fell asleep. **Meanwhile**, the dog kept barking.
    - Rule:
        - The conjunctive adverb is capitalized and is followed by a comma.

3. To combine two sentences
   - Examples:
     - If you want to use a conjunctive adverb, you don't have to put it in the middle of a sentence; **instead**, you can use it as a transition between two sentences.
     - Noah forgot to study for the test; **consequently**, he received a poor grade.
   - Rules:
     - Use a semicolon, do not capitalize the conjunctive adverb, and use a comma after it.
     - *Be sure that you have an independent clause on either side of the semicolon.*

For more information about the semicolon, see Section 14: Punctuation.

Note: Correlative conjunctions (e.g., either/or, neither/nor) are explained in Section 13: Parallel Structure.

SECTION 7: SENTENCE TYPES

Now that we've covered phrases, clauses, and conjunctions, it's time to put them all together and discuss how to create different types of sentences. When teaching sentence types or sentence construction, it is necessary to understand the types of clauses at work within a sentence. For each of the following examples, let's look at how to determine the number and type of clauses by first identifying the "working" verbs, connecting the verb (or verbs) to its subject as described above. As a reminder, a sentence must have at least one independent clause and must make sense to be considered a complete sentence.

Identifying Clauses: The Subject/Verb Pair

Holden Caulfield struggled with social interactions.

- Verb: struggled
- Subject: Who or what struggled? Holden Caulfield
- *One independent clause*

Holden Caulfield struggled with social interactions and disliked many people.

- Verbs: struggled, disliked (compound verbs)
- Subject: Who or what struggled? Who or what disliked? Holden Caulfield
- *One independent clause*; even though there are two verbs (struggled and disliked), they both share the same subject (Holden Caulfield)

Holden Caulfield struggled with social interactions, and he disliked many people.

- Verb 1: struggled; Subject 1: Holden Caulfield
- Verb 2: disliked; Subject 2: he
- *Two independent clauses* (compound sentence)

The number of subject/verb groupings that we identify equates to the number of clauses in a sentence. With this foundation, we can start thinking about how to manipulate independent and dependent clauses to achieve different sentence structures. By including a variety of sentence types in their writing toolbox, students can vary their writing style and utilize sentences as a vehicle for more complex thinking.

Combining clauses requires the appropriate use of conjunctions, commas, and semicolons. When teaching sentences, think of the conjunction and comma or semicolon as the glue that holds the sentence parts—phrases and clauses—together. There is a concrete way to join these parts, and that's how students internalize the comma rules and sentence construction techniques.

Simple Sentences

A simple sentence is made up of one independent clause.

- *The man* **jumped** over the bench.
- *Suzanne and Tiffany* **ate** lunch at Panera.
- *Christine* **ran** and **dove** into the wave.

Compound Sentences

A compound sentence is made up of two independent clauses joined by a comma + FANBOYS (or semicolon + conjunctive adverb). It is important to ensure that there is a complete independent clause on either side of the comma or semicolon.

- *The man* **jumped** over the bench, and *he* **fell** flat on his face.
- *The man* **jumped** over the bench; consequently, *he* **fell** flat on his face.
- *Suzanne and Tiffany* **ate** lunch at Panera, but *they* **were disappointed** with the new menu.

Note: The following sentence is a simple sentence. Even though it contains the glue "and," the second part of the sentence (fell flat on his face) is a phrase because it does not contain a subject. At its heart, the sentence reads "The man jumped and fell." Don't let the other details get in the way of the subject/verb pair!

- The man jumped over the bench **and** fell flat on his face.
    - Using a comma before "and" would be incorrect because this is not a compound sentence.

Complex Sentences

A complex sentence is made up of one dependent clause and one independent clause and can be structured either dependent to independent (D-I) or independent to dependent (I-D).

D-I: Dependent clause + Comma + Independent Clause

As a reminder, the dependent clause must contain a sentence destroyer, a subject, and a verb.

- **After** *the man jumped over the bench*, he sat down on the grass.
- **Because** *the storm was imminent*, the beachgoers ran for cover.
- **Even though** *the game ended*, the players stayed on the field to celebrate.

I-D: Independent clause (no comma) + Dependent Clause

At an early age, students begin speaking and writing complex sentences structured this way. They often utilize complex sentences with the conjunction "because," which allows them to explain why (e.g., I want a snack because I am hungry).

Structured this way, the sentence destroyer is the glue that holds the clauses together.

- The man sat down on the grass **after** *he jumped over the bench.*
- The beachgoers ran for cover **because** *the storm was imminent.*
- The players stayed on the field to celebrate **even though** *the game was over.*

Other types of complex sentences include dependent adjective clauses that describe the subject; the adjective clause begins with a relative pronoun* (who, whom, whose, which, that).

- She is the person **whom** *I respect most.*
- The author, **whose** *books have sold millions of copies worldwide,* will be in town signing autographs tonight.
- The book on the shelf is the one **that** *I borrowed yesterday.*

*See more on relative pronouns in Section 10: Pronouns Continued.

Compound/Complex Sentences

A compound/complex sentence is made up of two or more independent clauses and at least one dependent clause. We have discussed the "glue" for combining clauses (I-D and D-I), so it's now a matter of putting together three or more clauses using the same "glue" rules.

I-I-D: (Independent + Independent + Dependent)

This is a hybrid of a compound sentence (I-I) and complex sentence (I-D). We use the compound sentence comma rule (comma + FANBOYS) to combine the I-I and the complex sentence rule (no comma + sentence destroyer) to combine the I-D.

- He went to the mall, **and** he bought a pair of new shoes *because* his old Pumas were severely worn.
- Max rode his bike to the baseball field, **but** he couldn't play *because* the gate was locked.
- Christina and her friends bought iced coffees, **so** they could enjoy them *while* they walked in the park.

D-I-I (Dependent + Independent + Independent)

This structure is the reverse of I+I+D and allows students to vary their sentence structure by beginning with the dependent clause. We use the complex sentence rule (dependent + comma) to combine the D-I and the compound sentence comma rule (comma + FANBOYS) to combine the I-I.

- *Because* my sneakers were in bad shape, I went to the mall, **and** I bought a new pair.
- *After* the game ended, the players stayed on the field to celebrate, **but** it started to rain.
- *When* the game ended in a tie, the players yearned to keep playing, **yet** the referee refused.

Using their knowledge of combining clauses, students can also consider sentence structures that include different orders of clauses or even more than three clauses:

D-I-I-D (Dependent + Independent + Independent + Dependent)

- *When* the game ended in a tie, the players yearned to keep playing, yet the referee refused *even though* the players offered him money to keep playing.

SECTION 8: SENTENCE FRAGMENTS

Author created using Imgflip AI tool

We now know that a group of words must have a subject and a verb and make sense in order to be considered a complete sentence. Sentence fragments do not meet these criteria. Instead, they are typically phrases or dependent clauses that cannot stand alone.

Phrases

Example 1:

- Incorrect: My son enjoys many activities. For example, skiing and swimming.
  - The phrase (for example, skiing and swimming) does not have a subject/verb pair, so it cannot stand alone.
- Correct: My son enjoys many activities, including skiing and swimming.

Example 2:

- Incorrect: Running down the hall
  - As discussed above, this is a participle phrase; because it's only a phrase, we are left wondering who or what is running. We need to add the subject/verb pair to make this a complete sentence.
- Correct:
  - Running down the hall, Marco tripped.
  - Marco tripped running down the hall.

Dependent Clauses

Example 3:

- Incorrect: Because he was hungry
  - This is a dependent clause that acts as an adverb, but there is no subject/verb pair being modified. We must add an independent clause to complete this complex sentence.
- Correct:
  - Because he was hungry, Marco ran to get a slice of pizza. (D-I)
  - Marco ran to get a slice of pizza because he was hungry. (I-D)

If students read their sentences slowly, particularly out loud, they may be able to hear fragments, which often leave us wanting more to complete the thought. In addition, understanding subject/verb pairs, independent clauses, and phrases will also help to ensure that students are avoiding fragments in their writing.

SECTION 9: RUN-ON SENTENCES

Run-on sentences occur when two independent clauses are incorrectly joined together. They have the wrong "glue" combining them. A long, wordy sentence does not necessarily constitute a run-on (a common misconception). For example, the D-I-I-D compound/complex sentence in Section 7 has four clauses, but each clause is correctly "glued" to the others, making it a long but grammatically correct sentence.

Types of Run-On Sentences

There are three types of run-on sentences:

1. Two independent clauses are joined with no punctuation.
   - My neighbor's dog is barking I can't sleep.
2. Two independent clauses are joined with only a comma, which is known as a comma splice.
   - My neighbor's dog is barking, I can't sleep.
3. Two independent clauses joined with a FANBOYS conjunction but no comma.
   - My neighbor's dog is barking so I can't sleep.

Correcting Run-On Sentences

To correct a run-on or a comma splice:

- Separate the two sentences with a period.
  - My neighbor's dog is barking. I can't sleep.
- Add a semicolon
  - My neighbor's dog is barking; I can't sleep.
  - My neighbor's dog is barking**; therefore,** I can't sleep.
- Create a compound sentence (comma + FANBOYS)
  - My neighbor's dog is barking**, so** I can't sleep.
- Create a complex sentence
  - **Because** my neighbor's dog is barking, I can't sleep.

Fun With Comma Splices

In my experience working with students in Grades 3 and 4 in multiple school districts, the comma splice is a common issue when students are learning to combine sentences. If addressed early on (and with some playfulness), the comma splice can become a thing of the past for students. In teaching students to combine clauses, I remind them that two independent clauses (or simple sentences) can *never* be combined with only a comma. I then ask the class: *When can two independent clauses be joined with ONLY a comma?* A few students will say "never" with some uncertainty. I validate the response and ask the question again. This time, more students chime in and say "never" more confidently. Finally, I ask the question one more time and encourage the students to respond as loudly and with as much enthusiasm as possible. The students then all yell "never" together, which drives home the point. I repeat this over multiple class periods as a way to reinforce the glue (comma + FANBOYS) of correctly combining two sentences. Having fun with grammar in this manner furthers the sense of community in the classroom and reinforces the lesson expectations.

SECTION 10: PRONOUNS CONTINUED

Should I use "I" or "me" in this sentence?

I think I should say "myself" here, but should I?

Great, we're back to choosing who or whom again!

If I say "hers," it sounds possessive, but do I need an apostrophe?

These are only a handful of the questions we hear as educators regarding pronouns, which can be quite tricky to understand and teach. Pronouns take the place of nouns, and they fall into multiple categories that each have their own set of rules to follow. Some of these rules, of late, have been bent—others broken—and we'll get into that below.

To begin, Table P4.6 provides a breakdown of how pronouns are described in terms of three of these categories: **number** (singular or plural), **case** (subjective, objective, or possessive), and **person** (first, second, or third).

Number

Singular pronouns replace singular nouns and plural pronouns replace plural nouns; they must agree.

- **The girl** passed the exam. = **She** passed the exam. (singular girl = singular she)

Table P4.6 • Pronoun Chart Identifying Pronoun Number, Case, and Person

PRONOUN NUMBER, CASE, AND PERSON				
NUMBER	CASE			PERSON
	SUBJECT(IVE)	OBJECT(IVE)	POSSESS(IVE)	
Singular	I	me	my, mine	**First**
	you	you	your, yours	**Second**
	he	him	his	**Third**
	she	her	hers	
	it	it	its	
	who	whom	whose	
Plural	we	us	our, ours	**First**
	you	you	your, yours	**Second**
	they	them	their, theirs	**Third**

- **The girls** passed the exam. = **They** passed the exam. (plural girls = plural they)

Both of these examples include third-person pronouns. We will talk more about pronoun number and person below.

Pronoun Case: Subjective and Objective

Though subjective and objective might sound scary, they describe whether a pronoun is acting as a subject or as an object in a sentence. Without going into too much detail about objects, think of them as not-subjects; once you have a subject/verb pair in a clause, you cannot have another subject, so the pronoun choice will be an object. Here are two examples:

- **I** threw the ball into the tree.
    - **I** is the subject of the verb threw, so the pronoun must be subjective. This is also an example of a first-person pronoun with the speaker doing the action of the verb.
    - We would not say "**Me** threw the ball into the tree."
- He threw the ball to **me**.
    - **Me** is an object in this sentence because we already have a subject/verb pair in the clause: he (subject) threw (verb).
    - In this case, the pronoun must be objective. We would not say "He threw the ball to **I**."

A common source of confusion arises when a sentence contains multiple subjects or multiple objects. In both cases, even after learning the rule, take the other person out and check for agreement.

Multiple Subjects

When you (as the speaker) are part of a compound subject, use the subjective case pronoun "I" (not me) and put yourself second to the other person.

- Teresa and I went to the park.
    - ~~Teresa and~~ I went to the park.
    - Would you say "Me went to the park"?
- The other players and I skated on the lake.
    - ~~The other players and~~ I skated on the lake.

The following are additional examples of how to use subject pronouns with compound subjects.

- **He** and I *drove* to Boston.
- **She** and the other players *won* first place.
- **You** and I *should go* to lunch.

Multiple Objects

When you (as the speaker) are part of a compound object (not the subject), use the objective case pronoun "me" following the other person.

- Nisha threw the ball to Kai and me.
  - Nisha threw the ball to ~~Kai and~~ **me**.
  - You wouldn't say "Nisha threw the ball to I"!
- The coach blew the whistle at the other players and me.
  - The coach blew the whistle at ~~the other players and~~ **me**.

Other examples of objective case pronouns used in compound subjects:

- The email should be sent to Elizabeth and **him**.
- We brought **them** and their friends to the game.
- My sister planned the party for our neighbors and **us**.

Pronoun Case: Possessive

The third type of pronoun case outlined in the chart is the possessive group. As you might imagine, possessive pronouns are used to show possession, and they must agree in number and gender as outlined below.

Pronoun Agreement

When we talk about pronoun agreement, we must think in terms of the **pronoun/antecedent** relationship. The antecedent is the noun that comes before (and is referred to by) the pronoun. Let's look at an example that merges all four categories.

- The girl rode her bike to the ice cream shop.
  - **Pronoun/Antecedent:** "The girl" is the antecedent of the possessive pronoun "her."
  - **Pronoun Number:** Because "girl" is a singular noun, we must use the singular possessive pronoun "her."
  - **Pronoun Gender**: Because "girl" is a feminine noun, we use the feminine possessive pronoun "her."
  - **Pronoun Person:** "her" is a third person possessive pronoun.

Other examples of possessive pronouns:

- I rode **my** bike to the ice cream store. (singular)
- They rode **their** bikes to the ice cream store. (plural)
- We rode **our** bikes to the ice cream store. (plural)

Indefinite Pronouns and Agreement

Issues with agreement can come into play particularly with indefinite pronouns when gender is not clear. Indefinite pronouns are discussed in greater detail below in the context of subject/verb agreement (see Section 11), but the following is a brief summary in the context of pronoun agreement. Indefinite pronouns do not refer to specific people or things but instead to general groups, amounts, etc.

For the sake of pronoun discussions and agreement, the following indefinite pronouns are always singular: *everyone, anyone, someone, somebody, everybody, nobody, either, neither, each, one, no one.*

Because these pronouns are singular, any other pronoun in the sentence should also be singular to ensure consistency, but this is where rules have bent over time—in a good way.

- **Everyone** in the group did **his or her** part of the project.
  - This sentence is grammatically correct because the singular "everyone" agrees with the singular "his or her" (possessive) pronouns.
  - However, writing in this manner becomes quite wordy, having to repeat "his or her."

One option is to rewrite the sentence and make both pronouns plural:

- All of the students did their part of the project.

More recently, the plural pronoun "their" has become an acceptable partner with singular indefinite pronouns.

- **Everyone** in the group did **their** part of the project.
- **Anyone** who wants to buy lunch should bring **their** own money.

Shifts in Person

When using pronouns, ensure that pronoun person (first, second, third) remains consistent.

- Incorrect: When **a person** gets a new job, **you** have to learn many new skills.
    - Do not shift from the third person ("a person") to the second person ("you").
- Correct:
    - When **a person** gets a new job, **he or she** has to learn many new skills.
    - When **a person** gets a new job, **they** have to learn many new skills. ("They" is used as a singular third person pronoun, as described previously.)
    - When **people** get new jobs, **they** have to learn many new skills.

Reflexive Pronouns

The group known as reflexive pronouns consists of the following pronouns: *myself, yourself, himself, herself, itself, ourselves, yourselves,* and *themselves*. Importantly, they are used when the subject and the object of a sentence are the same.

- **I** fixed the bike chain **myself**. **She** fixed the bike chair **herself**.
- **You** must complete the assignment **yourself**. **They** must complete the assignment **themselves**.
- **We** should order **ourselves** dinner.

Another common issue is the use of the reflexive pronoun "myself" instead of me or I. Used correctly, "myself" is the object of a sentence with the subject "I."

- I fixed the broken sink **myself**. (*I* is the subject of the verb *fixed*.)
- I taught **myself** to play guitar. (*I* is the subject of the verb *taught*.)

However, "myself" should not be used as the subject:

- Myself and Priya will organize the fundraiser
- Priya and myself will organize the fundraiser.

In both cases, the subjective case pronoun "I" should be used. If you're unsure, apply the test of removing the other person. Which sounds better: "**Myself** will organize the fundraiser" or "**I** will organize the fundraiser?"

Relative Pronouns

Also discussed above with subordinate clauses (Section 5), relative pronouns relate one part of a sentence to another, describing the subject in more detail. The full group of relative pronouns consists of *who, whose, whom, which,* and *that.* In the context of pronoun case, let's clear up the confusion with who vs. whom.

Who vs. Whom

Who and *whoever* are used to replace subjects and *whom* and *whomever* are used to replace objects. Let's look at a few examples. For a test, replace *who* with "he" or "she" and *whom* with "him" or "her" and check with your ear. As a rule, *whom* follows prepositions.

- Who is winning the race?
  - *She is winning the race.*
- The tall boy, who runs very quickly, is a good basketball player.
  - The nonessential clause "who runs very quickly" has its own subject and verb. "Who" is the subject of "runs," so we use the subjective case.
    - *He runs very quickly*
- Whoever spilled the cereal must clean it up.
  - "Whoever" is the subject of the verb "spilled."
- Give the award to whomever you choose.
  - In a command, the implied subject is "you," so the objective case "whomever" must be used; in addition, following the preposition (to), the objective case is used.

Be careful with sneaky subordinate (relative) clauses:

- Jamie is the person who saw the movie.
  - "Who" is the subject of "saw" in the subordinate clause (who saw the movie)

- The man whom we met at the party is an architect.
  - The subordinate clause "whom we met at the party" has its own subject and verb. Since "we" is the subject of "met," use the objective case "whom" within the clause.

Who vs. That

Who is used to refer to people (often as part of an adjective clause) while *that* is used to refer to things (not people).

- She is the person **who** works the hardest.
- They are the players **who** try the most.
- Ford is a brand **that** is reliable.
- I need to find a snowboard **that** fits me.

Which vs. That

Which is used to add nonessential information to a sentence while "that" adds essential information. **Use a comma with *which* and no comma with *that.***

- I plan to play soccer, **which is my favorite sport**.
  - Nonessential: the gist of the sentence is about playing soccer; that it's my favorite sport is bonus information.
- My car, **which is in good shape**, still hasn't failed me.
  - Nonessential: adds information about the car.
- The belt **that I own** is brown.
  - Essential because otherwise it would be unclear whose belt the sentence references.
- She can't put down the mystery **that she is reading.**
  - Essential because we need to know that she is reading a mystery.

Vague Pronoun Reference

Another common issue with pronouns occurs when pronouns have ambiguous or unclear antecedents. The references are vague in the sense that the antecedent of the pronoun is not clear. As a reminder, the antecedent is the noun that the pronoun refers to:

- The girl rode her bike to the ice cream store. ("girl" is the antecedent of "her")

Ambiguous Reference

- Incorrect: Katherine and Jasmine went to lunch, and **she** ordered a chicken sandwich. (Who does "she" refer to: Katherine or Jasmine?)
- Correct: Katherine and Jasmine went to lunch, and Katherine ordered a chicken sandwich. *Or,* Katherine and Jasmine went to lunch, and they ordered chicken sandwiches.

Unclear Reference

- **They** say that soccer is the best game. (Who is "they"?)
- **This** is why I love watching soccer. (What does "this" refer to?)

To fix an unclear reference, add a specific noun or pronoun.

- **Many sports fans** say that soccer is the best game.
- **Teamwork** is why I love watching soccer.

SECTION 11: SUBJECT/ VERB AGREEMENT

Subject/verb agreement can be a challenging topic for students as there are a variety of factors to consider while ensuring that verbs and their subjects agree. As we've discussed previously, it is essential for students to be able to identify verbs and their subjects, which will come into play heavily in this section.

At the most basic level, singular subjects take singular verbs, and plural subjects take plural verbs. If students are struggling with agreement, have them use "she" to check for a singular subject and "they" to check for a plural subject.

- The student writes. (singular)
  - *Test: She writes.*
- The students write. (plural)
  - *Test: They write.*

The following is a nonexhaustive list of the most common issues that impact subject/verb agreement.

Complicating Phrases

With the exception of indefinite pronouns as subjects, phrases that come between the subject and the verb do not factor into subject/verb agreement; it can be helpful to have students cross out adjective phrases, prepositional phrases, etc. when checking for agreement.

- Andrew, the youngest on the team, swims faster than everyone.
    - Check: Andrew swims
- Andrew, the fastest of the swimmers, is the youngest on the team.
    - Though the plural noun *swimmers* immediately precedes the verb *is,* the subject of the sentence is *Andrew.*
    - Check: Andrew is
- The group of students in the back of the bus is the loudest.
    - Check: The group is
- The kids in the water are having fun.
    - Check: The kids are

Compound Subjects

As discussed above, a compound subject occurs when two or more people/things are connected to the same verb.

- When the items in a compound subject are joined by and, the verb is plural.
    - *Linda* **and** *Julie* walk to school every day.
    - As a test, replace Linda and Julie with "they" and check the verb: they walk (not they walks).
- When the subjects are both singular and are joined by **or/nor**, the verb is singular.
    - *The cat* **or** *the dog* is making a mess in the living room.
    - Neither *the cat* **nor** *the dog* is making a mess in the living room.
- When singular *and* plural items in a compound subject are joined by **or/nor**, the verb agrees with the item closest to the verb.

- Either the dogs or **the cat** is always making a mess. (singular)
- Either the cat or the **dogs** are always making a mess. (plural)

Indefinite Pronouns

Also described in Section 10 above, indefinite pronouns do not refer to a specific noun. They fall into three categories, each of which can be confusing for students until mastered. Indefinite pronouns also cause confusion with pronoun agreement in number and gender.

Always Singular

- Everyone, anyone, someone, somebody, everybody, nobody, either, neither, each, one, no one
  - *Everyone* on the team **contributes** equally.
  - *Someone* **is** standing behind me.
  - *Each* of the players **runs** hard to first base.
    - With indefinite pronouns in this group that are always singular, prepositional phrases do not impact subject/verb agreement; note that *players* is a plural noun, but the singular verb (runs) agrees with the singular subject (each).

Always Plural

- Many, both, several, few, others
  - *Many* of us **are** ready to eat dinner.
  - *Several* kids **play** on the swings at recess.
  - *Both* of the candidates **were** excited for the debate.

Singular or Plural (Depending on How They Are Used)

In this group, the prepositional phrase that follows the indefinite pronoun determines whether the verb is singular or plural. This is the exception referenced at the beginning of the section above on "Complicating Phrases."

- All, any, more, most, none, some
  - Example 1:
    - All of the players were hungry after the game. (players = plural)

        - All of the team was hungry after the game (team = singular)
    - Example 2:
        - More of the students are participating in class. (students = plural)
        - More of this show is necessary! (show = singular)

SECTION 12: MISPLACED AND DANGLING MODIFIERS

Modifiers provide additional information about items in a sentence. As described in detail above, modifiers include adjectives, adverbs, prepositional phrases, participle phrases, dependent clauses, and adjective clauses. Below are some examples:

- The **yellow** ball (adjective)
- He ran **quickly**. (adverb)
- He ran **to the park**. (prepositional phrase)
- **Running to the park**, she met her friend. (participle phrase - adjective)
- **After he ran to the park**, Roman ate lunch. (dependent clause - adverb)
- Roman, **who runs to the park daily**, is in great shape. (adjective clause)

Misplaced Modifiers

As a general rule, modifiers should be placed as close to the word they are describing as possible to prevent confusion. A misplaced modifier occurs when the modifier relates to the wrong word or phrase in the sentence, which impacts the meaning.

Example 1:

- Incorrect: Brett brought a sandwich to his friends covered in oil and vinegar.
    - Are the friends covered in oil vinegar or is the sandwich?

- Correct: Brett brought a sandwich covered in oil and vinegar to his friends.

Example 2:

- Incorrect: Mom almost drives us to school every day.
    - So every day, at the last minute, she changes her mind about driving?
- Correct: Mom drives us to school almost every day.

Dangling Modifiers

Issues with dangling modifiers occur most commonly with verbal phrases (participle, gerund, infinitive) when the modifying phrase does not connect to the correct noun (usually the subject of the sentence), which often results in confusion or amusement on the part of the reader. To correct a dangling modifier, rewrite the sentence so that the modifying phrase immediately precedes what it's describing.

Example 1:

- Incorrect: Hoping to buy a new suit, the store was closed when I arrived.
    - Who or what is hoping to buy a new suit? In this sentence, the phrase is modifying "the store" when it should be "I."
- Correct: Hoping to buy a new suit, I arrived at the store, but it was closed.

Example 2:

- Incorrect: Walking through Central Park, the hot dog carts caught my attention.
    - Were the hot dog carts walking through Central Park? Well, according to this sentence they were. Oops!
- Correct: Walking through Central Park, I focused my attention on the hot dog carts.

SECTION 13: PARALLEL STRUCTURE

As discussed above, it is important to maintain consistency with grammatical elements in writing, particularly verb tense and pronouns. Parallel structure relates to how specific elements in our writing remain in balance. Depending on the sentence structure, there are different ways to determine what needs to remain balanced or parallel.

Items in a Series

Consider the following examples of appropriate parallel structure and how to identify it:

Example 1:

- I plan **to buy** *apples*, *bananas*, and *oranges* at the store.
    - Three nouns (fruits) listed.
    - The nouns that need to be parallel come after the infinitive "to buy."
    - Ask, "To buy what?"

Example 2:

- The coach **told us** *to bring water, to wear our uniforms*, and *to arrive early*.
    - Infinitive phrases are listed consecutively and appropriately.
    - Parallelism begins after the pronoun *us*. Told us what?
    - The following would be a faulty parallel structure:
        - The coach told us to bring water, to wear our uniforms, and that we should arrive early.
        - The final clause "that we should arrive early" is not an infinitive phrase and is therefore not parallel with the previous two items.

Correlative Conjunctions

The correlative conjunctions *either/or, neither/nor,* and *not only/ but also* require a close focus on parallel structure given that they are utilized in pairs. The rule for correlative conjunctions is that if you use one part of the pair, you must use its partner. In the examples below, in addition to highlighting the correlative pairs, we also examine the parallelism rule that says the grammatical structure (e.g., adjective, phrase, clauses) that follows the first element in the pair must also follow the second element in the pair.

Example 1:

- Incorrect: Valentina wants to buy **either** *a new dress* **or** *shop for a new skirt.*

- In this example, the parallel structure is broken because the second element, following "or," includes the verb "shop"; as such, the elements are no longer parallel.

- Correct: Valentina wants to buy **either** *a new dress* **or** *a new skirt.*
  - Notice first that both *either* and *or* are used in this sentence, given their partnership.
  - Because "a new dress," which is a noun phrase, follows "either," a noun phrase must also follow "or."

Example 2:

- Incorrect: The Battle of the Bands **not only** *was held on the grass* **but also** *in the gym.*
  - In this version, what follows "not only" is a verb (was held) + prepositional phrase. Because only a prepositional phrase follows "but also," the sentence is not grammatically balanced.
- Correct: The Battle of the Bands was held **not only** *on the grass* **but also** *in the gym.*
  - Following "not only" is the prepositional phrase "on the grass," which means that a prepositional phrase must follow "but also" to keep the items grammatically balanced.

Think carefully about where the first part of a correlative pair is placed (e.g., before the verb, after the verb), and make sure the elements on both sides remain parallel.

Correlative Conjunctions and Compound Subjects

When either/or and neither/nor are used to separate compound subjects, be careful to ensure subject/verb agreement. If possible, it's best to keep both subjects singular or both subjects plural (notice the parallelism in this sentence).

- Either he or she **takes** out the garbage. (singular)
- Neither Cammy nor Hannah **is** hungry for lunch. (singular)
- Either the players or the coaches **make** the calls on the court. (plural)

As described above with indefinite pronouns, if one of the subjects is singular and one is plural, the verb agrees in number with the subject closest to the verb.

- Either the coach or *the players* **make** the calls on the court. (players = plural)
- Neither the players nor *the coach* **makes** the calls on the court. (coach = singular)

As a reminder, try to keep things simple and make both subjects singular or both plural.

SECTION 14: PUNCTUATION

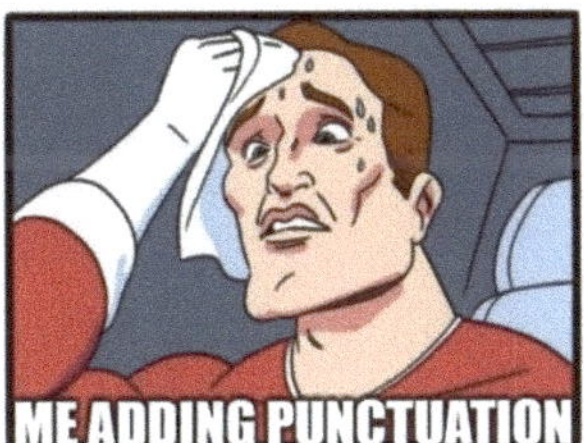

Author created using Imgflip AI tool

Commas and colons and dashes, oh my! Punctuation, in all its forms, is critical for clarity, meaning-making, and effective communication. Through continued exposure to and practice with punctuation, students will learn to leverage various forms of punctuation both accurately and stylistically. The following is an overview of all things punctuation.

Marks of End Punctuation

- Period: completes a declarative sentence (statement of opinion or fact).
    - He drives a blue car.
    - The Rangers are the best hockey team.
- Question Mark: completes an interrogative sentence.
    - Where are we going tonight?

  - To whom do I owe this honor?
  - Sarah asked if we are going to dinner tonight.
    - This is called an indirect question (not an interrogative sentence), so it takes a period and not a question mark.
- Exclamation Point: completes an exclamatory sentence.
  - This is the best day ever!
  - We're going to Disney World!

The Semicolon

The semicolon deserves its own space here because it's often misunderstood or—in some cases—avoided altogether by writers who are not sure when to utilize it. A hybrid of a period and a comma, the semicolon provides neither the full stop of a period nor the phrase/clause combining "glue" of a comma. It is used to combine independent clauses that share a close relationship in meaning. The word that follows a semicolon is not capitalized.

- I like kittens; they are cute.
- Jake's favorite animal is a cat; he desperately wants one as a pet.

The semicolon is often utilized along with conjunctive adverbs to combine independent clauses, with the conjunctive adverb expressing a type of relationship between the clauses (addition, contrast, etc.), as mentioned previously. As a reminder, the rule is

- Independent clause + semicolon + *conjunctive adverb* + comma + independent clause.
  - I went to the mall to buy new shoes; *however*, the store did not have my size.
  - The swimmers trained hard all season; *consequently*, they won the championship.

Semicolons are also used to separate items in a list that contain commas:

- My bucket list includes trips to Boston, Massachusetts; San Francisco, California; and Aspen, Colorado.
  - Using only commas would make this look like one long list of cities and states, rather than three groups of city/state pairs.

The Colon

The colon is primarily used to introduce a list or explanation; it must be preceded by an independent clause.

When introducing a list, make it clear to the reader that a list is coming.

- The basketball coach's letter told me to bring the following: a water bottle, new sneakers, and a basketball.

If the list is part of the action of the sentence, do not use a colon.

- I brought a water bottle, new sneakers, and a basketball to practice.

The colon is also used, for example, to denote hours and minutes (4:00), to follow a salutation (To Whom It May Concern:), and to separate titles from subtitles (*Wings of Fire: The Brightest Night*).

The Dash

First and foremost, a dash is not the same thing as a hyphen. In fact, a dash is twice as long as a hyphen. Dashes are used to interrupt sentences and provide additional information. They offer a more pronounced interruption than commas, and they alert the reader that a side-thought or some commentary on the information in the sentence is coming. They usually work in pairs, surrounding the additional information—though a single dash can be used at the end of a sentence. Students should use dashes sparingly as they can become overwhelming for readers if used too frequently.

- As the thieves fled through the woods, Harry—oh, poor Harry—slipped and fell in a ditch.
- The sunset—pink, yellow, and purple—slowly painted the night sky.
    - Use dashes particularly when listing items that are separated by commas.
- We have everything we need for our camping trip—a tent, sleeping bags, and baked beans.

Consider the following example from Thomas Hardy in his famous novel about a hay trusser turned mayor:

> The desire—sober and repressed—of Elizabeth-Jane's heart was indeed to see, to hear, and to understand.

- In this sentence, "sober and repressed" modify the noun *desire* and is offset by dashes.
- Elizabeth-Jane is a hyphenated name.
- For fun: The items in a series at the end of the sentence are infinitives (but you know that already).*

*Detail added within parentheses can provide bonus information or a commentary on the topic of the sentence. As with dashes, if the parentheses are removed, the sentence must still be grammatically correct. Here are two more examples:

- Edgar Allan Poe (1809–1849) was a prolific writer and poet.
- The student's grade point average (GPA) increased by two points last year.

The Ellipsis

The ellipsis is a punctuation mark that lets the reader know that words have been omitted. It consists of three periods with spaces between (i.e., . . .). If the omission spans more than one sentence, four periods are used (e.g., "The ellipsis is . . . . four periods."). Ellipses can also be used to indicate a pause or an unfinished thought.

Example 1:

Original: Celina ran at a lightning-quick pace with sweat on her face until she reached the finish line.

Ellipsis Added: Celina ran at a lightning-quick pace . . . until she reached the finish line.

- Here, the ellipsis indicates an omission from the original text; the sentence, however, must remain grammatically correct after the text is omitted.

Example 2:

In "The Love Song of J. Alfred Prufrock," T.S. Eliot creates a character who is trapped in his own thoughts:

"I grow old . . . I grow old . . . I shall wear the bottoms of my trousers rolled."

- Here, the use of the ellipses conveys the hesitation in Prufrock's thinking.

Commas

Many of the following comma rules have been discussed above in the context of specific grammatical components. The following is a summary:

1. Separate three or more items in a list (items in a series) using a coordinating conjunction.
    a. I brought *food, water,* and *blankets* when I went camping.
    b. I saw the chipmunk *run into the garage, jump over the bucket,* and *slide through the window.*
2. Separate independent clauses (comma + FANBOYS).
    a. The swimmers trained hard all season, and they won the championship.
    b. I opened the package, but it was empty.
3. Separate a dependent and an independent clause in a complex sentence.
    a. Because the swimmers trained hard all season, they won the championship.
    b. When the team arrived at the field, they were greeted by the cheers of their enthusiastic fans.
4. Add nonessential information (nonrestrictive/parenthetical).
    a. Omar, a hard worker, earns a great living.
    b. The Lincoln Memorial, my favorite monument, is a powerful symbol of American history.
    c. My sister, who is a talented horseback rider, trains her own horses.
    d. I ordered the osso bucco, which was delicious!

5. Separate introductory words and phrases from the main clause of the sentence.
   a. Furthermore, I demand to see the manager.
   b. Hoping to get a refund, I demanded to see the manager.
   c. Before school, I take a walk around the block.
   d. Yes, I would be happy to meet you for lunch!
   e. Josephine, I can't believe that you said that!
6. Surround interjections.
   a. The restaurant, however fancy, failed to impress me.
   b. She did, indeed, win the race.
7. Separate coordinate adjectives.
   a. My kids ate all of the delicious, homemade brownies.
   b. The old, abandoned house became an eyesore for the town.
8. Separate parts of dates and addresses.
   a. Let's meet on Friday, November 12, 2024 in Central Park, New York.
   b. My favorite restaurant is located at 311 Park Drive, Nowheresville, New Jersey 07862.
9. Set off quotations.
   a. Beth said, "Let's have dinner at the French restaurant."
   b. "This is my favorite movie," she said.
   c. "The result of the game," the referee said, "is a tie!"
10. Following salutations in letters
    a. Hi Sophia,
    b. Dear Dr. Smith,
11. Following closings in letters
    a. Sincerely, Mr. Anderson
    b. With sympathy, Michele

Quotation Marks and Punctuation

Quotation marks are used to punctuate dialogue (direct speech) and quotations, to punctuate the titles of short works (e.g., short stories, poems, episode names, chapter titles, essays), and to imply a sarcastic or ironic tone.

As a set of rules, consider the following when adding punctuation with quotation marks:

1. Periods and commas go **inside** quotation marks.
    a. With dialogue, place a dialogue tag at the beginning or end of the sentence.
        i. Arjun whispered, "I am excited to meet our new neighbors."
            - Comma before the quote and period inside.
        ii. "I am excited to meet our new neighbors," Arjun said.
            - Comma inside the quote and period at the end of the sentence.
    b. Dialogue tags can also interrupt the sentence/quote.
        i. "The result of the game," the exhausted referee said, "is a tie."
        ii. "Watching the rain storm," Lindsey said, "makes me happy."
    c. Titles of short works are quoted (not underlined or italicized).
        i. My favorite musical album is "Before These Crowded Streets."
        ii. When I finished reading the poem "My Last Duchess," I immediately read it a second time.
2. Semicolons and colons go **outside** quotation marks.
    a. My favorite musical album is "Before These Crowded Streets"; indeed, it's the best!
    b. Jake's favorite animal is a cat; "I want one as a pet," he said.
3. Question marks and exclamation points are placed either inside or outside quotation marks depending on the

structure/meaning of the sentence. This can be tricky! The following is an overview of question marks; the same rules apply to exclamation points.

a. If the quoted material itself is a question, then the question mark goes **inside** the quotation mark.

   i. Mary asked, "Are we going to dinner tonight?"

   ii. The children said, "Can we swim in the deep end?"

b. If, however, the entire sentence is a question—not just what's being quoted—then the question mark goes **outside** the quotation mark.

   i. Did Mirabel say, "Let's go to dinner tonight"?

   ii. Did the children yell, "We're going to swim in the deep end"?

   iii. Have you read the poem "Sailing to Byzantium"?

c. What happens when the entire sentence is a question and the quotation is a question too? The question mark goes **inside** the quote to avoid the ever-awkward double question mark.

   i. Did the children ask, "Can we swim in the deep end?"

4. Don't use quotation marks with indirect speech—when someone is not actually speaking even though it might initially appear as though someone is.

   a. John said that he was hungry.

   b. After the party, Simone told me that she was tired.

5. Quotation marks can be used to emphasize the tone of a word or phrase—think "air quotes"—often with an implied sarcastic or ironic meaning.

   a. Though John was "working late" yesterday, I saw him at the concert.

   b. My roommate's "brilliant" idea was to adopt a pet alligator.

6. Quotes within quotes use a single quotation mark.

   a. "When Simone yelled, 'The rain just started,' I ran to close my car windows," said Christina.

b. "John claimed that he was 'working late' yesterday," said Peter.

Punctuating Dates

1. Add a comma between the day of week and the month.
   a. She played her first softball game on Friday, April 26.
   b. Thursday, January 18 was a snow day.
   c. My first day of work was Monday, October 23, so I started training on Wednesday, October 18.
      i. In this compound sentence, the comma after October 23 is used to separate the two independent clauses.
2. Add a comma between the day of the month and the year.
   a. We last went to Central Park on October 21, 2021.
   b. On May 2, 2016, we went on vacation to Disney World.
      i. The comma after 2016 separates the introductory phrase from the rest of the sentence.

Possessives

To show possession—that someone or something owns something—we use an apostrophe. The age-old question is "But where does the apostrophe go?" The following rules will clear that up.

1. Put an apostrophe + *s* after singular nouns.
   a. The student's backpack is new.
   b. The store's name recently changed.
   c. Carolyn's favorite pet is a hermit crab.
2. Put an apostrophe after plural nouns that end in *s*.
   a. The students' backpacks are on the floor.
   b. The players' uniforms need to be washed.
   c. The birds' song woke me up early.

3. For irregular plural nouns, add an apostrophe + *s*. Let's look at two examples closely since this can be confusing for students.
   a. Child = singular; children = plural
      i. The child's bike fell over.
      ii. The children's bikes are in the driveway.
   b. Woman = singular; women = plural
      i. The woman's dress is sparkling in the moonlight.
      ii. The women's meeting will be held at the library.
4. For singular nouns ending in *s*, use either an apostrophe after the *s* or add an apostrophe + *s*. Though you can get away with either, the more accepted option is apostrophe + *s* to avoid confusion with proper names.
   a. Chris's saxophone needs a tune-up.
   b. The class's project involved the study of chaos vs. order.
   c. Mr. Jones's wish is to be a little more funky.

Contractions

Speaking of apostrophes, they are also used to form contractions—two words merged into one. Because they mimic casual speech, contractions are considered informal when used in writing. Some contractions lead to usage errors, as we'll see in the next section. Here are some examples:

- I'm (I am)
- We're (we are)
- They're (they are)
- It's (it is)
- Should've (should have—not should of)
- Would've (would have)
- Can't (cannot)
- We've (we have)
- You're (you are)

Capitalizing Words in Titles

In addition to knowing how to punctuate (quotes or italics) the title of a work (poem, short story, novel, film, TV show, etc.), students must also learn which words in titles are capitalized. The following rules apply if students are citing the name of a text or creating a title for their own piece of writing. Though some style guides vary slightly, the following expectations are largely accepted in terms of capitalizing words in titles:

1. Capitalize the first and last word in the title.
2. Capitalize nouns, pronouns, verbs, adjectives, and adverbs.
3. Do not capitalize the following (unless they are the first or last word in the title):
    a. Articles: a, an, the
    b. FANBOYS: for, and, nor, but, or, yet, so
    c. Short prepositions (fewer than five letters): in, on, by, to, at, of, up, with, from

Here are some examples:

- *Diary of a Wimpy Kid*
- *An Extraordinary Journey*
- *The Cat in the Hat*
- *Dog Man: For Whom the Ball Rolls*

SECTION 15: COMMONLY CONFUSED WORDS

Author created using Imgflip AI tool

No discussion of grammar and usage would be complete without a quick overview of the most commonly confused words, including my greatest pet peeve of late: regard vs. regards.

It's vs. Its

- **It's** (it is) time to feed the chickens.
- The chicken ate **its** lunch.

Who's vs. Whose

- **Who's** (who is) coming to the beach with me?
- **Whose** dog is on my lawn?

They're vs. There vs. Their

- **They're** (they are) coming to the beach with me this weekend.
- Look at the waves crashing over **there**.
- The kids left **their** bikes in the street.

To vs. Two vs. Too

- We should go **to** the movies.
- The bottle of juice costs **two** dollars.
- I want to go to the beach **too**. (also)
- The tea is **too** hot to drink. (degree)

You're vs. Your

- **You're** (you are) going to regret that decision.
- Please bring me **your** homework.

Lead vs. Led

- Please **lead** the students slowly down the hall.
- The teacher **led** the students slowly down the hall.
- The old pipes in the house are made of **lead**.

Regard vs. Regards

- I'm calling in **regard** to the advertisement you posted.
    - A person *cannot* be calling (or doing anything, for that matter) in **regards** to something.
- Please send my **regards** to your family.

References

Alber, R. (2014). Using mentor texts to motivate and support student writers. *Edutopia*. https://www.edutopia.org/blog/using-mentor-text-motivate-and-support-student-writers-rebecca-alber

Amplify. (2024a). *Science of writing: A primer*. Retrieved December 12, 2024, from https://amplify.com/pdf/uploads/2024/09/SoR_Collateral_SoR-Primer-3_091724-1.pdf

Amplify. (2024b, October 8). *The writing chapter: Sparking the writing revolution with the latest insights and research* [Video]. YouTube. https://www.youtube.com/watch?v=c_PX7TT-Cvc

Anderson, J. (2023). *Mechanically inclined: Building grammar, usage, and style into writer's workshop*. Taylor & Francis.

Anderson, J., & La Rocca, W. (2023). *Patterns of power, grades 1–5: Inviting young writers into the conventions of language*. Taylor & Francis.

Bernabei, G. S. (2015). *Grammar keepers: Lessons that tackle students' most persistent problems once and for all, grades 4–12*. Corwin.

Bjork, R. A., & Bjork, E. L. (2019). Forgetting as the friend of learning: Implications for teaching and self-regulated learning. *Advances in Physiology Education, 43*(2), 164–167. https://doi.org/10.1152/advan.00001.2019

Black, P., Harrison, C., Lee, C., Marshall, B., & Wiliam, D. (2003). *Assessment for learning: Putting it into practice*. Open University Press.

Black, P., & Wiliam, D. (1998). Assessment and classroom learning. *Assessment in Education, 5*, 7–74. doi:10.1080/0969595980050102

Braddock, R. R., Lloyd-Jones, R., & Schoer, L. (Eds.). (1963). *Research in written composition*. National Council of Teachers of English.

Bransford, J. (2000). *How people learn: Brain, mind, experience, and school*. National Academies Press.

Bruno, E. K. (2012). *Punctuation celebration*. Macmillan.

Cleary, B. P. (2007). *Slide and slurp, scratch and burp: More about verbs*. Millbrook Press.

Crystal, D. (2004). *Making sense of grammar*. Longman.

Dewey, J. (2008). 1933: Essays and how we think. In J. A. Boydston (Ed.), *The collected works of John Dewey* (Vol. 8). Southern Illinois University Press.

Distefano, P., & Killion, J. (1984). Assessing writing skills through a process approach. *English Education, 16*(4), 203–207.

Dorfman, L., & Dougherty, D. (2023). *Grammar matters: Lessons, tips, & conversations using mentor texts, K–6*. Taylor & Francis.

Dreyer, B. (2020). *Dreyer's English: An utterly correct guide to clarity and style*. Random House Trade Paperbacks.

Ehrenworth, M., & Vinton, V. (2005). *The power of grammar*. Heinemann Educational Books.

Essberger, J. (n.d.). *What is grammar?* Englishclub.com. Retrieved December 12, 2024, from https://www.englishclub.com/grammar/what.php

Graham, S. (2006). Strategy instruction and the teaching of writing: A meta-analysis. In C. A. Macarthur, S. Graham, & J. Fitzgerald (Eds.), *Handbook of writing research* (pp. 187–207). The Guilford Press.

Graham, S., Harris, K. R., & Santangelo, T. (2015). Research-based writing practices and the common core: Meta-analysis and meta-synthesis. *The Elementary School Journal, 115*(4), 498–522. https://doi.org/10.1086/681964

Graham, S., & Hebert, M. (2011). Writing to read: A meta-analysis of the impact of writing and writing instruction on reading. *Harvard Educational Review, 81*(4), 710–744. https://doi.org/10.17763/haer.81.4.t2k0m13756113566

Graham, S., Kim, Y.-S., Cao, Y., Lee, J. W., Tate, T., Collins, P., Cho, M., Moon, Y., Chung, H. Q., & Olson, C. B. (2023). A meta-analysis of writing treatments for students in grades 6–12. *Journal of Educational Psychology, 115*(7), 1004–1027. https://doi.org/10.1037/edu0000819

Hare, R. L., & Dillon, R. (2016). *The space: A guide for educators*. Edtechteam Press.

Harris, R. J. (1962). *An experimental enquiry into the functions and value of formal grammar in the teaching of English, with special reference to the teaching of correct written English to children aged twelve to fourteen* [Doctoral thesis, Institute of Education, University of London, London, UK].

Hattie, J. A. C., & Donoghue, G. M. (2016). Learning strategies: A synthesis and conceptual model. *Npj Science of Learning, 1*(1), 16013. https://doi.org/10.1038/npjscilearn.2016.13

Hillocks, G. (1986). *Research on written composition: New directions for teaching*. National Council of Teachers of English.

Hillocks, G., & Smith, M. W. (1991). Grammar and usage. In J. Flood, J. M. Jensen, D. Lapp, & J. R. Squire (Eds.), *Handbook of research on teaching the English language arts* (pp. 591–603). Macmillan.

Hochman, J. C., & Wexler, N. (2024). *The writing revolution: A guide to advancing thinking through writing in all subjects and grades* (2nd ed.). John Wiley & Sons.

Hochman, J., Wexler, N., & Lemov, D. (2017). *The writing revolution: A guide to advancing thinking through writing in all subjects and grades*. Jossey-Bass.

Holub, J. (2013). *Little red writing*. Chronicle Books.

Koutrakos, P. (2018). *Word study that sticks: Best practices, K–6*. Corwin.

Lyons, S. (2009). *If you were an apostrophe*. Picture Window Press.

Maizels, J., & Petty, K. (1996). *The great grammar book*. Random House.

McGrath, K. (2015, September 28). *A vision for every student: Exploration-based learning*. Getting Smart. https://www.gettingsmart.com/2015/09/28/a-vision-for-every-student-exploration-based-learning/

MIND Education. (2024). *Productive struggle & math rigor*. Stmath.com. Retrieved December 12, 2024, from https://www.stmath.com/productive-struggle-math-rigor

Myhill, D., Jones, S., Watson, A., & Lines, H. (2013). Playful explicitness with grammar: A pedagogy for writing: Place of grammar within the teaching of writing. *Literacy, 47*(2), 103–111. https://doi.org/10.1111/j.1741-4369.2012.00674.x

National Assessment of Educational Progress. (n.d.). *Assessments – writing*. Retrieved December 12, 2024, from https://nces.ed.gov/nationsreportcard/writing/

Popham, W. J. (2014). *Transformative assessment in action: An inside look at applying the process*. Association for Supervision & Curriculum Development.

Reynolds, J., & Kiely, B. (2015). *All American boys*. Atheneum Books for Young Readers.

Roberts, K., & Roberts, M. B. (2016). *DIY literacy: Teaching tools for differentiation, rigor, and independence*. Heinemann.

Rosenthal, A. K., & Lichtenheld, T. (2022). *Exclamation mark*. Scholastic.

Rothman, S., & Oswald, P. (2020). *Attack of the underwear dragon*. Random House Children's Books.

Sedita, J. (2023). *The writing rope: A framework for explicit writing instruction in all subjects*. Paul H. Brookes.

Smith, M. W., & Wilhelm, J. D. (2007). *Getting it right: Fresh approaches to teaching grammar, usage, and correctness*. Scholastic.

Truss, L. (2006). *Eats, shoots & leaves: The zero tolerance approach to punctuation*. Gotham.

VanDerwater, A. L. (2020). *Write! Write! Write!* Wordsong.

Vardy, M. (2020). *TimeCrafting: A better way to get the right things done.* Mango Media.

Vygotsky, L. S. (1967). Play and its role in the mental development of the child. *Soviet Psychology*, *5*(3), 6–18. https://doi.org/10.2753/rpo1061-040505036

Weaver, C. (1996). *Teaching grammar in context.* Boynton/Cook.

Weaver, C., & Bush, J. (2008). *Grammar to enrich & enhance writing.* Heinemann Educational Books.

Weeks, S. (2013). *Pie.* Scholastic.

Wiggins, G. (2012). *What is transfer?* Jaymctighe.com. Retrieved December 12, 2024, from https://jaymctighe.com/wp-content/uploads/2021/05/What-is-transfer-Grant-Wiggins.pdf

Woodson, J. (2023). *Remember us.* Nancy Paulsen Books.

Index

CORWIN

To help every educator help every student

We believe that every single student deserves a great education

We believe that knowing our impact is both a privilege and a responsibility

We believe that a fair, stable, and thriving society is built on education

Ready to add even more flavor to your grammar instruction?

There's so much more to savor in the world of language learning!

When you join authors Patty McGee and Tim Donohue's ***Not Your Granny's Grammar*** online community, you'll discover fresh classroom ideas, digital resources, and expert guidance that will transform how your students experience grammar. As a community member, you'll gain access to a thoughtfully prepared collection of educational goodies, delivered to you weekly by email.

And as a token of appreciation for reading the book and joining the community, Patty and Tim would like to offer you your first goodie: a BONUS grammar unit not included in the book that you can put to use in your classroom right away!

Just scan the QR code below to grab your copy.

In subsequent months, you'll receive a whole toolbox full of innovative teaching tools that make grammar more appealing to everyone.

Want to take your exploration of effective grammar instruction to the next level? Patty and Tim can work with your district in a variety of ways, including:

- **Grammar Makeover Workshops & Keynotes (where traditional approaches get a fresh, modern twist)**
- **On-site Professional Learning in Your District (bringing expertise directly to your teaching team)**
- **Classroom Coaching Collaborations (working side by side to enhance instruction)**
- **Curriculum Revisions and Writing (refreshing your approach to language learning)**
- **Custom Created Webinars and Thinktanks (collaborative spaces for professional growth)**

Scan the QR code now to join Patty and Tim's fast-growing Not Your Granny's Grammar online community and receive your BONUS grammar unit.

pattymcgee.org/NYGG

Zeitfracht Medien GmbH
Ferdinand-Jühlke-Straße 7
99095 Erfurt, Deutschland
produktsicherheit@kolibri360.de